CHANGING SCHOOLS

4-2-93

For Robert & Ruth

fondly

Art

CHANGING SCHOOLS

Progressive Education Theory and Practice, 1930-1960

Arthur Zilversmit

The University of Chicago Press
Chicago and London

Arthur Zilversmit is professor of history at Lake Forest College.

The University of Chicago Press, Chicago 60637
The University of Chicago Press, Ltd., London
© 1993 by The University of Chicago
All rights reserved. Published 1993
Printed in the United States of America

02 01 00 99 98 97 96 95 94 93   1 2 3 4 5 6

ISBN (cloth): 0–226–98329–3
ISBN (paper): 0–226–98330–7

Library of Congress Cataloging-in-Publication Data
Zilversmit, Arthur.
    Changing schools: Progressive education theory and practice /
Arthur Zilversmit.
        p.   cm.
    Includes bibliographical references and index.
    1. Progressive education—United States—History—20th century.
2. Educational change—United States—History—20th century.
I. Title.
LB1027.3.Z55 1993
370.11—dc20   92–21402
                                                                              CIP

♾ The paper used in this publication meets the minimum requirements of the
American National Standard for Information Sciences—Permanence of Paper for
Printed Library Materials, ANSI Z39.48–1984.

For Charlotte

Contents

Illustrations

Preface

*H*istory speaks most powerfully when it deals with questions that are immediate and personal. In 1966, when my wife and I sent our five-year-old son off for his first day in public school, my interest in the history of American education suddenly assumed a new weight; it became immediate and personal. As we left the modern suburban school building, I wondered why schools were still being run in the familiar ways I recalled from the days I attended an old-fashioned New York City public school, with its dry over-heated air, smelling of chalk dust and a special brand of disinfectant. In those days, during World War II, I was always worried that I might violate one of the school's many arcane rules, that I might be reported for going up the wrong staircase or be sent to the principal for talking too much in class.

I was reminded of my own school days again a few years later when I sat uncomfortably in a small chair and watched my daughter's third grade teacher struggle as she tried to teach an arithmetic lesson. At least half of the pupils were bored—some because they already knew what the teacher was explaining, others because they had given up. I recalled the boredom of my own classes at New York's P.S. 6, and I wondered why schools still prized order over creativity, why they still seemed incapable of meeting the needs of individual children.

As a young adolescent, I spent most of the year within the dreary, fortresslike walls of P.S. 6, but during the summers I attended a wonderfully liberal camp, run on the principles of progressive education. Later, as a student and then as a teacher, I read and admired the works of John Dewey and recognized the philosophy that had animated my summer experiences. Now, when my own children were enrolled in public schools, I wondered what had happened to these humane and liberating ideas.

This question was in the back of my mind for a number of years and when I met with a group of teachers to talk about teaching history, I took advantage of a break to ask them what they thought had happened to progressive education. One of them told me about the public schools of Winnetka, Illinois (a wealthy suburb just a few miles away), where progressive education had prospered in the 1930s. I began to study the history of the Winnetka schools. My research on progressive education in Winnetka led to a broader study of the ways in which John Dewey's philosophy affected individual schools.

I learned that in sharp contrast with my own experience and what I had seen in my children's schools, the most influential historian of modern American education maintained that progressive ideas had been accepted by most of the leaders of American education and that they had resulted in a *Transformation of the School*. Lawrence Cremin argued that by the 1950s progressivism had, in fact, become a stultifying new orthodoxy.[1]

In an important study of American education after World War II, Diane Ravitch echoed Cremin's conclusion—progressivism *was* the dominant educational ideology by 1945. But Ravitch carefully noted that while these ideas had become orthodox for professional educators, "[w]hether progressive practices were equally commonplace is another issue . . ."[2]

That question is the focus of this study.

Let me briefly describe my approach. While we know a great deal about the theories of progressive educators and their claims that these ideas were influencing the programs of thousands of schools, we know little about how progressive principles fared in individual schools. To understand the real impact of progressive education, we need to look at specific schools and classrooms. Accordingly, this study moves between descriptions of progressive education at the national level and close studies of several local school systems in the Chicago area. The focus is on elementary schools because these were most likely to be influenced by progressive ideas. The first half of the book centers on progressivism in the 1930s, when its influence was at its height. The second section deals with progressivism in the post-World War II period, when it was on the defensive.

Chapter 1 provides a definition of progressive education, largely centered on the thought of John Dewey. The next chapter examines several public school systems that adopted progressive principles in the 1920s and 1930s, with the major focus on the schools of Winnetka. Chapter 3 assesses the impact of progressivism on the nation's classrooms in the 1930s.

Chapter 4 centers on several school systems in the Chicago area in the 1930s. The schools of these communities (unlike those of Winnetka) were not well-known, but these towns were each very different and they can be taken to represent more typical American schools. Like Winnetka, Lake Forest was a wealthy suburb. In sharp contrast, Waukegan, only a few miles to the north, was an industrial city hit hard by the depression. Mundelein, located several miles west of Lake Forest, was a small community with a two-classroom school, typical of many rural villages before World War II.

Chapters 5 and 6 focus on the impact of the baby boom and the Cold War on American schools. Chapters 7 and 8 look in detail at the reverberations of the trends of the 1950s in the same Chicago area schools we looked at in the 1930s. I present my conclusions in the last chapter, and I also discuss the implications of this story for educational reform.

The history of the ways in which progressive ideas influenced individual schools is relevant to the current debates about school reform. Understanding the relationship between educational ideas and practices provides a sobering perspective on educational reform and, most important, it can help us see how we might transform our schools into John Dewey's "Schools of Tomorrow."[3]

Acknowledgments

My interest in educational reform began many years ago at Buck's Rock Work Camp in Connecticut where a group of talented teachers, especially the late Bill Cotton of New York's Walden School, exemplified progressive education at its best.

I began work on this project during a stimulating year as a member of the Shelby Cullom Davis seminar at Princeton University. Lawrence Stone, who was then the director of the seminar, and my fellow seminar members provided an intellectually exciting atmosphere of free-ranging discussions of issues in the history of education; I am indebted to them for their comments and for their encouragement.

I owe a great deal to my friends and colleagues at Lake Forest College. Charles A. Miller gave my manuscript careful consideration and made valuable suggestions. Michael Ebner not only read the manuscript at several stages and gave good advice, but at several crucial points kept me moving along.

My friend, Leon Litwack, listened to me talk about my work in progress and read several chapters; as always, I benefited from his advice. Robert Church facilitated my access to the Northwestern University Library. Several conversations over lunch with him and Michael Sedlak helped me to clarify my thinking on a number of points. Professor Church read three chapters early on and made many useful suggestions.

It is impossible to study the history of progressive education without relying on the work of the late Lawrence Cremin, whose *The Transformation of the School* is the seminal work in this field. David Tyack's work in the history of American education, too, has been crucial. Beyond that, I profited from Professor Tyack's careful reading of the manuscript; his suggestions have been enormously beneficial.

Early on in my research on Winnetka's schools I met Janet Stevenson. She had attended the Winnetka public schools during the heyday of Carleton Washburne's experiments in progressive education in that unusual community. Stevenson told me a great deal about the village and its schools. Her enthusiasm helped spark mine and gave me a sense of that elusive but crucial element, the feelings of those involved in Carleton Washburne's schools. Through her, I met her mother, the late Mrs. John Marshall, who remembered a lot of wonderful town gossip about Washburne. Stevenson introduced me to a number of retired Winnetka teachers who shared their memories with me.

A number of Lake Forest College students have assisted me in important ways. Katherine Amato-Von Hemert helped research the story of the Mundelein schools in the 1930s. Christine MacLennan dug through the Waukegan and Lake Forest school records for the 1930s. Mara Way helped on the study of these schools in the postwar period. Jennifer Quinn assisted me by going through periodicals and newspapers of the postwar period. Mary A. Dolce shared with me her research on the schools of Mundelein. Vicki Kimmel carefully reviewed my annotations and checked quotations against the original sources.

I am especially grateful to the staff of the public libraries and the schools of Winnetka, Lake Forest, Waukegan, and Mundelein. In each community, they graciously made their records available and suggested new avenues for research. The staff of the Lake Forest College Library deserves special thanks for going beyond the call of duty in helping me track down obscure books and articles. The staff of several other libraries also made important contributions: Northwestern University, Princeton University, Rutgers University, Teachers College of Columbia University, the United States Department of Education, Stanford University, and the Universities of California at Berkeley and Los Angeles.

A number of people shared with me and my research assistants their memories of teaching in the schools of the communities I studied. In Winnetka: former teachers, Don and Mary Boyer, Francis Murray, Mr. and Mrs. Soren Ostergaard, and the former superintendent of a neighboring school district, Frederick L. Redefer. Alex Baskin kindly sent me a recording of his wide-ranging interview with Washburne.

In Lake Forest, former teachers we interviewed included Valada Hayward, Robert Vandervoort, and Mr. and Mrs. Orville B. Peterson. In addition, the late Ned Reichert, former chair of the Education Department of Lake Forest College (assisted by his wife, Hazel), gave me a valuable perspective on his friend, superintendent

Frederick Quinlan. My colleague, Rosemary Hale, provided me with the views of a parent of Lake Forest school children while Philip L. Speidel gave me the perspective of a member of the Lake Forest School Board. Allen Klingenberg, who until recently was superintendent of Lake Forest schools, helped me gain access to school records.

I learned a great deal about Waukegan schools from H. R. McCall. I also appreciate the help of Lawrence Pekoe and Lynn Pekoe, who helped me gain access to Waukegan school records.

In Mundelein I learned a great deal from former superintendent Albert Kroll; he not only spent time reminiscing with me, but also gave me access to his files. Among the former Mundelein teachers we interviewed were Abbie Dolton, Genevieve LaMadegleine, and Ruth Rouse. We also spoke with former students Vance Ray and Stanley Rouse.

I want to publicly thank Lake Forest College for its generous sabbatical leave policy and for providing funds for research expenses.

Early versions of parts of this book were presented as papers at a number of seminars and conferences: The Shelby Cullom Davis Historical Seminar, 1972, 1973; The American Studies Association, 1975; and The History of Education Society, 1980, 1981, and 1986. I am grateful to those who commented on these early efforts—especially Ronald Cohen and Jennings Wagoner, Jr.

My editor at The University of Chicago Press, Doug Mitchell, provided a splendid audience for my developing ideas and provided a great deal of encouragement. I also want to thank members of the professional staff of The University of Chicago Press who have made the publishing process as smooth and worry-free as possible.

Finally, I want to express my gratitude to Charlotte Zilversmit for her patience and support, her careful reading of the manuscript, and most of all her many thoughtful comments and insightful ideas. It is altogether fitting that this book is dedicated to her.

1

PROGRESSIVE EDUCATION:
A DEFINITION

When John Dewey died in 1952, *The New York Times* announced
the death of the "Father of Progressive Education." For sixty years,
Dewey had called for a radical transformation in schooling. He had
inspired a movement to establish new schools that would be democratic rather than authoritarian, that would make learning meaningful and pleasurable by focussing on the needs and interests of
children. Dewey advocated a radical change in school methods,
shifting from memorization and recitations to learning activities
based on experience.[1]

Dewey had begun his long career as a school reformer in the
1890s, one of those periods when school reform was prominent on
the national agenda. At that time, a number of educators and community leaders were working to change schools. Some of them
shared Dewey's views: they too wanted schools that would reject
rote learning and authoritarian discipline and would, instead, use
the interests of children to promote learning in a democratic setting. These progressive educators wanted to make schools into humane institutions that respected childhood, and they hoped that
the children who were educated in these schools would, as adults,
create a better society.

Although progressive education aroused widespread interest
and sometimes passionate debate, it is a difficult movement to define. Indeed, Lawrence Cremin, its leading historian, saw progressive education as so diverse that his important study of educational
reform, *The Transformation of the School*, avoided a definition.[2] Yet,
despite the fact that the movement was complex, I believe it can be
defined. Clearly, in the 1920s and 1930s, when progressive education had reached a high point in its influence, there was general

agreement on what differentiated a progressive school from others. Despite diversity, progressive education was based on a clearly identifiable cluster of ideas.[3]

In arriving at a definition, it is important to recognize that progressive education was only one of several contemporary educational reform movements. Each was an effort to adapt education to a nation that was being transformed by industrialization, urbanization, and immigration. As Americans faced these major challenges, many hoped schools could play a role in helping the nation cope with rapid change.

Educational reformers believed new forms of schooling could help meet new pressures and new demands. But while they agreed that schools needed to change, these reformers differed widely in their prescriptions. Some wanted schools to devote more attention to developing skilled workers to meet the needs of a society that was growing more and more dependent on highly evolved technologies. They called for a vocational component in the curriculum to prepare young people to enter modern industrial occupations. Others reformers were concerned with the problem of absorbing new immigrants from eastern and southern Europe; they wanted the schools to be a major force in unifying the nation and producing loyal citizens. Both groups saw education as a form of social control. In the face of rapid changes that were eroding traditional social institutions such as the family and the church, they hoped schooling could become a new stabilizing force.

A third group of reformers (whose goals overlapped with the other two groups) was primarily concerned with applying principles of efficiency, centralization, and bureaucratic decision making, based on the example of modern business, to the schools.[4] They deplored the conventional curriculum as inefficient. They called for testing and standardization. At the same time, they wanted to rescue urban schools from hopelessly inefficient and corrupt ward politics.

Each of these educational reform groups wanted to change schools and adapt them to modern society. Moreover, each of them was part of the progressive movement prominent in American politics and social reform in the years before World War I. The focus of these reformers was on social rather than individual needs.

While the movement to establish progressive schools, which developed at the same time, was also was concerned with social goals, its focus was on meeting the needs of individual children. Dewey and his followers also wanted to accomplish social reform through schooling, but theirs was a distinct movement with its own agenda. Their first priority was to create schools in which children would find a nurturing environment that would allow them to develop their individual capacities.

Progressive educators shared a common core of beliefs, but it was not, of course, a monolithic movement. Its leaders emphasized different aspects of their aims and, over time, the movement stressed different aspects of its agenda. Yet there is a central core of ideas and practices that were widely recognized in the 1920s and 1930s as part of a movement that stemmed from the educational and philosophical writings of John Dewey. These formed the essential core of progressive education.

John Dewey grew up in rural Vermont and attended the tiny University of Vermont. After graduation, he taught high school briefly and then went back to school and earned his Ph.D. at the nation's first professional graduate school, The Johns Hopkins University. From there he embarked on an academic career in philosophy and psychology at the University of Michigan and then, in 1894, he accepted a position at the new University of Chicago, where he added the department of pedagogy to his professional concerns.

Even before he came to Chicago, Dewey was dissatisfied with a philosophy that treated ideas as abstractions, unrelated to daily living. He had been concerned with finding ways in which academic philosophy and psychology could play a larger role in dealing with broad social questions. He had begun to expand philosophical discussions by bringing social issues, such as the ethics of participating in a strike, into his classrooms.[5] He argued that it is only "[w]hen philosophic ideas are . . . used as tools to point out the meaning of phases of social life" that "they begin to have some life and value."[6] Dewey's philosophy supported a new approach to the discipline, providing a link between the world of ideas and the social world. By the time he got to Chicago, Dewey had rejected philosophical idealism and developed a philosophical position that denied the separation between the spiritual world of thought and ideals and the natural world of human action.[7]

Crucial to Dewey's new position was his reading of the larger meaning of Darwin's revolution in biology. For Dewey, *The Origin of Species* "introduced a mode of thinking that in the end was bound to transform the logic of knowledge, and hence the treatment of morals, politics, and religion."[8] Darwin had shown that all living forms, including humans, are constantly undergoing change and, most important, that these changes tended in no particular direc-

tion, with no discernible purpose except the continuation of life
itself. Therefore, Dewey argued, Darwin's discoveries meant that
ultimate truths could not be found outside the flux and change of
this world. It was this ever-changing world itself that provided the
only source of meaning. In keeping with his rejection of any transcendental source of values, Dewey believed that philosophy
should reject "inquiry after absolute origins and absolute finalities
in order to explore specific values and the specific conditions that
generate them."9 And, by turning away from questions about a
hypothetical transcendental reality, philosophy could turn to the
concrete ways by which we could "improve our education, . . .
ameliorate our manners . . . [and] advance our politics."10 Philosophy would come down to earth and be available to those who
sought to improve the human condition.

Chicago in the middle of the last decade of the nineteenth century was an ideal place for a young philosopher to integrate academic talents and social concerns. The city itself exemplified the
new social forces changing the face of the nation. The new industrialism and the growth of the new cities could be seen here firsthand.
Furthermore, William Rainey Harper was assembling an innovative faculty at the new University of Chicago; many of the people
he brought there were interested in social reform and they, too,
were finding fresh ways of looking at their disciplines. At the same
time, Jane Addams, at Hull House, was pursuing innovative methods of examining and alleviating the problems of industrial, urban
America.

Addams played an important role in shaping Dewey's ideas.
When she decided to live among the poor at Hull House, it was not
in order to serve as merely another source of charity. She recognized that "the dependence of classes on each other is reciprocal"
and that the members of the middle classes had much to learn from
the poor; that a life cut off from contact with the poor was devital-
izing.11 Education was to be a central theme at Hull House, but it
was to be a process in which teacher and student frequently exchanged roles. The middle class residents had much to learn from
the people of the neighborhood. Thus Hull House was to be "the
living embodiment of an alternative view of education," a view
that stressed how education could serve the needs of people of
many different backgrounds and, at the same time, could foster a
new sense of community.12

Dewey was deeply involved with Hull House from its beginning. He was a member of its first board of directors. (Addams
once said that the "philosopher" was included "to keep us from

becoming either hard-boiled or sentimental in this new undertaking.")[13] It was in the context of the University of Chicago and Hull House that Dewey developed the principles of his philosophy of education.[14]

Education played a central role in Dewey's philosophy. Because humans are part of nature, they must strive to adapt; adaptation is the price of survival. Learning is an essential part of the adaptation process. The individual encounters new situations and copes with them by learning new behaviors. Dewey saw learning as a process of problem solving. For genuine learning to take place, it must be real to the student, the process must actively engage the learner. The fault with the traditional school is the passivity of the learner, who is expected to absorb, without question, the prescribed curriculum through drill and rote exercises.

Shortly after his arrival in Chicago, Dewey, in collaboration with his wife Alice, established an experimental elementary school. Here he believed he could follow a scientific approach to test and refine his ideas about human nature and individual psychology and education. At the University of Chicago's laboratory school he could experiment and develop sound principles of pedagogy.[15]

In 1899 Dewey issued his first comprehensive statement of his educational philosophy—the basis of progressive education—in a series of lectures to the parents of the children enrolled in his school. These lectures (published as *The School and Society*) enunciated the main principles of the new education.[16]

First, from his vantage point as a Darwinian, Dewey posited the goals of education in purely naturalist terms as continuing individual growth, physical as well as mental. The child should be viewed as a complex organism, not as just a mind, and schools should recognize that "the care and growth of the body are just as important as the development of the mind."[17] Respect for the growth of the individual also meant a recognition by the school that not all children learn at the same rate and in the same way. The goal of individual growth called for a respect for childhood and a recognition that the activities of children could be valuable in themselves, for their own sake, without reference to later adult life. "[I]f we identify ourselves with the real instincts and needs of childhood," Dewey said, "and ask only after its fullest assertion and growth, the discipline and information and culture of adult life shall all come in their due season."[18]

Second, Dewey regarded the school child not only as a distinct individual but also as one who came to school with a number of important assets: an "interest in . . . communication; . . . in finding

out things; in making things, . . . and in artistic expression." These
he called "the natural resources . . . upon the exercise of which
depends the active growth of the child."[19] While a child does not
have "much instinct for abstract inquiry," the child does have a
"constructive impulse" and an "art instinct."[20] The school should
use these resources; education should be regarded as an active pursuit that makes use of the child's native curiosity. The experiences
that a child brings to the classroom could be used by the school but,
instead, Dewey argued, the child "has to leave his mind behind,
because there is no way to use it in school. If he had a purely
abstract mind, he could bring it to school with him, but his is a
concrete mind, interested in concrete things."[21] In the progressive
school, therefore, learning would come as the result of activities
that involved the child's natural interests.

It is important to note, however, that for Dewey this did not
mean that the teacher simply stood back and let nature take its
course. According to Dewey, the teacher had a crucial role, for the
child's interest had to be directed: "Through direction," the child's
interests "tend towards valuable results, instead of scattering or
being left to merely impulsive expression."[22]

Dewey tied the "new education" to broader patterns of social
change—the emergence of an industrial society. He introduced the
idea of school as the "legatee" institution, one that had to take on
socialization functions that had previously been the responsibility
of institutions that were disintegrating under the pressures of industrialism. Dewey argued that under the old "household and
neighborhood system" (that was disappearing) "[t]he entire industrial process stood revealed." Now the learning that took place and
the character traits that were developed by observing and participating in the productive process had to be found somewhere else.
In the face of the radical changes wrought by industrialism "only
an equally radical change in education suffices." The school would
have to assume new functions; its curriculum would have to en-
compass much more than the "three R's."[23]

Finally, although Dewey believed that the goal for the individual
was growth, this was not the ultimate purpose of the new school.
Individual growth was important not only for the sake of each
child but even more important for the good of the larger community. The ideal of community permeated Dewey's educational
thought. He repeatedly referred to the new school as "an embryonic community" and in his well-known formulation maintained:
"When the school introduces and trains each child into membership within such a little community, saturating him with the spirit

of service, and providing him with the instruments of effective self-direction, we shall have the deepest and best guaranty of a larger society which is worthy, lovely, and harmonious."[24] For Dewey the school was to become the key to reforming society.

Dewey's educational philosophy is often described as child-centered, as opposed to subject-centered. In some ways, this is true. For Dewey, education had to begin with the interests and capacities of the child, not with the formal curriculum. But Dewey did not throw out the curriculum. He recognized the importance of "the traditional or three R's curriculum" and conceded that it represented "the keys which will unlock to the child the wealth of social capital which lies beyond the possible range of his limited individual experience."[25] But Dewey believed the essential skills and knowledge that children needed could be taught by enlisting their active cooperation. The teacher, therefore, needed to have a carefully developed curriculum, but this course of study had to remain flexible so that the teacher could use the activities that engaged the natural curiosity of the child to promote the necessary learning. Second, with maturity, Dewey believed, a child developed an increasing capacity to see long-term goals. Therefore, as the child advanced in school, the curriculum could be more and more formal; it did not have to appeal to the immediate experience and interests of the student. In short, schooling could become more subject-centered in the later grades without doing violence to the principle that the schooling process should be based on using the interests and experiences of individuals.[26]

Dewey's philosophy of education must be seen as part of a larger philosophical outlook. Two major threads that permeated his thought were a devotion to scientific methods and to the idea of a democratic community. As a Darwinian, Dewey saw humans as part of nature. Therefore, the proper approach to understanding human behavior was similar to the methods that had been so successful in the study of other parts of the natural world. But for Dewey science was more than chemistry and biology; science was a method, a broad approach to solving human problems. It meant first ascertaining as objectively as possible what the facts were, then developing hypotheses and projecting these into the future to see the possible results of following one or another hypothesis and, finally, choosing one hypothesis and testing it in action or in the imagination. As Richard Bernstein has pointed out, Dewey believed that "scientific knowledge of man gained through the social sciences . . . [could] play an enormous role in intelligently determining our decisions, choices and actions."[27]

But for Dewey, science was directly related to questions of value. In education, for example, science could be the basis for the testing and measurement helpful to traditional schools "in which marks, grading, classes and promotions are important" and where the "aim is to establish a norm." On the other hand, in a progressive school, science could be the basis for "a study of the conditions favorable to learning." Here a pedagogy based on science could find the conditions that would permit learning to take place "naturally and necessarily," conditions that would "call out self-educative activity, or learning." In this setting, the scientific method could discover ways to cooperate "with the activities of the pupils so that they have learning as their consequence."[28] For Dewey, science could not define the problem, nor by itself, offer solutions—its power lay in its ability to clarify options and allow intelligent choices.

Dewey clearly linked his scientific approach to human affairs with his ideal of a democratic community. "It is of the nature of science," he said, "to welcome diversity of opinion, while it insists that inquiry brings the evidence of observed facts to bear to effect a consensus of conclusions." Public discussion and consensus about the conclusions of scientific investigation were essential. "[F]reedom of inquiry, toleration of diverse views, freedom of communication, the distribution of what is found to every individual as the ultimate intellectual consumer, are involved in the democratic as in the scientific method."[29]

The ideal of an open, democratic community is basic to Dewey's philosophy. While Dewey's Darwinian model suggested that the evolutionary process we are part of does not point to any final goals, the model does emphasize the importance of continuing adaptation and growth. Dewey believed continuing individual growth required a special kind of community. The "object and reward of learning is continued capacity for growth" but "this idea cannot be applied to *all* the members of a society" except in a democratic community.[30] For Dewey (as for Jane Addams), a democratic society was "more than a form of government" it was "primarily a mode of associated living, of conjoint communicated experience," and real communication could only be possible with the destruction of the "barriers of class, race, and national territory." A society in which people learned from each other had to be an open society.[31] Dewey's program for education was a crucial part of a philosophy that looked to the use of scientific method to achieve a democratic community.[32]

Dewey's ideas about schooling did not, of course, stand alone.

At the turn of the century, when he wrote *The School and Society*, other people were also developing new approaches to education. In fact, only a few miles from Dewey's Lab School, Colonel Francis W. Parker's Cook County Normal School promoted many new practices that fit into Dewey's philosophy of education. Parker believed the school should be organized as "a model home, a complete community and embryonic democracy."[33] Like Dewey, Parker recognized the importance of starting with the natural interests of children. His child-centered pedagogy called for integrating material from the different school subjects. In the practice school at Cook County Normal, reading and writing were taught by having children create their own "Reading Leaflets." Field trips formed the basis of nature study and geography "began with first-hand knowledge of the surrounding countryside."[34] Lawrence Cremin sums up the prevailing spirit at the school: "The job of the teachers was to start where the children were and subtly lead them . . . into the several fields of knowledge, extending meanings and sensitivities all along the way."[35] Dewey visited Parker's school and obviously liked what he saw. He sent his own children there for two years before he opened his own school at the university. Although he and Parker were never close friends, Dewey recognized the value of Parker's work and he hailed Parker as the "father of progressive education."[36]

But Parker was not a philosopher like Dewey and others who were developing new theories with broad implications for schooling. One of the most important of these thinkers was the pioneer psychologist G. Stanley Hall, one of Dewey's teachers at Johns Hopkins. Like Dewey, Hall's approach to education was based on a naturalist philosophy. He also approached schooling by examining the natural needs of the child, and he was the founder of the child study movement. Hall objected to the "standardized, lockstep organization of the schools" and wanted to individualize the curriculum. But, as his biographer, Dorothy Ross, points out, Hall was a social conservative who was not "willing to abandon the authoritarian, competitive classroom."[37]

A more important contributor to thinking about schooling was the psychologist Edward L. Thorndike. Thorndike had a deep faith in science, and believed that anything that exists, including intelligence and learning, could be measured. He was one of the pioneers of the educational testing movement and one of the most significant champions of the movement to enhance the efficiency of schooling.[38]

Like Dewey, Thorndike was deeply influenced by Darwinism

and was sharply opposed to the traditional curriculum. He, too, believed that pupils learned by doing and that school problems should be devised based on the children's daily experience and on what engaged their interest.[39] One of Thorndike's best-known studies proved to be a crucial weapon for those who wanted to change the curriculum. It undermined a major argument for teaching traditional school subjects—their supposed ability to strengthen mental "faculties." In a series of experiments Thorndike demonstrated that skills developed in one specific course were not transferable to other subjects; learning Latin verbs could not improve a pupil's general ability to remember.[40]

Accordingly, like Dewey and Hall, Thorndike was highly critical of the traditional school, but he differed from Dewey in his belief that human learning was based on "simple, semi-mechanical phenomena . . . which animal learning discloses" and in his claim that these phenomena could be understood in purely neurological terms.[41] More important, Thorndike regarded intelligence as essentially fixed at birth and he was highly pessimistic about education's ability to modify individuals.[42] He differed sharply from Dewey in the elitist conclusions he drew from his thinking about intelligence. Thorndike maintained that "in the long run it has paid the 'masses' to be ruled by intelligence" and that "the natural processes which give power to men of ability to gain and keep it are not . . . unmoral." While he, too, supported the ideal of democracy, he differed radically from Dewey in his political philosophy. "The argument for democracy," Thorndike held, "is not that it gives power to all men without distinction, but that it gives greater freedom for ability and talent to attain power."[43]

Thus, while progressive education, the essential core of which was formed by Dewey's ideas, was part of a general movement to change American education in the twentieth century, it differed in important ways from other reform efforts. The quest for "efficiency," represented by Thorndike's thinking, was an important aspect of twentieth century educational reform, but the progressives were not primarily concerned with efficiency. Dewey did criticize "waste" in education, but his emphasis was quite different from that of those who promoted businesslike methods; for him the question was not "one of the waste of money . . . the primary waste is that of human life."[44]

Further, while Dewey emphasized a broad scientific approach to education, he differed from other educational reformers who defined the role of science much more narrowly. For example, one important thread in twentieth-century educational reform was the effort to construct a curriculum scientifically by basing it on surveys of the information and skills children would need as adults. These efforts of "scientific" curriculum specialists to build a new, more efficient school program were fundamentally flawed from the viewpoint of the progressives. The curriculum experts were intent on building the schools' program on the basis of what was seen as useful for functioning in society as it was. This was contrary to the fundamental thrust of Dewey's thought, with its basic premise that all aspects of life were constantly changing. Furthermore, while progressive educators wanted the curriculum to include skills that would be useful to the learner, this was not enough. Dewey aimed at building a better society and this could not come from a program that prepared children to adjust to present conditions. Attempts to "select subject matter by wide collection and accurate measurement of data" were only appropriate, Dewey said, for those who "want schools to perpetuate the present order," not for schools that believed that a "social order different in quality and direction from the present is desirable and that schools should strive to educate with social change in view."[45]

Progressive educators were also suspicious of another educational reform that invoked the prestige of science, the burgeoning educational testing movement.[46] Dewey and other progressives were interested in identifying individual differences and in promoting the needs of the individual child (which could be determined by careful testing), but their emphasis was quite different. Unlike those who drew their inspiration from Thorndike's scientific psychology, they were wary of using tests to assign pupils to special classes. More important, they were hostile to the idea that IQ tests measured an unchangeable entity.[47]

In the 1920s, two decades after Dewey wrote *The School and Society*, a number of schools were attempting to carry out his ideas. The newly formed Progressive Education Association provided an institutional framework for spreading the ideas of those committed to progressive pedagogy. It adopted a statement of purpose made up of seven principles, most of which were fully congruent with the principles Dewey had announced twenty years earlier. For example, the organization stood for the idea that in a progressive school "Interest [should be] the Motive of All Work" and it saw a progressive teacher as "a Guide, Not a Task-Master." The organization, like Dewey, viewed the progressive school as "a laboratory" where new ideas could be tried out, thereby becoming "a leader in educational movements."[48]

Yet the emphasis of the progressive education movement in the 1920s was somewhat different from Dewey's. While Dewey had recognized the importance of art in the curriculum, some progressive schools now made this the very core of their curriculum. They centered their program in the arts and emphasized the school's role in promoting creative self-expression. As Lawrence Cremin points out, this "pedagogical version of the expressionist credo" reflected a broad attack on Victorian aesthetics and the "Puritanism" of American culture in the 1920s.[49]

Second, while the progressives of the 1920s agreed with Dewey that the school should recognize that the child came to school with interests that were not exclusively academic, they differed from him by standing the traditional curriculum on its head. Instead of neglecting the nonintellectual interests of their pupils, they were in danger of leaving academics out of the schools' programs.

A third important new aspect of progressive education in the 1920s was an intense concern for the psychological development of children.[50] An interest in the emotional needs of children was implicit in Dewey's call for a recognition that the child came to school with a well-developed curiosity and certain skills and interests and, indeed, Dewey played an important role in the founding of the Child Study Department in the Chicago public schools.[51] But in the 1920s some progressive schools went much further. Reflecting the new American awareness of the work of Freud, they focused on the emotional needs of children and some progressive schools began to blur the distinction between lessons and therapeutic interventions.[52]

The emphasis in progressive education in the 1920s on the artistic and psychological needs of children reflected the new concerns of American intellectuals in the period after World War I. Equally reflective of the period was the virtual disappearance from the progressive agenda of Dewey's notion that the school was to play an important role in the reform of the larger society. Social reform had no place in the seven principles of the Progressive Education Association.

In the 1930s, when organized progressive education matured and reached a high point in its influence, it underwent further changes. One of these was very much in harmony with Dewey's thought. In the midst of the depression, some progressive educators embraced Dewey's hope for social reform through education, and the 1930s marked a high point in the history of attempts to reform society through its schools.

On the other hand, as Dewey's educational ideas were adopted by more and more professional educators in the 1930s, they were subtly altered in the process of their wider dissemination. Increasingly, administrators used the language of progressive education to justify policies that were not in harmony with Dewey's goals. More important, as aspects of progressivism became part of educational orthodoxy, the potential anti-intellectualism of the movement came to the fore.

One way of describing some of these changes in progressive education is through an examination of the career of one of its most important leaders, William Heard Kilpatrick. Born in 1871 in the rural South, Kilpatrick was the son of a Baptist minister.[53] He grew up with a deep commitment to religion, but as a student at Mercer University he was profoundly influenced by Darwin's *Origin* and moved far from the fundamentalist creed in which he had been raised. Like Dewey, Kilpatrick did graduate work at Johns Hopkins. But unlike Dewey, he did not move directly into the college classroom; he became an elementary and high school teacher and principal in rural Georgia. Although he had had no formal preparation for teaching, Kilpatrick revealed a natural talent for it and an instinctive empathy and respect for children. He enlisted their cooperation rather than punishing them and innovated in a number of ways, including eliminating report cards as devices that only encouraged destructive competition and a focus on grades rather than learning. The ambitious young Kilpatrick soon accepted a faculty position at Mercer and finally moved to Teachers College of Columbia University, first as a student and then as one of its most influential faculty members.

Kilpatrick acknowledged the influence of many of the men who were shaping educational thought at the time, including Francis Parker and G. Stanley Hall, but Dewey's teachings were crucial. Dewey (who had come to Columbia in 1905), "remade [his] philosophy of life and education."[54] An extremely popular teacher and an influential writer and lecturer, Kilpatrick was to be the major interpreter of Dewey's educational philosophy.[55] While Dewey was never regarded as a sparkling teacher, Kilpatrick attracted so many students that his classes were always overcrowded. Students reported that Kilpatrick's courses changed their lives: "I see things differently now, the whole world is different." During summer sessions, so many teachers wanted to take Kilpatrick's courses that no classroom or auditorium at Columbia could accommodate them all. One of his students reports that "[s]tudents in his classes became imbued with a missionary zeal, with a desire to act and live differently, to go back to their own environments and to change things . . . [T]he enthusiasm and the love that Kilpatrick begot from his students were beyond all imagination."[56] In the 1930s many teachers identified progressive education with the thought of William Heard Kilpatrick.

Although Dewey accepted Kilpatrick's interpretation of his thought, and wrote an introduction to a laudatory biography of Kilpatrick, there are differences in emphasis in the two men's versions of progressive education.[57] Kilpatrick was a great popularizer, but he was not a philosopher and he showed a marked aversion to abstract thought. Lacking Dewey's subtlety, Kilpatrick emphasized the practical and the anti-intellectual aspects of Dewey's thought, thereby distorting it in crucial ways.

Kilpatrick's most important contribution to educational practice was the project method in which children would learn what they needed to know as they pursued a topic that interested them. This provided an important way of overcoming the passive model of learning that both he and Dewey had rejected. In an activity curriculum, projects, chosen by children with the help of their teachers, would necessarily enlist their interests and would encourage their active participation in learning. With the project method, the artificial barriers between school subjects would be broken down. Children would learn reading, writing, arithmetic and other areas of the curriculum as they worked on a large project as, for example, the children of New York's Lincoln School did when they spent a year studying boats. The project method, as originally described by Kilpatrick in 1918, provided a balance between meeting the needs and interests of children. It recognized that teachers could play an important role in leading children to discover new interests, even resorting temporarily to compulsion "if compulsion will result in such learning that sets free some self-continuing activity . . . before harmful concomitants have been set up."[58] In his subsequent writings, however, Kilpatrick increasingly denigrated the importance of traditional school subjects. In 1936 Kilpatrick still echoed Dewey when he said the "new curriculum must . . . put first things first. The child must for us come before subject matter as such." But, in a parenthetical phrase, he revealed a crucial difference in emphasis: "Subject matter—*if any reader be concerned for it*—will be called this way better into play than is usual now."[59]

Kilpatrick's anti-intellectual stance is clear in his discussions of his own academic field—mathematics. The problem with the teaching of mathematics was that it had been "taught . . . to too many." While he recog ized that algebra and mathematics based on algebra were "essential to civilization," he emphasized that they were "practically useless to most citizens." Certain kinds of mathematical training, he argued, were actually harmful in that they promoted the wrong kind of thinking. For example, since geometry is a closed system it requires deduction from accepted principles, a kind of reasoning that, according to Kilpatrick, is misleading when applied to the problems of daily life.[60]

Kilpatrick and Dewey differed sharply in their views of the role of academic subject matter. While Kilpatrick claimed that the proponents of the "newer type of curriculum are not . . . indifferent to subject matter" and maintained that "they need it and expect to use it," his emphasis was clearly different from Dewey's.[61] For Dewey, subject matter was important. It represented "the essential ingredients of the culture to be perpetuated in . . . an organized form" and he held that a thorough knowledge of subject matter would "protect" teachers from "the haphazard efforts" they might make if "the meaning had not been standardized." Good teachers, Dewey argued, needed to understand children but they needed first to have such a deep understanding of subject matter that it was always ready to be used in "interaction with the pupils' present needs and capacities."[62] Kilpatrick, on the other hand, put love of children first in his list of the requirements for being a good teacher.[63]

Moreover, for Dewey, as children matured they came closer and closer to being able to understand subject matter as adults did and the curriculum could become more subject-centered.[64] Kilpatrick, on the other hand, argued that the program of "teaching . . . by activities, not by subjects" was not only applicable to elementary education, but that it should replace the subject-centered curriculum of secondary schools for most students.[65]

Kilpatrick also differed from Dewey in his acceptance of the increasing emphasis of post–World War I progressivism on the role of schooling in promoting "mental hygiene," that is, creating classroom settings that promoted psychological health. According to Kilpatrick, an important result that derived from a "well-managed regime of purposeful activity . . . freed from artificial and external demands of subject matter requirements" was to prevent "personality maladjustment." The activity curriculum, he argued, followed "nature's road to mental health."[66] This was an important shift in emphasis. While Dewey argued that education should foster personal growth and that schools should be concerned with the needs of the whole child, he did not identify teaching with psychother-apy. In his support for an increasingly psychologized school pro-gram, Kilpatrick's version of progressive education was more anti-intellectual than Dewey's.

Kilpatrick did, however, support Dewey's thought on educa-tion's role in social change and he played an important role in reviving progressive education's social reform agenda. In 1933, Kil-patrick, with a group of like-minded colleagues (including Dewey), published *The Educational Frontier,* a collection of essays which ar-gued that the crisis of the depression challenged schools to play an important role in the required restructuring of society.[67] A year earlier, George Counts had challenged progressive educators to make their schools institutions that would "Dare . . . [to] Build A New Social Order." Kilpatrick and his group of "frontier" theorists enthusiastically supported this call, arguing that the schools should help to reshape society to make America more equal and more democratic.

The frontier group represented the most radical version of Dewey's vision. Although their efforts aroused a campaign against progressive education by political conservatives, they were quite ineffectual in achieving their goal of transforming America through the schools. Despite rhetoric proclaiming the dawn of a new age of collectivism, their naive premise that teachers could lead a social revolution against the interests of powerful business-men and established classes understandably failed to attract many teachers. Even at the height of the movement, their journal, *The Social Frontier,* attracted fewer than four thousand subscribers. As David Tyack has noted, "[t]he everyday life of administrators and teachers did not much reflect the aspirations of educational revolu-tionaries."[68] But Kilpatrick and the other Social Frontier thinkers did help to restore a balance within the progressive education movement. They led an effort to recover Dewey's vision of the progressive school as an institution concerned with social reform, a vision that had been all but lost in the individualistic, child-cen-tered, progressivism of the 1920s.

Despite the changes in emphasis, it is possible to provide a work-ing definition of progressive education. The movement changed over time and it had distinct and somewhat different meanings for different people; it represented a constellation of ideas, not a set program. Yet it differed markedly from other contemporary educa-tional movements, such as the drive for educational efficiency, just as the thought of Dewey differed sharply from that of Hall and Thorndike.

The movement's philosophical basis hinged on Dewey's premise that all aspects of life are constantly evolving and that all human goals must, therefore, be regarded as provisional. This led to a belief that the schools' ultimate task was to prepare people for life and for change. Because life is flux, no single stage is superior to another; childhood should not be regarded as mere preparation for adulthood. Children have the right to live fully as children. Schools must recognize that the joys and opportunities of childhood should not be subordinated to future goals. They should use children's native curiosity, not subordinate it to an arbitrary, preselected curriculum.

Dewey's devotion to idea of continual change and his belief that individuals could play a role in molding evolutionary forces to create a better society gave schools a crucial role. But his theories stood in direct contrast to the traditional view that education was to be a tool to help children become part of the existing social system. Thus, from its beginnings, progressive education was tied to social reform. Specifically, it had a genuine compassion for immigrants and it shared Jane Addams's commitment to bettering the lot of the poor and dispossessed. It rejected the fatalism of William Graham Sumner and Herbert Spencer and held that a more humane society could be achieved through a program of action directed by informed intelligence.

While Dewey's philosophy was the basis for progressive education, behind it stood a well-established pattern of American thought. Progressives shared Horace Mann's vision of a messianic role for education, the belief that the common school could provide the alternative to social turmoil and could mitigate the effects of economic inequality. Progressive education shared the traditional American belief in progress and its liberal faith that all conflicts could be resolved by people of goodwill. Conversely, it lacked a vision of the darker side of human nature. It had no clear sense of evil. The progressives inherited the vision of Ralph Waldo Emerson rather than the darker views of Emerson's Calvinist ancestors. In the words of Reinhold Niebuhr, progressive educators were "Children of Light," laudable for their devotion to promoting the social good, but weakened by their failure to recognize the reality of evil.

While progressives were sometimes viewed by their enemies as dangerous radicals who threatened the American way of life, they saw themselves as devoted to democracy, representing the genuine American ideology of Jefferson and Lincoln. Their social radicalism was limited by their acceptance (for the most part) of technology and industrialism as well as the private ownership of the means of production. Their political radicalism was limited by their fervent belief in reform though education rather than through conflict.

How the progressive's ideas were applied to schooling varied over time and among different educators. But in the 1920s and 1930s there was some agreement on a definition of progressive schools. First, progressives agreed that a progressive school was one that followed a child-centered rather than a subject-centered curriculum, a school which mobilized children's natural desire to learn.

Second, they agreed that it was a school concerned with meeting the needs of the "whole child," promoting children's emotional and physical needs as well as their intellectual development. This agreement, however, masked a great deal of controversy about the ideal balance between intellectual concerns and meeting other needs within the school program and on how much emphasis on subject matter should remain.

Third, there was agreement that a progressive school was one in which children would play an active role in determining the content of their education. Here, too, educators disagreed on how much real responsibility the schools could give to pupils. There was less agreement, even superficially, on a final point. Some progressives believed that a progressive school should have a program that would help children to develop in ways that would lead them to become reformers, to improve the world outside of the classroom.

Yet these disagreements were like quarrels within a family in which the members share a core of common assumptions. Even when they disagree, they appeal to this common core to justify their position on any issue. It is possible, therefore, despite disagreements, to recognize a distinct movement that was progressive education and, given this general definition, determine its influence on American classrooms.

2

OLD WINE, NEW BOTTLES

*I*n the fall of 1940, seven-year-old Tony Bailey, a refugee from war-torn Europe, arrived in Oakwood, Ohio, a posh suburb of Dayton. Tony had been sent to America by his parents to escape the German bombardment of London. Now he was off to his first American school, Harman Avenue Grade School. He was initially assigned to the second grade, but was advanced to the third after a few days (probably reflecting the fact that the American school had not pushed young children as fast as the English school Tony had left). He has warm memories of his American school days. "Our class project that year was Indians. We made wampum with beads and string, drew tepees, wigwams, pueblos and long houses. Miss Seitner directed us in a play called *How an Indian Chief Is Chosen*, and took a photograph . . . showing me and my boy classmates doing various heel-and-toe exercises in the guise of being Indian braves." Tony spent two years in a Catholic school and then returned to Harman: "When I reached the sixth grade," he recalls, "our class project was maps. (I had missed dinosaurs in fourth grade and volcanoes in fifth.)"[1]

The school Tony attended in suburban Dayton had developed a curriculum that united the traditional subjects around significant topics that could engage the interests of their pupils. The school he attended was an example of the successful dissemination of the ideas of progressive education. For Tony, Harman Street school represented American public education, but how typical was his school? To what degree had the progressives changed American public schools?

Progressive educators of the 1920s and 1930s had aimed at nothing short of a transformation of American education. Although many of them worked in private schools, their aim was to restructure public education as well as private. Lawrence Cremin has argued that progressivism had a profound effect on the public schools: "The twenties and thirties were an age of reform in American education, as thousands of local districts adopted one or another of the elements in the progressive program."[2] But Cremin devoted only a few pages of his larger study of progressivism to its impact on public schools; he made little attempt to assess the impact of the ideas of progressive educators at the local, classroom level in typical American schools. Since he concentrated on a few examples of progressive education in outstanding school systems, Cremin's evidence led him to exaggerate the impact of progressivism.[3] Diane Ravitch's history of American education after World War II also claims that progressive education transformed the educational aims of American schools. On the basis of a "sampling of diverse districts," Ravitch concludes that the progressive curriculum revision movement of the late 1930s led to "a profound shift in the stated goals of schooling, away from concerns with intellectual development . . . to concern for social and emotional development."[4] A careful look at actual classrooms, however, shows that progressive ideas had little effect on what went on in typical American elementary schools.

Determining the impact of progressive education on American public elementary schools is a process that is fraught with difficulty. To begin with, there is the sheer size of the American educational enterprise—in 1940 over eighteen million children attended 183,000 public American elementary schools, housed in buildings ranging from ill-ventilated hovels to impressive architectural monuments. Furthermore, control over American schools was extremely localized. Traditional suspicion of state (let alone federal) intervention meant that most decisions affecting the education of American children were made at the local district level, either by one of the approximately 117 thousand administrative units responsible for the functioning of public schools or by local administrators and teachers.[5] Although by the 1930s, there was, as David Tyack has pointed out, "considerable uniformity of educational ideology . . . and pedagogical programs" as well as "strong pressures toward homogenization," the locus of power over the curriculum and teaching methods was still at the district level.[6] Accordingly, the federal and state governments collected few statistics on the curriculum or teaching methods; their interest was largely the financial aspects of education and certain programs (such as vocational education) that had attracted special support.

Moreover, in the absence of sound data on what was actually being done in American classrooms, the facts have been obscured by the rhetoric of educational advocacy. In an effort to persuade schools to adopt innovations, progressives often described educational experiments in glowing terms, as did John and Evelyn Dewey in *Schools of To-Morrow*. Educational journals of the interwar period were filled with descriptions of innovative schools, but few articles attempted to depict what was going on in more typical classrooms. This "Schools of Tomorrow" educational journalism gives a false impression of the degree of innovation in American education. On the other hand, those who favored retrenchment in the face of the fiscal crisis of the 1930s also exaggerated the extent of innovations in the schools as they decried the cost of "fads and frills" that had been added to the curriculum. The cumulative effect of reading these ideologically motivated discussions gives the impression of great ferment in the American classroom—a conclusion that other evidence does not support.

Finally, the degree of educational innovation is obscured by an understandable willingness on the part of educators to head off criticism by giving old practices new labels. If a combined social studies course used the same materials previously taught as separate history, geography, and civics courses, the change was likely to conceal the nature of the school's commitment to educational innovation.

Despite these difficulties, however, there are ways of establishing the nature of the impact of progressivism on American public elementary schools in the interwar period. (The emphasis is on elementary schools because it is clear that secondary schools were far less likely to substitute child-centered for subject-centered curricula.) While chapters 3 and 4 assess the impact of progressivism by looking closely at a few schools, concentrating on four districts in the Chicago area, the present chapter uses the scattered information that is available about school practices on a national level.

Although it is difficult to measure exactly a concept as illusive as child-centered education, there are indicators that suggest the degree of progressivism in a school system. For example, while the ratio of fixed to portable school desks is not by itself an index of progressivism, there is a relationship between the kind of seats a school board chooses to purchase and its attitude toward education: a school system that continued to purchase fixed, bolted-down desks was not interested in a child-centered curriculum. Similarly, although a teacher who received her training in a thoroughly orthodox normal school might still become a dedicated progressive teacher, there is a relationship between the educational philosophies of teacher-training institutions and the views of their graduates. The relationship is not sufficiently direct to establish an accurate index of progressivism, yet here is another indicator that is suggestive and which, with other such indicators, allows us to form some assessment of the progressivism of American public education.

If children were to be at the center of progressive education, progressive reformers clearly saw it would take highly trained, sensitive teachers to place them there. If rote learning and a rigidly subject-centered curriculum were to be eliminated, the role of the teacher would be crucial. For progressives, then, there was no such thing as a progressive classroom without a progressive teacher. There is no doubt that there were talented progressive teachers in the 1920s and 1930s—teachers who used the spontaneous enthusiasm of their pupils as an important factor in establishing the setting for significant learning experiences, teachers who were able to differentiate the needs of individual children and who could structure situations that would allow all children to achieve and attain a sense of self-worth. But if such teachers were typical, we would expect to find that teacher-training institutions were at least attempting to foster this kind of education. There is little evidence that they tried.

To begin with, in the early 1930s American elementary school teachers were not highly trained. An overwhelming majority of them had no more than two years of normal school education, while fully one-fourth had even less professional training. Only ten percent of elementary teachers had sufficient training to earn a B.A. Moreover, they could not claim that professional experience made up for their lack of formal training since public schools "were taught predominantly by young, unmarried women with little teacher experience." The training of faculty members of the teacher-training institutions was also singularly unimpressive; over fifty percent of the faculty members of state teacher colleges and normal schools had one year or less of graduate work, and most of them had no personal experience in elementary education.[7]

The typical normal school and teachers' college was not a center for progressive education. Even the best of the teachers' colleges and normal schools were remarkably traditional in their teaching methods.[8] Moreover, the educational philosophy of faculty members at teacher-training institutions was, in large part, quite traditional. A detailed study of the educational philosophy of teachers of teachers made in the early 1930s reveals that although the majority of faculty members had "acquired the vocabulary of various trends and movements in education," they had "failed to gain a deeper understanding of the philosophy which underlies them." Despite the general impression that "the traditional school" had disappeared, a study of teachers' colleges and normal schools found that faculty members "in significant degree . . . hold to those purposes, ideals, and practices which are in basic agreement with the older philosophy underlying the traditions of American education." The study concluded that faculty members represented "an influence which makes for continuance of a large part of the traditional in education rather than a break with it."[9]

If teachers were to be in the vanguard of educational change, they needed the power that comes from the ability to see themselves as respected professionals. During the 1920s and especially in the 1930s, while there was a surplus of teachers, many communities began to require additional years of preparation for candidates for teaching positions. These efforts to restrict entry supported teachers' aspirations and desires for professionalization. But despite efforts to change the public image of teachers and to make teaching into a profession, public school teachers found they still lacked respect and they were still subject to humiliating restrictions. A sociologist who studied the "typical" midwestern community of "Elmtown" noted that one of the major objectives of the town's board of education was "seeing that teachers conform, in the classroom and in their personal lives, to the most conservative economic, political, religious, and moral doctrines prevailing in the local culture." In the larger community of "Middletown," teachers were seen as "meager souls, out of touch with life, the sort of people one can hire for the wages of a clerk in a retail store." They were "people who couldn't make good in business."[10]

By the end of the decade, although the rhetoric of progressivism had permeated educational discourse, classroom teachers, like their instructors in normal schools and teachers' colleges, often revealed through their teaching practices that there was a large gap between a theoretical progressivism and their activities in the classroom. Just before World War II, the superintendent of a small Massachusetts school district reported on educational theory and practices in his schools. He noted that while teachers had "learned the words of modern education" they did not, in fact, carry out these ideas and their classrooms were "teacher-centered" rather than "child-centered." He speculated that this might be due to "faulty understanding," to conflicts between newer ideas and "old and thoroughly learned patterns of behavior," or to a simple "failure of the teachers to recognize that what they do is not what they say is best." Despite the teachers' acceptance of the principles espoused by the progressives, these ideas had not noticeably affected the way they taught.[11]

Although the progressive teacher would be the most important factor in establishing a progressive classroom, the official course of study, whether developed by individual teachers or by a school system, set parameters for the progressivism of any classroom. On the eve of World War II, an analysis of some eighty-five thousand courses of study by a group from Teachers College, Columbia University, reached conclusions that were clearly disappointing to those who had hoped that progressivism had made important inroads in American classrooms. While recognizing a significant trend to find new patterns for organizing materials and experiences—a "trend to find new bottles, if not new wine"—the study concluded that "in most cases the content remains more or less the same." Moreover, "the majority of courses still reveal no significant change in organization from the traditional separate subject matter point of view." When activities had been added to course material, "the activities and experiences seem to be merely addenda appended in an effort to rejuvenate a more formal academic outline of content." Most "new" courses of study did not reflect a change in educational philosophy, but represented a superficial change in traditional academic subjects.[12]

Classroom furniture provides another clue to the progressivism of American elementary schools. Progressive education could, of course, take place in the most unlikely setting, but progressive educators favored portable furniture over the older, bolted-down, desks because teachers could rearrange these desks to suit the needs and activities of the pupils throughout the day. Portable desks facilitated dividing a classroom into small groups and informal instructional settings. Although a progressive teacher could obviously function in a room with stationary furniture, and a traditional school system could use portable furniture as if it were still bolted to the floor, the decision to purchase portable instead of fixed furniture offers some clue to a school system's educational philosophy. According to statistics of the school seating industry, it was not until 1931 that a majority of new desks sold were portable, and as late as 1934 stationary school desks still accounted for almost forty percent of new desks sold. The single most popular kind of seating sold in 1934 was still the fixed, nonadjustable combina-

1. A school in a community built for farm workers by the Farm Security Administration, Eleven Miles Corner, Arizona, ca. 1940. While the classroom is brightly lit and modern, the children's desks have been bolted to the floor, making it difficult to use them for the kinds of group activities that progressive educators promoted. Photograph by Russell Lee. Farm Security Administration. United States Library of Congress, Department of Prints and Photographs. (Negative number: LC-USF 34-71960-D.)

2. Before World War II, thousands of students attended one-room schools like this one, which was a converted two-room dwelling near Taos, New Mexico. The photographer noted, "Of fifteen pupils, six were absent the day picture was taken" (December 1941). Photograph by Irving Rusinow. Records of the Bureau of Agricultural Economics, National Archives. (Negative number 83-G-41768.)

tion seat and desk.[13] Although the trend in school seating was clearly toward portable furniture, in the mid-1930s many school systems were still purchasing old-fashioned desks suited to the traditional classroom, and as late as 1940 school seating manufacturers were still advertising bolted-down models. (For the segregated schools southern blacks attended in the 1930s, even bolted-down desks would have been a major improvement—forty percent of these schools had no desks at all.)[14]

Increasingly in the 1930s, the progressive concern for the well-being of the whole child involved a serious commitment to the mental health of pupils. For progressives like Carleton Washburne, "mental hygiene" was a crucial aspect of progressive education. This concern was expressed in the Winnetka, Illinois, schools by having a team of psychiatrists, psychologists, and social workers to counsel with children and to aid teachers by making them aware of the psychological needs of their pupils.

Although a few other communities provided similar facilities, they were clearly exceptional.[15] The rarity of public school employment of school psychologists and social workers in the 1920s and 1930s is evidenced by the almost total lack of statistics on the number employed. In 1940, the national professional school social work association had only 209 members. There are no estimates of the number of school psychologists in this period, but the fact that New York State only had sixty-seven qualified school psychologists in 1939 is suggestive of the national picture. Even in those school systems which established guidance programs, the impact of these programs was often minimal. For example, in "Middletown" the guidance program was "primarily concerned with academic guidance, leaving social guidance and job guidance largely untouched."[16] An extensive commitment to the provision of psychological services for pupils came only after World War II.

The picture of American educational practice that emerges from the scattered statistics and studies of the 1930s shows that American schools had not made very significant steps toward implementing John Dewey's vision of child-centered education. These observations are reinforced by a more detailed examination of one state, New York, for which an excellent comprehensive survey is available. New York is not a typical state; it might well be expected to be in advance of other states in instituting progressive educational innovations. Therefore, the prevalence of progressive practices in the elementary schools of New York can serve as an important clue to the impact of progressivism on the schools of other states.

From 1935 to 1938, a group of educational experts under the

direction of Luther Gulick undertook an extensive investigation into the "character and cost of public education in New York State," culminating in over twelve separate volumes and numerous articles. Professor Gulick calls it "the last of the great surveys."[17] Although the Regents' Inquiry (as the study was officially named) was not concerned with the impact of educational ideas, the volumes and manuscript records of the survey are a rich source for understanding education in New York in the last of the prewar years and contain valuable information on the extent of progressive innovations in the state's schools.

The inquiry is an unusually useful source for several reasons. First, the study was not done by the state education department, but by educational experts who came from outside the state, so that those who conducted the study had few personal axes to grind. Second, it was aimed at finding what was happening in typical schools rather than reporting on exceptional cases. Finally, the survey provided a rich source of data by concentrating on an extended analysis of a limited number of topics. Rather than amassing reams of statistics on the whole state, the inquiry staff began by making a detailed study of the social and economic characteristics of the communities of New York and then selected fifty of these which could be considered typical of the state's diverse school districts.[18] The schools of these communities became the subject of detailed investigation (including classroom observations) and analysis. The thoroughness of the study was unsurpassed in American education.

The state's elementary schools were the focus of a series of studies under the direction of Leo J. Brueckner of the University of Minnesota. The title of his summary volume—*The Changing Elementary School*—may have been ironic, for the whole thrust of the study was the degree to which elementary education had not been adapted to current educational theory. Brueckner's staff examined courses of study, curricula, and teaching methods and in each case noted their failure to conform to the standard of progressive educational theory.[19] They found that the elementary curriculum was dominated by state syllabi (many out of date) and textbooks. "The purpose of instruction appears to be largely to get pupils to master organized bodies of formalized, inert subject matter." Generally, the academic subjects were kept in their own separate compartments and not linked (as progressive educators had urged). Furthermore, "[l]ittle is done by many teachers to relate much of what is taught to the experiences of every day life." The survey staff found that "most of the teaching observed was very formal and along traditional lines," emphasizing "the acquisition of bodies of materials . . ." Because of their "undue stress on the teaching of specific facts and skills," these schools tended to "neglect the development of social understanding, rich interests, effective study habits, and worthy use of leisure time."[20]

The more detailed studies by subject-matter specialists supported these conclusions. William S. Gray and Bernice Leary examined reading programs, visiting 310 classrooms in 72 schools. They rated these programs on a five-point scale and found that over sixty percent were in the lowest category: "A narrow, formal type of instruction which was provided during the reading period two and three decades ago, and which gave major emphasis to mastery of the mechanics of reading rather than to the broader ends which reading may serve in child life." As an example of the type of instruction offered by a school in the lower part of this category, they described a classroom where the children were required to sit "in position, hands folded, eyes on blackboard"; their only relaxation from the drill was "through a different kind of formality, when windows were opened and all stood erect breathing 'in-out, in-out' to the teacher's formula." In most classrooms the reading period was devoted to oral reading from a basic text; very little time was devoted to "voluntary, independent reading," and adjustment for individual differences was "more frequently hoped for than attained."[21]

Arithmetic instruction was also dominated by traditional ideas and implemented in old-fashioned methods. Typical arithmetic instruction ignored the social aspects of the subject and its relevance to the world outside the classroom, emphasizing instead computational skills. "In many of the lessons observed the pupils merely copied long lists of examples from the blackboard and worked them at their seats, a deadly routine procedure." Fewer than ten percent of the teachers observed made any attempt to "relate the arithmetic being studied to local situations."[22]

The review of the state's program in English gave further evidence of the absence of progressive education in the elementary schools. Dora V. Smith, the inquiry's expert on English instruction, described one of the classes she observed:

> A first grade class sat bolt upright in straight rows and in seats nailed to the floor. At a signal from the teacher that the "language" lesson was about to begin, each child clasped his hands on the edge of his desk, set his feet squarely on the floor, and prepared for a ten minute solo

performance of the story of *The Three Bears* by a child
obviously superior to the rest of them in attainment in
language.

Smith acknowledged that such an English lesson seemed "incred-
ible"—except to those who had "spent considerable time in . . .
classrooms"—but, she maintained, "this formula for the development of language power . . . is still the most generally practiced
procedure in use."[23] She found that over sixty percent of New
York's teachers "still adhere to a program of segregated, non-func-
tional teaching of English skills." Moreover, teachers made very
little effort to adjust material to the individual needs and abilities
of students: "No basic philosophy of individual need seemed to
prevail, but rather a sense of the necessity for coaching certain
weak pupils so that they might meet an arbitrary standard set."[24]
  In the social studies, the inquiry staff found a mixture of progressive and old-fashioned practices. On the one hand, the investi-
gators reported that social studies teachers were, for the most part,
quite imaginative and were able to lead discussions in which they
asked more "thought questions" than questions designed to elicit
factual material. They made extensive use of field trips and conducted relatively democratic classrooms: "The prevailing practices
can probably be described as 'guidance without domination.'" The
report went on to suggest that "an investigator who knew schools
of thirty years ago might well be impressed with the degree of
pupil freedom."[25] On the other hand, as in the other subjects, the
state syllabi were rigid, and few local syllabi were better. In most
cases the social studies were not integrated (as the progressives
maintained they should be) but consisted of parallel courses in
history and geography, with little reference to the other social sciences. "The curriculum as pupils experience it," the report pointed
out, "is largely a matter of acquiring factual information. While
such information may be justifiably memorized, the higher objectives of understandings, attitudes, and skills are not adequately
emphasized."[26] The report did not attempt to reconcile its praise of
the quality of teaching with its low estimate of the curriculum as
experienced by pupils.
  A careful reader of the reports of the Regents' Inquiry is forced
to conclude that the movement for a more child-centered school
had failed to make a great impact on the New York schools. In the
late 1930s, the elementary schools of New York still offered a relatively traditional subject-centered curriculum, and they were

staffed by teachers who, for the most part, adhered to traditional philosophies of education.

New York's failure to adopt progressive ideas was by no means unique. A study of innovation in Pennsylvania schools concluded that the process of diffusing new educational ideas was extremely slow. The report recognized that recent controversies in education left "the general impression . . . that the schools, by and large, have adopted the practices that are debated." But, despite the charge that the ills of society are a result of "progressive education," schools had not changed a great deal. "[I]n the schools of Pennsylvania today and, the authors venture to say, in the schools of America, we find little manifestation of the practices subject to controversy. As a matter of fact, the succeeding waves of 'reform' which have come and passed in this century have left discouragingly little mark."[27]

Yet advocates for a more child-centered school could point to some hopeful signs in the 1930s. Increasingly, educators with a progressive orientation were moving into influential positions in the hierarchies of state education departments. While their roles there were largely advisory, they could use their positions to disseminate progressive principles. Accordingly, the curriculum bulletins of state education departments frequently advocated progressive ideas.

The role of a progressive state department of education can be seen in the most famous attempt to change the schools of a single state, the Virginia curriculum project. Begun in 1931 under the direction of Hollis P. Caswell of George Peabody College for Teachers, the project was based on using classroom teachers to revise the curriculum. The process eventually involved fifteen thousand Virginia teachers. They completely changed the state courses of study. Especially at the elementary level, the new courses tied the curriculum to both the interests of children and "social functions," such as "Communication and Transportation of Goods." Yet, although the project attracted national attention, it is not clear how much these changes affected classroom practices in Virginia.[28]

A more modest effort to promote educational progressivism at the state level began in 1935 in Alabama when the state superintendent appointed C. B. Smith to the newly created post of state director of the Division of Instruction. Significantly, Smith chose to prepare himself for his new duties by going to Columbia University Teachers College, the most important center for the dissemination of progressive educational ideas.

Beginning in 1936 and working closely with faculty members from Peabody, the state began issuing curriculum bulletins that took a progressive approach. Like the Virginia project, the Alabama program centered on "individual growth within the context of social aims." The approach was cautious. While a 1937 bulletin suggested that the interests of pupils should be taken into account, it refused to allow the interests of pupils define the curriculum. It cautioned that "[p]upil purposes should not be thought of as educational aims." Although the new state elementary course of study called for activity programs, it also called for skill development. But, according to the historian of progressive education in Alabama, there was no place in this conservative state for the radicalism of the Social Frontier thinkers. As was the case in Virginia, it is difficult to measure the impact of these state efforts. Some schools changed substantially, while in others the effects were "meager."[29]

At the same time that progressives were exerting more influence in state education departments, they were also beginning to have a significant effect on teacher-training institutions. By the eve of World War II, teachers' colleges had changed a great deal. A generation earlier, most normal schools were provincial institutions whose course of study bore little resemblance to the curriculum of liberal arts colleges or universities. Faculty members at most of these institutions rarely had much education beyond the B.A. In the 1920s and 1930s, however, most two-year normal schools became four-year teachers' colleges. During this transition they were subject to great pressure by accrediting associations to send their faculty to graduate schools for additional education. This pressure proved to be a significant factor in bringing new approaches to education to their campuses.

Because Teachers College of Columbia University had achieved a national reputation, a large number of faculty members from former normal schools chose its Morningside Heights campus for the graduate courses they needed. Thus Teachers College became a major center for the dissemination of the ideas of progressive educators. At Columbia, teachers of teachers took courses from such leading progressives as John Dewey, George Counts, and Harold Rugg and they were part of the standing-room-only audience for Kilpatrick's lectures on philosophy of education.

An example of the ways in which teacher training institutions changed can be seen by looking at one of them, Northern Illinois Normal School in DeKalb. In the early twentieth century, Northern, like other midwestern normal schools, was struggling for the right to train high school teachers; state universities were demanding

that high schools require at least a bachelor's degree for new teachers. In 1920, Northern responded by becoming a state teachers'
college and offering a four-year program. But for a number of years
the school continued to be primarily a two-year normal school.
(Until 1943, Northern continued to offer a two-year normal school
program for elementary teaching.) In 1926, it had a faculty of forty-
five. Less than half held bachelor's degrees and twenty percent of
the faculty members had received at least part of their education at
Northern. Four faculty members had attended Columbia Teachers
College. Despite the fact that it now offered a bachelor's degree to
some of its students, Northern's degrees were not accepted at face
value by universities; they required Northern's graduates to do
additional work before being accepted as candidates for higher degrees.

In 1935, however, the college won accreditation by the North
Central Association. As part of the accreditation process, the school
began to offer faculty members leaves of absence to work on higher
degrees. Significantly, many faculty members chose to take graduate courses in education rather than in the academic subject they
taught; these professional courses in educational philosophy and
methods were most likely to inculcate progressive principles. The
new policy resulted in a significant change in the status of the faculty. By 1940, ninety-six percent of the sixty-three faculty members
at Northern held at least a master's degree; eighteen (twenty-eight
percent) had attended Columbia Teachers College.[30]

Western Illinois State Teachers College showed a similar pattern.
According to Western's historian, the period from 1920 to 1940 was
one of increasing attention to professional methods courses and the
"latest educational doctrine out of Teachers College at Columbia"
soon found its way to the Western campus.[31]

Yet, the changing nature of the teachers' colleges had little effect
on the public schools of the 1930s, when jobs for newly trained
teachers were very scarce. Even when young teachers, inspired by
newly learned progressive ideas, found positions, they might face
a hostile superintendent, principal, or school board. Virgil Scott's
thinly disguised autobiographical novel quotes the superintendent
addressing the teachers of a small town in Ohio in 1936:

> Those of you who teach your first Shenkton class
> tomorrow have come directly from the college campus,
> from the classrooms where you learned a lot of theory.
> . . . Others of you have been away to school for the
> summer, and you have come back filled with ideas about
> project methods and core curricula and other Columbia

theory. And some of you . . . are hoping, perhaps, to put
a lot of that theory into practice . . . I don't want you to
get the idea that I have a quarrel with so-called
progressive education.

But, he continues, these methods simply won't work in his school.
The main job for teachers here is "[t]o keep three hundred and fifty
potential hoodlums quiet enough so that you can teach the remaining hundred something."

When the junior high school social science teacher nonetheless
proposes a project for his geography class, the principal tells him
that that isn't a good idea because the children would have to get
out of their seats: "You can't afford to let them get out of their seats
. . . They'd tear the place apart . . . brick by brick." Although he is
taken aback, the young teacher presses on, pointing out that if the
children are busy and interested they will not get out of control.
"Why don't you just take it easy?" the principal asks. "Why don't
you just let them read their books and then ask them questions?"

"I was thinking about motivation."

"Give them tests every day . . . That motivates them, and it kills
fifteen minutes of every class."[32]

Despite the impassioned discussions of progressive education in
the 1920s and 1930s, despite the marked progressivism of a few
school districts and the increasing importance of progressive ideas
in state education departments and teachers' colleges, it is clear
that by 1940 progressive education had not significantly altered the
broad pattern of American education. The call for a child-centered
school had, for the most part, been ignored. How do we account for
progressive education's lack of impact in most schools and explain
its success in a few school districts?

The role of the depression in discouraging educational innovation was of obvious importance. Many school districts found themselves cutting back and in no position to experiment with new approaches and programs. Everywhere music, art, and other
"nonessentials" were under fire from hard-pressed taxpayers, and
school boards were forced to retrench.[33] Under these circumstances, widespread adoption of progressive practices was extremely unlikely.

Moreover, the depression exacerbated previous problems.
School districts overcrowded in the 1920s found they had to defer

building programs in the 1930s. Schools operating on double shifts and concerned with the basic problem of finding enough seats for their pupils could not commit themselves to finding answers for less immediate problems.

For some elementary schools, particularly in rural areas, the problems were even more acute. In the early 1930s, Helen Hussman, fresh from her high school graduation, began teaching in a one-room school in western Oklahoma. She had few teaching supplies and no guidance from the county superintendent, yet she knew that she would be evaluated by her students' performance on the countywide annual exams. Accordingly, she spent most of her time in traditional ways—listening to recitations and outlining the required textbooks so that the older children could copy the information into their notebooks. For Helen, as for other rural teachers, an important concern was to maintain a building that approached the basic standards of health and safety.[34]

Thousands of schools, particularly in the South, lacked even basic sanitary facilities. Blacks attended schools of unbelievable squalor. A "typical" black school in east Texas was "a crude box shack built by the Negroes out of old slabs and scrap lumber." Its single classroom had "a few rough hewn seats," only enough for half of the fifty-two pupils. Because of the condition of the roof, school was dismissed whenever it rained. The only supplies provided by the school district was a broom.[35] For these schools, operating below the standards of the nineteenth century, progressive education was not a relevant concern.

Aside from economic considerations, other factors complicated the transformation of the schools. Although the philosophy of progressive education was beginning to be increasingly influential in teacher-training institutions, most classroom teachers before World War II had had their professional training when a more traditional approach prevailed. It was not until the postwar period that a large number of teachers who had received their training in progressive teacher-training colleges would enter the public schools.

Finally, it is important to recognize the genuinely radical implications of progressive rhetoric. Even if we discount the importance of the Social Frontier group, which urged a complete restructuring of American society, a genuine educational progressivism would challenge tradition in many ways. As Robert and Helen Lynd pointed out, to the people of "Middletown," the educational program that called for "education for individual differences" was generated by "remote 'philosophers' in university graduate schools of education." It was "no more consonant with certain

3. The One-Teacher Negro School in Veazy, South of Greensboro, Greene County, Georgia, 1941. The segregated schools of the rural south made a mockery of the American promise of equality of opportunity. Photograph by Jack Delano. Farm Security Administration. United States Library of Congress, Department of Prints and Photographs. (Negative number: LC-USF-46248-D.)

dominant elements in Middletown . . . than was the philosophy of Socrates with that of the Athens of his day." If such a program were implemented, it would lead thinking children to look behind cultural clichés, to "poke a finger through the paper wall and look in at the realities within."[36]

3

PROGRESSIVE SCHOOLS IN
THE 1930s

*I*n the period between the two world wars, progressive education was closely associated with independent schools. Such private schools as Margaret Naumburg's Walden, Francis Parker School in Chicago, and Lincoln School of Columbia University Teachers College were among the best-known exemplars of the new education in the 1930s. Freedom from bureaucratic regulation, as well as the ability to deal with a select group of students (and parents), allowed private schools to be flexible and receptive to innovation. A single individual, with a vision of a new kind of education, would find it easier to start a small, private school than to change a public school system. For Dewey, however, the schools' almost messianic role in building a better society could not be performed in these small niches. Dewey's commitment to an egalitarian society meant that the schools that served all the people, the public schools, had to be infused with progressive principles.[1]

Dewey's ideas were, of course, applied to some degree in public schools, and educators in the 1930s often used Dewey's language, pointing, for example, to the necessity for educating the "whole child." A few public school systems, such as the one Tony Bailey attended, went further. High on any list of progressive public schools, were those of Winnetka, Illinois. This chapter focuses on progressive education in Winnetka, with brief looks at several other progressive public school systems. The story of these schools shows how Dewey's ideas could operate within public school systems.

Located twenty-five miles north of downtown Chicago on Lake Michigan, Winnetka, Illinois, was (and still is) one of Chicago's wealthiest suburbs. The town was dominated by members of a wealthy elite, but Winnetka's residents were imbued with a special vision for their community. They sought to preserve in this wealthy suburb the idealized values of a New England village.[2] Accordingly, the town was permeated by a spirit of neighborliness, community, and a tradition of public service. Winnetka proved to be a natural setting for an experiment in progressive education in a public school system.[3] From 1919 to 1940, Winnetka schools embarked on a series of educational innovations that included such progressive features as an emphasis on art, student self-government, student-run business enterprises, and a large Department of Educational Counsel, ministering to the psychological needs of students (and staff). In the period between the two world wars, Winnetka's public schools achieved international recognition as centers for progressive education.

The story of Winnetka's commitment to innovative education began in the winter of 1911–12 when a group of wealthy Winnetka parents, most of whom had attended eastern prep schools and colleges, met to consider founding a new private school so that their children could attend a first-rate school close to home.[4] According to the story, as it had been passed on in the folklore of the village, one of the participants, Edwin Fetcher, proposed that instead of promoting a new private school, the group could work to improve the public schools and make them so outstanding that they would be proud to send their own children there.[5] The others agreed, providing Fetcher would run for school board president; he acceded, insisting, however, that several others also become candidates. The reformers rapidly won control of the board and proceeded to the task of reform.

In 1913 the board moved to fill the newly created post of superintendent and chose E. N. Rhodes, a principal in another suburban community, Oak Park. Under Rhodes, a number of progressive reforms were instituted, but it is not clear whether Rhodes or the board was responsible for most of these. Within a few years, board members, especially Fetcher and a Chicago pump manufacturer, Edward Yeomans, were convinced that Rhodes did not have the dynamism or the persuasive ability to make the Winnetka schools truly outstanding. Impressed by Frederic Burk's work in individualizing instruction at San Francisco State Normal College's Demonstration School, the board asked Burk to recommend a new superintendent. The man he recommended, Carleton Washburne, became the dynamic force behind educational reform in Winnetka.

Washburne was himself a product of progressive education. His mother, Marion, had been dissatisfied with the Chicago public schools and enrolled her children first in Parker's demonstration school at Cook County Normal and then in the private school that was later to be named Francis Parker. An enthusiastic participant in the child study movement, Marion Washburne was the first editor of Colonel Parker's journal, *The Course of Study*. She became a close friend of Parker, as well as of John Dewey and his wife, and Carleton grew up in a household in which the ideas of these leaders of progressive education were enthusiastically proclaimed. He had fond and vivid memories of his days in Parker's school.[6]

After earning an undergraduate degree at Stanford, Washburne (who had not planned to become a teacher) got his first job teaching in a rural one-room school in California. This experience, trying to teach a group of children who differed markedly in age, ability, and background, convinced him that the curriculum had to be adapted to the needs and capacities of the individual child. His interest in individualizing the curriculum brought him to San Francisco Normal School, where he joined Burk's faculty in pioneering individualized instruction. Like Washburne, Burk recognized that the graded classroom was hopelessly ineffective; children of greatly varying abilities, sharing only a common chronological age, were asked to learn the same material at the same rate. This "lock-step" system forced fast learners to waste time while dooming slow learners to frustration and failure. Burk and Washburne began to develop an alternative program, using individualized, programmed texts and diagnostic tests.[7]

In 1919, Burk sent Washburne to Winnetka to be the new superintendent, with the cheering words: "You're a very young man. Winnetka is a very small town. If you fail it won't make a big splash."[8]

Ultimately, Washburne was to make a big splash in Winnetka. The most important asset he brought with him was his boundless energy and his enthusiasm for educational reform. Within a few months of his arrival, Washburne, a warm and inspiring leader, enlisted his teachers in a concentrated effort to reorganize the curriculum. He began by asking teachers to list the specific goals they wanted students to learn in each subject. Then, with the help of the teachers, the new superintendent began to write individualized texts, based on these goals, in such "tool" subjects as arithmetic and spelling. Washburne's enthusiasm and evangelical fervor captivated the Winnetka teachers. Convinced that they were participating in a historic development in education, teachers responded with great enthusiasm and even volunteered to work vacation days to prepare the new materials.

The "Winnetka Plan," as developed by Washburne in these early years, relied on the individual approach for learning the "common

4. Winnetka's superintendent, Carleton Washburne (center), in front of Skokie Junior High School with a group of teachers who had accompanied him to the New Education Fellowship Conference (an international gathering of progressive educators) in Locarno, Switzerland, in 1927. Photograph by J. R. Marshall. Courtesy of the Carleton Washburne Memorial Library, Winnetka Historical Museum.

essentials"—the skills and information which, Washburne believed, any person growing up in modern society would need. The ultimate goal for each child was one hundred percent mastery of the step-by-step goals in each of these "tool" subjects, but the rate at which the children completed these goals could vary tremendously. Within one nominal fourth-grade classroom, some children might be doing second-grade arithmetic while others were doing sixth-grade work. A child who was doing third-grade arithmetic might be doing fifth-grade spelling—students advanced at their own rate in each subject independently. After learning a specific task from a self-instructive text, the student would take a self-corrective, diagnostic test. If there were any errors, the pupil was directed by the text to do an exercise which stressed the kind of problem that had not been solved correctly. After this, the student would take another diagnostic test. When this was completed without an error, the teacher would administer a test, check the answers and, if it was also error-free, would mark on the student's record card that a specific "goal" had been accomplished. The student would then go on to the next task.[9]

Washburne was not only concerned that the students be permitted to learn at their own pace, he was also determined to discover what the components of the common essentials really were. He wanted to know as exactly as possible what basic skills and information were absolutely essential for all members of society. For example, the young superintendent and his staff launched an ambitious survey of all allusions in the popular media to historical and geographical facts. He then built an individualized social studies program around these "essential" facts.[10]

A third aspect of Washburne's concern for efficiency in learning was his attempt to discover at what point in their education children should be introduced to a subject. As a result of extensive research, he determined at what stage a child could most effectively be taught each of the arithmetic skills, and the Winnetka curriculum was adjusted accordingly.

Washburne's program of individualized instruction was compatible with Dewey's idea that children should be treated as individuals and also with his idea that children needed to master certain subject matter as the "keys" to "the wealth of social capital," but it did not reflect Dewey's emphasis on the school as a community. The picture of each child following a process of "programmed learning" was antithetical to Dewey's progressive classroom as a community. Winnetka's individualized program owed a great deal to G. Stanley Hall's concern for individualism (Washburne's mentor, Burk, had studied with Hall). Furthermore, the emphasis on identifying "common essentials" was in harmony with the goals of the efficiency movement in education and was similar to the work of E. L. Thorndike, who supplied teachers with a list of the ten thousand most frequently used words.[11]

Although Washburne's first priority was individualizing instruction, this represented only part of the Winnetka program. The efficiency of individualized instruction in the common essentials, which took up roughly half of the school day, made it possible to devote the rest of the school day to "group and creative activities." This part of the curriculum, which was closer to Dewey's vision of education, included art, music, discussions of current events, student self-government, and field trips. The philosophy that sustained these activities echoed Dewey's concerns. The "Philosophy of the Activity Program" in the Winnetka schools argued, as Dewey did, that the complexities of modern communities obscured the ways in which society functioned. Schools, therefore, could offer children surrogate experiences—"a chance in some way to *live through* simpler forms of community life" that would "help them to interpret present day living and lay the foundation for a larger social consciousness." As a guide for the second-grade units on Southwest Indians put it, "[t]he gap between present-day child life and complex, sophisticated adult society requires a bridge. We are attempting to build this bridge by using enriched, adapted *play* experiences based on the life of the local community, or primitive peoples, peasant types, and early civilizations." The group and creative activities also echoed Dewey's emphasis on using the interests of children for pedagogical needs. Through these activities, the school would "seize and use the vigorous and vital interests of present-day child life for ends that are valuable for the child and society." To Washburne, these activities were crucial. They were "the vital, life giving part of the curriculum" and "the great advantage of handling the common essentials on an individual basis" was that it provided "time for these free activities."[12]

By the mid-1930s, the group and creative activities represented a highly sophisticated program. They were most highly developed in Skokie Junior High School under the direction of S. R. Logan, who came to Winnetka as assistant superintendent in 1926. Rae Logan brought with him from rural Montana a populist heritage of egalitarianism and democracy. An outspoken critic of Montana's large corporations, he had long been active in promoting rural cooperatives. Logan's educational philosophy was based on his deep devotion to community and democracy. He considered himself a loyal disciple of Dewey and a picture of the philosopher of progressive education hung on his wall. Like Dewey, Logan believed that democratic citizenship could only be taught by allowing children to practice it, not through "vain exhortation."[13] After bringing Logan to Winnetka, Washburne put him in charge of the junior high school program. Here Logan developed the well-known Skokie miniature community, in which students reproduced on a small scale the institutions of the larger society.

At Skokie, students not only participated fully in self-government, but, with Logan's help, they wrote, and repeatedly reviewed and revised, the Skokie Constitution. (The preamble used familiar language: "We, the people of Skokie School, in order to form a more perfect union . . ."). Article III provided for the organization of "Clubs, Corporations and Labor Unions" and the children organized a variety of enterprises.[14] Some were corporations with student shareholders, others were cooperatives.

For example, a group of children in one class decided to raise rabbits as pets and formed a corporation for this purpose. All went well for awhile but then disease struck and the company's assets were wiped out. The "Livestock Corporation" decided to hold a raffle to raise money to pay its debts. This led to an intense discussion on the morality of raffles and ultimately the junior high school community government voted to forbid the raffle; the livestock company declared bankruptcy.

The activities at Skokie arose directly out of the needs of the members of the miniature community. A credit union assisted children who had forgotten their lunch money. To help children pay for broken dishes in the cafeteria, students organized a mutual insurance company. In a more controversial move, student dishwashers united in a labor union and then declared the Skokie cafeteria a closed shop. The decision to charter the union aroused a great deal of debate that included discussions of the roles of unions in the national economy and a debate over their merits. In this way, the miniature institutions at Skokie Junior High School led to an examination of the institutions and problems of the larger society.[15]

The primary emphasis in the group and creative activities was not on developing skills—that was the focus of the individualized instruction program—but rather on fostering creativity and the development of "social consciousness." Yet there was a great deal of what Washburne called "incidental learning" in the group and creative activities; it was there that art, music, social studies, science, and literature found their places in the curriculum. Although the individualized portion of the curriculum received much wider

5. The student-run Credit Union at Skokie Junior High School, Winnetka, in the 1940s. This was one of the many economic enterprises of the Skokie miniature community. Photographer not known. Courtesy of the Carleton Washburne Memorial Library, Winnetka Historical Museum.

attention in educational circles, for Washburne the two parts of the curriculum were complementary.

Under Washburne, the Winnetka schools pioneered a number of other innovative practices, including mainstreaming of handicapped children. The individualized curriculum made it possible for "slow" children to work at their own pace within the regular classroom while, at the same time, allowing unusually gifted children to move through the curriculum at an accelerated rate. Deaf children had their own special teacher, but they were integrated into the group and creative activities. With the help of a philanthropic Winnetka family, the public schools established a nursery school within the junior high school building that served as a laboratory in family living for junior high school students.

Washburne was deeply committed to promoting "mental hygiene," and Winnetka pioneered in bringing psychological consultation into the school system with a Department of Educational Counsel that by 1939 included a psychiatrist, a psychologist, and two psychiatric social workers.[16] Washburne's concern for balancing the emotional and academic needs of children is illustrated in his concern about a very bright young girl, "J. M.," who, by the time she was nine, had completed Winnetka's sixth-grade curriculum. Should she be sent to the junior high school even though she was "smaller and younger" than any of the other children? Washburne's initial solution was to let her move up, but to slow her down academically. This proved to be a failure. "The general feeling of the teachers, and of J. M. herself, who was charmingly frank about it, was that she had 'loafed on the job' a good deal . . . when the stimulus of rapid advancement was taken away." Washburne found a larger meaning in the failure of this plan, however, noting that it "gives some inkling as to what would have happened to her in a regular school system, where the class lock-step is the rule." Moreover, the experiment was not a failure from a psychological perspective: "Socially, J. M. has grown greatly in the last year."[17]

The most ambitious innovation was the Graduate Teachers College of Winnetka. Progressive educators had long recognized that their less-structured curriculum put extraordinary demands on teachers. Progressive teachers not only needed to have a thorough grasp of subject matter and to understand the varied needs of children, but they also had to know how to take advantage of unanticipated teaching opportunities. Progressive education required well-prepared teachers. Convinced that the success of the Winnetka program depended on assuring a reliable source of teachers with appropriate training, Washburne, in cooperation with leaders of two private schools, established the teachers' college in 1932. In many ways, the college anticipated the MAT programs that flourished after World War I. College graduates were accepted for the program solely on the basis of their "quality as persons and potential teachers." Previous course work in education was not required.

The school's curriculum was the embodiment of the progressive principle of learning by doing, and students spent most of their time as interns working with experienced classroom teachers. As one of the three directors of the school, Washburne was able to hire some of its most able graduates.[18]

The progressivism of the Winnetka public schools was clearly evidenced in their educational philosophy, which Washburne described as embodying four basic principles. The first two focused on the needs of children. They held that "every child has a right to master those knowledges and skills which he will probably use in life" and that "every child has a right to live naturally, happily, and fully as a child." The third and fourth principles linked the needs of the individual and the community: "human progress depends on the development of each individual to his full capacity" and "the welfare of human society requires the development of a strong social consciousness in each individual."[19]

All but the first of these propositions place Washburne and the Winnetka schools in the tradition of progressive education. Although individualized instruction and matching the curriculum to each pupil's capacities reflected progressivism's concern for the needs of the individual, the individualized parts of the program did not include the premise that the child's own interests should be the basis for schoolwork. This aspect of Washburne's philosophy of education owed more to Hall and Thorndike than it did to Dewey. The group and creative activities, however, were firmly based on progressive principles. Here learning proceeded from activities that engaged the interests of the child. This part of the curriculum emphasized the progressives' commitment to fostering creativity and a sense of community. Washburne's and Logan's concern for developing a "strong social consciousness" clearly fulfilled Dewey's vision of the school as an agency for helping to create "a more lovely society."[20]

What led to the acceptance of progressive education in Winnetka? Why did it flourish here? An important factor was the nature of this community, which thought of itself as a "special place," with a long tradition of "community mindedness." Since its founding in the middle of the nineteenth century, Winnetka had displayed an unusual dedication to public service, which can be traced to its founders, especially Charles and Sarah Peck and Artemius Carter, each of whom was deeply influenced by a reform-minded Chicago Unitarian minister, Robert Collyer.[21] Carter and the Pecks were New Englanders and were part of what historian Lee Benson has identified as the "Yankee" reform tradition. Accordingly, Winnetkans resembled the citizens of such outposts of New England as Chautauqua, New York, who, as Benson describes them, differed from their neighbors in their belief "in self-improvement in all respects, in man's responsibility to make the world virtuous and moral, and in social progress." In keeping with this New England reform tradition, Winnetka had a deep commitment to promoting public education.[22]

Winnetka's tradition of public service was furthered by one of its most famous residents, Henry Demarest Lloyd. Lloyd was already a well-known social reformer when he settled in the village in 1878. He came to regard Winnetka as "a laboratory where he tested his theories about the practice of democracy."[23] Under Lloyd's influence, the village developed a nonpartisan government and experimented in municipal ownership of its public utilities. Accordingly, although its population was considered safely conservative in matters of national economic policy, Winnetka owned its electric company and resisted efforts of public utility corporations to buy it out.

The fullest expression of Winnetka's commitment to public service was its community house. Begun in 1911, the same year that the reformers took over the school board, it served the town in much the same way that settlement houses catered to the needs of poor immigrants in the city.[24] According to Helen Hood, who described Winnetka in the early 1920s, the community house "brings together all types of people, it prevents class cleavages. Its functions all bring into contact rich and poor, employed and employers . . . welcoming the president of a corporation and his gardener, or his maid, on equally friendly terms. It stands for social democracy." Even if we discount the hyperbole, it is clear that this rosy picture represents the way in which the community wanted to see itself. Social democracy was a goal in Winnetka, an ideal that would make residents unusually receptive to John Dewey's vision of the school as an agency for building a new, more lovely community.[25]

Yet the explanation that Winnetka was "a special place" does not account entirely for the village's receptivity to progressive education. One reason Washburne had been hired was because Winnetka was the kind of town in which a small group of influential men held a great deal of power. These men could run the board of education and the schools according to their own ideas. The way in which Rhodes was fired is an example of how these men, acting alone, could make decisions that affected the whole community. Although Rhodes was a shy man, he apparently had won the confidence of many people in town; yet the board was able to discharge him with a minimum of fuss. The elitist nature of the political process in Winnetka enabled reformers to retain control of the school board with little opposition. Traditionally, when vacancies occurred, the board itself nominated replacements and these nominees ran unopposed in general elections.[26]

The school board was not completely independent of public opinion. Shortly after Washburne's arrival, the board's decision to build a junior high school in the western section of the village created a heated controversy and an opposition slate for the school board put up a stiff fight. Opponents of the junior high school argued (unsuccessfully) that the site was much too far from the center of town and that the proposal of the wealthy supporters of the plan was much too expensive.[27] Yet, for the most part, the school board was able to perpetuate itself despite the formality of submitting to periodic elections. Although it would encounter increased opposition in the 1930s, during the 1920s the board was secure in its own power and it gave Washburne a free hand in all educational matters. Ironically, progressive education, with its reverence for democratic values, was sustained by an undemocratic political system.[28]

The undemocratic nature of the political process is not, of course, a sufficient explanation for the success of progressive education in Winnetka—the political structure could have just as well lent itself to the imposition of an authoritarian educational program. Moreover, there is no evidence of widespread dissatisfaction with the schools (at least before a contested school board election in 1933). For many years, the Winnetka Plan, as it came to be called, elicited widespread support throughout the village.

One reason for this support was undoubtedly local pride. Winnetkans shared in the honor of supporting a school system that was attracting national and even international attention. They were used to having the best—Washburne's program gave them the feeling that their children were getting high-quality public education.[29]

But the most important reason for the support given the schools in these years was the nature of the program that Washburne developed in Winnetka. The combination of the progressive group and creative activities with efficient individualized instruction in the common essentials could satisfy a broad clientele.

The Washburne program appealed to educational liberals who believed with Dewey that schools should use a child's natural curiosity in the classroom and offer a broad program whose scope went beyond the academic needs of children. Those who supported "progressive" causes in the 1930s and were concerned with the need to restore a sense of community to American life could take pride in the development of the miniature community at Skokie Junior High. The group and creative activities program was attractive to Winnetka parents who were committed to promoting creativity and the arts. In addition, those who were concerned with healthy psychological development were impressed with Winnetka's counseling program.

At the same time, traditionalists, who believed that schools should emphasize teaching the "3 R's," could see that Winnetka's schools devoted a great deal of attention to the basic skills. Washburne's research activities demonstrated that Winnetka's children did as well or better at learning the basic subjects as the children from neighboring communities.[30] The charge that an emphasis on creativity and socialization could come only at the expense of basic skills could not be applied to the Winnetka schools. Ambitious parents could take satisfaction that under the Winnetka Plan a bright child's learning was not restrained by the teacher's need to let the slower children set the pace.

Washburne's emphasis on scientific research and testing was undoubtedly welcomed by the enlightened businessmen of the community in an age that celebrated business efficiency. The broad concerns that led to the cult of the engineer and the interest in Taylorism in industry supported the scientific aspects of Washburne's educational program.

The Winnetka Plan skillfully combined progressive goals with the efficient teaching of basic skills, thereby appealing to several diverse audiences. Like a good political platform, it won the support of people who disagreed on important aspects of the curriculum but still found that their special interests were taken into account.

Washburne was himself a crucial reason for the acceptance of his program. Although he made some enemies, he made many more friends, and his enthusiasm for what he was doing, his evangelical zeal, won many converts in the village. He had a genuine gift for soothing outraged parents and calming his opponents. He was a remarkable asset in promoting interests of the schools. For example, when a problem in the Cook County assessor's office delayed tax bills almost a year, Washburne persuaded many Winnetkans to pay their tax bills early. He was an eloquent spokesman for his program and an important influence in stimulating support for progressive education in Winnetka.

Even more than his role in the community, Washburne's success depended on his leadership within the schools. Many efforts at educational reform fail because schools, like other social systems, are remarkably adept at avoiding change. Washburne, who was a charismatic leader, overcame the natural conservatism of the schools by the sheer force of his energy and commitment. He convinced Winnetka's teachers that they were engaged in a historic movement to improve, not just the local schools, but American education. Framing his ideas in these momentous terms, he inspired the staff to do their utmost. Teachers willingly worked overtime to insure the success of the program. Most important, he won the support of the teachers by showing that he respected them. For example, when he came to Winnetka in 1919, fresh from a college faculty, his doctoral degree in hand, he did not assume that he already knew what needed to be done. "Being younger and less experienced than most of the 40 or so teachers . . . I knew that I had much to learn from them." The Winnetka program was, he recalls, developed in a "group process" in an atmosphere of "mutual respect."[31] Since teachers helped develop the new curriculum, they had a vital interest in assuring its success. Moreover, through the Winnetka Teachers College, Washburne was assured of a supply of excellent new teachers committed to his vision of progressive education.

By giving the teachers an important role in the development of the Winnetka Plan, Washburne dealt with two major causes of teacher dissatisfaction—a sense of loneliness and isolation from other adults and the strong feeling that they are not respected by administrators. Winnetka's superintendent avoided the mistakes of a later group of reformers, the university-based people who, in the post-Sputnik era, produced "teacher-proof" curricula only to see them abandoned within a few years.[32]

Washburne's ideas were rarely challenged in the 1920s. He convinced board members that all educational decisions should be made by the professionals running the schools and the board gave him a free hand to try new policies. In the early 1930s, however, opposition to the Winnetka program was building up. By then, the president of the school board recalled, "[n]o dinner party was complete without a wordy battle over the schools and Carleton Washburn [sic] . . . If Johnny couldn't spell, Washburn was at the bottom of it." In 1933, the school board faced its most important political challenge when a slate opposed to Washburne's policies entered the election. Now, for the first time, progressive education was a clear issue in Winnetka and the fight was bitter.[33] The opposition claimed that the Winnetka schools were too expensive and that the curriculum included too many "frills" and "fads"; they decried the lack of discipline and argued that Winnetka should return to a traditional curriculum.[34] Although the pro-Washburne slate won, thereafter the process for nominating candidates for the school board was taken away from the board and assigned to the town caucus, the community's committee for nominating candidates for other village posts. In the years after the contested election, the caucus made sure that there was always one anti-Washburne representative on the board. More significantly, after 1933 the school board exercised much closer supervision over Washburne and thereafter the emphasis in Winnetka was no longer on innovation.[35] After Washburne resigned in 1945, the board clearly indicated its preference for a less controversial replacement.

Why did the town change its attitude toward Washburne and educational innovation in the 1930s? Obviously, the depression and the general concern for greater economy in running public services contributed to the board's new orientation; other suburban school systems were forced to cut services drastically in the face of declining revenues. But there were other factors at work—factors which may shed some light on the conditions influencing the acceptance of progressive education in other communities.

Changes in the population of Winnetka were significant in accounting for the board's new attitude. In the 1920s, the population of Winnetka almost doubled—from slightly over five thousand in 1920 to nearly ten thousand in 1930. (After 1930 there was little change in the number of people living in the village.)[36] Although the ethnic composition of the population did not change significantly, some people moving into the village were not imbued with the same ideals as the older residents. This was a period when suburban living began to appeal to a broader group of people. They were looking for a better life in the suburbs; some of them may not have paid much attention to the subtle differences that separated Winnetka from its neighboring communities. While many of the new residents had chosen to live in Winnetka because it had a reputation for providing good schools, some of them probably defined "good schools" in quite traditional terms.[37]

The changing population alarmed some longtime residents. One "old resident" told an interviewer in 1928 that the village did not want "people coming in too fast. We want them to trickle in, so that they can be brought to appreciate and accept our point of view." Now, he feared, "the newcomers are almost getting ahead of us. . . . We just can't keep the old village as it used to be." The village president warned that Winnetka was in a period of transition. It was, he said, no longer a town "where everyone knows everybody else. We have had and are having right now an influx of people who don't know the village traditions and ideals." These residents, coming in "from some crowded section of Chicago" had had no experience in living in a community like Winnetka. "If we're to maintain the village on the principles with which it was founded, then it's up to us to educate them to the aims of the village." The old tradition of community service was endangered.[38] The newcomers did not share the attitude of upper-class social reform that marked Winnetka in the period when a few men took over the public schools with the attitude that they could, in a disinterested manner, best serve the needs and interests of all the people.

Moreover, as the population stabilized after 1930, public school enrollments began to decrease. In the 1930–31 school year, the schools had enrolled 1,929 pupils; by 1940 the enrollment had declined by over twenty-five percent to 1,422. Spending for schools also declined (although not quite as much as enrollment). These conditions undoubtedly led to closer supervision by the board and to demands that schools economize. Winnetka had spent $191.27 per pupil in the 1930–31 school year; by 1935–36 per pupil expenditures had been reduced to $160.55.[39]

Winnetka was also responding to an altered national climate of opinion in the 1930s. America's faith in leadership by experts, which had been an important characteristic of prewar political progressivism and of the political culture of the 1920s, was giving way to a more participatory model of politics. This contrast could be symbolized by the change from the presidency of Herbert Hoover, the engineer who would solve America's problems, to the presidency of Franklin Roosevelt, who, through his "Fireside Chats," invited the people to share his thinking. In the 1930s, the board recognized that government *for* the people would have to be modified to include government *by* the people.

Another reason that Washburne met increased opposition in the 1930s was the changing political orientation of the progressive education movement nationally. In the 1920s, Washburne had argued that schools should strive to build a "social consciousness," but it was clear that what he meant by this was a broad and humane internationalism and a sense of the interdependence of all people—doctrines that were unlikely to offend the people of Winnetka. During the economic crisis of the 1930s, however, some progressives called for a more radical agenda. In 1932, when George Counts startled the Progressive Education Association with his challenge to teachers to "Build a New Social Order," he placed a heavy burden on public school members of the organization.[40] The call for progressive teachers to enlist in a fight to reform the capitalist system linked progressive education with political and economic radicalism. Throughout the decade, Washburne, who was one of the leaders of the association, found that he had to defend himself and his staff against shrill and persistent charges of sympathy for communism. Winnetkans who had been tolerant of Washburne's vague internationalism and the kind of social radicalism implicit in the child-centered school were alarmed at the political and economic radicalism that marked progressive education in the 1930s.

A further consideration in accounting for the changing attitude toward progressive education in Winnetka is that the curriculum itself was changing. Washburne always disliked the description "Winnetka Plan" because, he said, there was no set plan—the curriculum and teaching methods were constantly evolving. In the early years, Washburne's emphasis was clearly on individualized instruction. The development of group and creative activities lagged behind. Washburne was more interested in the individualized portion of the curriculum, and it would have been impossible to devote adequate time to developing both aspects of the program. By the late 1920s, however, the group and creative activities program became increasingly important. Also, the relationship between the two parts of the curriculum gradually shifted. In the 1920s Washburne had argued strenuously with William Heard Kilpatrick, who maintained that the group activities should be used as a means of teaching the basic skills as in his project method. Washburne argued that the two parts of the curriculum should be kept separate because using group projects as a way of teaching basic skills involved too much hit-or-miss teaching—there was no guarantee that class projects would lead to teaching all the needed skills. Moreover, Washburne maintained, using group and creative activities to teach skills tinged those activities, making them less creative and spontaneous.

In the 1930s, however, the rigid dichotomy weakened.[41] By 1940, Kilpatrick's project method was much more nearly realized than in 1920. Moreover, in the 1930s the emphasis on individualized instruction in the common essentials (which had never been stressed in the junior high to the same degree as in the lower grades) was further weakened within the junior high. Rae Logan, to whom Washburne delegated direction of the junior high program, emphasized preparing children to live and work in groups. Skokie Junior High School became the frequent target of critics of the schools in the 1930s as being insufficiently concerned with promoting discipline.

Washburne and his staff also put an increasing emphasis on the

6–9. Four views of classrooms at Crow Island School, Winnetka.

6. Children in the brightly lit work area of one of the "L"-shaped classrooms in 1941. Note the sink and the lavatory that were included in every classroom. Hedrich-Blessing photograph, courtesy Chicago Historical Society. (Negative number 6184D.)

7. A tepee erected in the main area of an identical classroom, 1941. Both the boys and girls are weaving. Note the comfortable portable furniture. Hedrich-Blessing, photograph courtesy Chicago Historical Society. (Negative number 6184J.)

8. Crow Island students working at their desks and at the blackboard in another part of the main classroom area, ca. 1950. The Winnetka schools took pride in the fact that their students learned the traditional subject matter as well or better than children in more traditional schools. These classrooms were designed to facilitate both the Winnetka plan's individualized instruction program and the group and creative activities. Photographer not known. Courtesy of the Carleton Washburne Memorial Library, Winnetka Historical Museum.

9. The Pioneer Room in the basement of Crow Island School, Winnetka, ca. 1950. Children from other Winnetka schools visited and spent time living the lives of pioneers in this well-equipped room in the basement of Crow Island. Photographer not known. Courtesy of the Carleton Washburne Memorial Library, Winnetka Historical Museum.

school's role in preventive mental health work in the 1930s. Under the influence of the Department of Educational Counsel, Winnetka teachers became more sensitive to their role in helping children make a good adjustment to school and ultimately to life. The suggestion that, in some cases, part of the school's role in mental health work was to undo the pernicious effects of the home environment undoubtedly angered many critics of the schools.

The gradual shift from the "hard" pedagogy of the individualized instruction to the "softer" pedagogy of the emphasis on group activities and mental health probably alienated some of Washburne's constituents. If Washburne's initial success was sustained by the image of heavy concentration on the "3 R's," it may well be that the dilution of that image eroded the base for his support.[42]

But despite the fact the Washburne could no longer count on the wholehearted support he had enjoyed in the 1920s and despite the economic constraints of the depression, he was able to maintain his program intact. Although there were few dramatic innovations, the curriculum continued to evolve and the progressive tradition of the schools continued after Washburne left Winnetka for military service in 1943.

The most tangible record of the Washburne years in Winnetka is Crow Island school, designed by Eliel and Eero Saarinen and Lawrence Perkins in cooperation with Washburne and the Winnetka teachers. This "astonishing building" provides an ideal setting for carrying out a progressive program.[43] Each classroom has direct access to the outdoors and has its own workroom with a sink and its own bathroom; Washburne described these classrooms as "separate cottages, connected by the hallway inside."[44] Crow Island included special rooms designed to support group and creative activities as well as a children's museum. Its basement still houses a pioneer room, where social studies classes come to live like early Americans. The building continues to impress visitors interested in promoting the ideals of progressive education.

Winnetka was not, of course, the only public school system that innovated by introducing progressive educational practices. In 1915, when John Dewey and his daughter Evelyn set out to identify *Schools of To-Morrow* and to describe the ways in which these schools were implementing new ideas, they found a great deal to commend in the schools of Gary, Indiana.[45] Under the direction of superintendent William A. Wirt, who had studied with Dewey at the University of Chicago, the Gary schools had become a show-place for educational innovation and attracted national attention.[46] It is not surprising, therefore, that one of the first steps the small group of educational reformers in Winnetka had taken was to en-gage Wirt as a consultant.

Although Winnetka and Gary are not far from each other geo-graphically, the contrast between them is dramatic. In sharp con-trast to Winnetka, Gary in the 1920s was a heterogeneous working-class city with a large immigrant population and, in later years, a large number of black migrants from the rural South.[47] Gary's schools faced problems typical of urban schools, with only ordi-nary financial resources. But, according to the Deweys, they were achieving extraordinary results.

Gary was an "instant city," built by the United States Steel Cor-poration to house the people who worked in its mills. It opened its first schools in 1906 and hired Wirt as their first superintendent.[48] Wirt was in a position to develop a school system without restraint from tradition. Like Washburne, Wirt found a board of education that was willing to give him free rein.

The most distinctive feature of the Gary schools was the "pla-toon" system—a way of doubling the capacity of the schools by taking advantage of the fact that when one group of students was using the well-equipped auditoriums, shops, laboratories, or play-grounds, another group could occupy the classrooms. The platoon system doubled the capacity of the school while at the same time allowing the children to spend a great deal of time in laboratories and shops. While most schools stood empty part of the day, the Gary schools remained open in the late afternoon and even into the evening, so that they could promote adult education programs.

The ways in which this system—sometimes called the work-study-play school—provided for educational opportunities out-side of the formal classroom obviously appealed to the Deweys. The schools' laboratories and shops were places where children learned by doing. But while the schools were well endowed with workshops, the Deweys were careful to point out that these "were not instituted to turn out good workers for the steel company . . . but for the educational value of the work they involved." This was not narrow vocationalism.[49]

For the Deweys the ultimate value of the Gary program was not the efficiency of the ways in which the school plant was used. They were most impressed with the "social and community idea" that lay behind these features. In Gary, "[t]he School is a small commu-

nity in its discipline, and a democratic one," where children of
different ages learned from each other.[50] The Deweys were enthusiastic about the public service aspects of the program. Not only
did the schools enrich their neighborhoods through adult education programs, but they worked to improve the conditions of immigrant workers by having children bring home information to promote better health, hygiene, and ways to improve living conditions.

While Wirt's schools reflected many of Dewey's educational ideals, the progressivism of the system did not continue as long as that
of Winnetka. In 1915, the same year that Dewey published his
glowing account of the Gary system, its board of education, in an
economy move, forced Wirt to trim the program. Three years later,
a survey by the General Education Board of the Rockefeller Fund
reported that teaching practices in Gary were often quite traditional.[51]

In 1940, two years after Wirt died, a new survey of the Gary
schools described a system that had become stultified in routine.
The report noted "an almost religious devotion to the past" and a
"creeping dilapidation of many aspects of a system that but a few
years ago was among the most glorious of educational triumphs."
Gary's teachers, the survey charged, were more concerned with
subject matter than with the needs of children and it condemned
their old-fashioned teaching methods.

> The concern for subject matter exhibited in a great many
> Gary classrooms results in much work being done which
> is lacking in vital meaning to pupils. Applications of
> learning in school to life situations are often too
> perfunctory and superficial. As in too many schools, an
> academic classroom is still regarded in Gary schools as a
> recitation room requiring little else but neat rows of seats
> and a teacher's desk in the center of the stage.

The report depicted an inbred and complacent system. It pointedly
noted that while Gary had attracted a great deal of attention in the
past, now "[i]t is only in your fancy . . . that the educational world
is watching Gary."[52]

Denver provides another example of a large public school system that was widely respected for its progressivism in the 1920s
and 1930s. Under the leadership of Jesse Newlon and later A. L.
Threlkeld (both of whom had studied at Columbia University
Teachers College), the Denver schools embarked on a program of
continual curriculum revision. As educational historian Larry Cuban points out, the superintendents "were especially keen on de-

veloping organizational methods that would turn curriculum revision into a tool for changing teacher practices."

The curriculum development process they devised was unique in the ways in which it involved classroom teachers. Between 1920 and 1930 over seven hundred teachers and principals, organized into thirty-seven committees, created thirty-five courses of study. Teachers were granted released time to work on curriculum projects and classroom teachers chaired the committees (which included administrators). By 1927 thirty to forty percent of the entire instructional staff had participated in a revision committee.

Curriculum revision proved to be an excellent way of introducing new ideas to classroom teachers; the superintendents brought in leading exponents of educational progressivism to work with the revision committees. Even teachers who did not serve on these committees were involved in the revision process by assessing new programs.[53]

In the absence of surveys of the schools by outside agencies, it is difficult to assess the degree to which progressive ideas affected actual classroom practice in Denver. However, by using contemporary descriptions and photographs of classrooms, Cuban concludes that the Denver schools, especially at the elementary level, made a significant shift to student-centered instruction. Fully ninety-four percent of the descriptions of classroom activities in the elementary schools, he found, were student-centered.[54] Progressive education had clearly made an impact on this city's schools.

Pasadena, California, was another city that was well known in the period before World War II for the progressivism of its public schools. Californians have often taken the lead in innovation and, in the 1930s, California schools were generally considered more progressive than those of other states. Helen Hefferman, chief of the state's Bureau of Elementary Education from 1925 to 1965 was deeply committed to Dewey's ideas and helped to spread progressive ideas throughout the schools of the state. Accordingly, as a historian of progressivism in California has noted, while Columbia University Teachers College "was the philosophical and inspirational center of the movement, . . . California was the implementation center."[55]

Even within the context of this state's commitment to Dewey's ideas, the schools of Pasadena stood out as exemplars of progressivism. During the 1920s, Pasadena adopted many innovative practices. The schools began a junior high school program in 1922, and in 1928 it extended public schooling by integrating two years of college into the public school program. Under this unique 6-4-4 system, pupils spent six years in elementary school and then went on to a four-year program in a school that combined two years of junior high and the first two years of high school. The curriculum of the final four years represented the last two years of high school and the first two years of college. The schools introduced other progressive ideas. Like Winnetka, they established a sophisticated counseling program that was recognized in 1932 as one of five best counseling programs in the nation.[56]

The community took pride in its schools and the innovations, which, like Washburne's activities in Winnetka, brought national recognition to Pasadena. Although Pasadena was much larger, it resembled Winnetka in that its wealthy founders (many of whom had come from the Midwest) were imbued with an ethos of community building. It was appropriate, therefore, that when board members were looking for a new superintendent, they first tried to hire the superintendent of Winnetka.[57]

In the 1930s, the new superintendent, John A. Sexson, faced not only the financial crisis of the depression but also the challenge of an extensive rebuilding program, mandated after the Long Beach earthquake of 1933. As elsewhere, the schools were under great pressure to reduce salaries and eliminate programs. Sexson, however, was a shrewd politician who was able to preserve most of the progressive innovations. In the early 1930s, when the California Taxpayers' Association, which had been studying the agencies of city government, turned its attention to the public schools, Sexson dealt with this potential threat by welcoming the study, provided that it be conducted by professional educators. The resulting survey, under the direction of faculty members from the University of Southern California, turned into a ringing endorsement of Pasadena's schools and their progressive practices.

While most school surveys of the period found that schools did not meet the standards of progressivism of the professors of education who made up most survey teams, the Pasadena study is filled with praise. The schools provided for an "extensive recognition of individual pupil differences." They were commended for "adjusting the school program to the needs of the students more completely than the majority of California cities." The curriculum gave "evidence of a modern philosophy of education" and encouraged "modern methods of teaching." The schools used "a progressive promotional policy," moving children through the grades with their age groups. While the schools had adopted an activity program, this had not resulted in lower achievement in the formal school subjects. The progressivism of the school system was thorough, extending into the individual classrooms. According to the survey, "a large majority of teachers" demonstrated in "their actual classroom procedures" that they were "conscious of the basic educational objectives."[58]

Sexson maintained the educational program through his shrewd work with community groups, meeting informally with community leaders and compromising with them before issues ever came to the board. In order to maintain the school programs, Sexson was willing to allow salary cuts for teachers—cuts which ultimately led to a great deal of hard feeling because they were not restored as times got better.

The seeds of another potentially divisive issue could be seen in the 1931 survey. By almost every measure, the predominantly Mexican and black schools of Pasadena were not doing very well. The survey team accepted segregated schooling and was willing to attribute inferior performance to the background of the pupils. But one of the students, Jackie Robinson, had a different perspective; he did not work hard in school, he remembers, because although his older brothers and their friends had "studied hard" they still wound up as "porters, elevator operators, taxi drivers, bellhops."[59] In the postwar period, this racial isolation would help to spark a crisis when progressive educators tried to apply Dewey's democratic principles across racial lines. These issues of discontented teachers and segregation would contribute to Pasadena's becoming the battlefield for a dramatic campaign against progressive education in the 1950s.

Analysis of the success of progressive education in Winnetka, Gary, Denver, and Pasadena reveals a number of common factors.[60] Strong educational leadership was important in each of these communities. In Gary and Winnetka the superintendents were unusually strong. Washburne and Wirt ran their schools with little outside interference. They had developed the new programs which distinguished their schools, and their reputations were closely linked to that of "their" schools. Both men won national recognition. Although Pasadena's superintendent was not as well known, he too was a strong leader with a national reputation among professional educators. Even more than the other two, Sexson worked very closely with the groups who held power in the community, anticipating possible difficulties before they resulted in challenges.

As a result, he, too, was able to exercise a decisive role in governing the community's schools. While Denver had four different superintendents from 1920 to 1940, it also benefited from strong and sustained leadership. Jesse Newlon's influence continued long after he had left because men whom he had hired carried on his approach.

As these men attracted national attention to the schools, bringing honor to their communities, their ability to dominate the school system was enhanced. In Denver, Pasadena, Gary, and Winnetka, residents took pride in their acclaimed school systems. Since the schools were closely identified with their superintendents, these communities gave them a great deal of power and latitude in setting goals.

Progressive education also succeeded when the schools' program could appeal to a number of different groups in the communities. In Winnetka, Washburne's innovations won widespread support because he could appeal to at least two distinct groups. His individualized instructional program won the support of those who wanted the schools run on an efficient basis while the group and creative activities appealed to those who supported Dewey's goals.

The Gary program also appealed to several different audiences. While the Deweys celebrated its extended curriculum and its democratic and communitarian goals, others (and especially business people) praised the system's efficiency. Platoon schools that could make better use of school facilities were an attractive alternative to building expensive new schools. Similarly, while the Deweys were impressed with Gary's shop program as liberating, rather than vocational, others could see it as a way of preparing the children of immigrants to become good workers.[61] The dual nature of the program in Gary is illustrated by the differences between its major proponents. Wirt's longtime associate, Alice Barrows, a tireless advocate of the platoon school, always emphasized the "creative and humanistic side of the Gary plan." Wirt, on the other hand, increasingly celebrated the system's efficiency.[62]

In Denver, Newlon and his successors, too, not only accepted progressive pedagogy but also embraced the goals of the administrative progressives—social efficiency and scientific management. One of the reasons Newlon and Threlkeld gave teachers a major role in curricular revision was because they saw it as an inexpensive way of bringing teachers in touch with the new ways of thinking about education.

The role of teachers was another important factor in accounting for the success of progressive reforms. In Denver, Newlon's program of making teachers the principal agents of curricular innovation was similar to the way in which Washburne initiated individualized instruction in Winnetka. Newlon recognized that no program of curricular innovations would work that had not "evolved to some extent out of the thinking of the teachers who are to apply it."[63] Not only did this process insure the enthusiastic cooperation of the teachers in implementing curricular reforms, it provided additional benefits. By being asked to head these committees and by being given released time to work on them, teachers received the recognition and respect they needed. Furthermore, the curriculum committees served as an important antidote for the sense of isolation that often demoralizes teachers.[64]

The importance of teacher involvement is highlighted by looking at the Gary schools. A weakness of the Gary program was that Wirt did not involve teachers in developing the Gary system. As a result, these teachers lacked a commitment to its success. The 1918 survey of the Gary schools found that many them were confused and overwhelmed and therefore reverted to the conventional teaching methods they had learned in normal school.[65]

As the story of these school systems shows, progressive innovation was possible in a public school system. As in Winnetka, it required the belief by community leaders, who saw themselves as "progressive," and who believed that schooling was important and that innovation was as desirable in education as it was in business. It also required unusually strong educational leaders who could lead the school staff as well as members of the community and convince them of the importance of their program for the schools. Instituting a progressive program and maintaining it demanded superintendents who were astute politicians, building support for their programs by demonstrating how they could enhance community prestige. This program worked best when these superintendents were willing to temper their commitment to Dewey's progressivism with a pragmatic concern for efficiency.

It is clear that these factors did not often come together. But when they did, progressive education did work in public school systems. Dewey's ideas were visionary but they were not out of reach.

4

PROGRESSIVE EDUCATION IN THE 1930s: THE LOCAL PERSPECTIVE

In the 1930s school officials often described their goals in rhetoric that resonated with progressive phrases such as "meeting the needs of the whole child." Although most schools were not deeply affected by progressive education, this rhetoric was not completely divorced from reality. A number of schools, such as those in Winnetka, implemented progressive principles. But what impact did these ideas have on other schools? A close look at a number of individual schools and school systems can provide a valuable perspective on the extent of progressive practices in typical schools of the 1930s.

Recapturing a picture of the daily routines of the classrooms of the past is a difficult process; records are hard to find. While schools maintain files of board minutes and financial transactions, materials relating to the curriculum are quickly discarded. Each time a superintendent's office is moved or remodeled, boxes of records are relegated to the garbage. Lesson plans and other curricular materials are among the first to go. Interviews with former teachers can provide some insight into past school practices, but anyone who has used oral history interviews knows that these sources are inherently problematic—How typical were these individuals' experiences? How well do they remember?

Yet, with these limitations in mind, a look at a number of schools in the 1930s can deepen our understanding of the impact of progressivism. Accordingly, this chapter explores the relationship between Dewey's ideas and classroom practices in three communities in the Chicago metropolitan area, communities close to Winnetka geographically but with markedly different traditions and disparate responses to progressive education—Lake Forest, Waukegan, and Mundelein.

Located only a few miles north of Winnetka on the shores of Lake Michigan, Lake Forest then, as now, shared Winnetka's wealth and social status. Lake Forest was characterized by grand mansions, many with magnificent views of Lake Michigan. These estates, with their large servant staffs, were often the sites of opulent parties, and the social milieu of Jay Gatsby's Long Island was duplicated on Lake Michigan's north shore. (It is no coincidence that F. Scott Fitzgerald depicted Daisy's socialite husband, Tom Buchanan, as coming from Lake Forest.)[1] There were, of course, smaller houses in the community; many of these were the homes of servants, former servants, and tradespeople.[2]

In the 1930s, Winnetka and Lake Forest were the homes of equal numbers of families listed in the Chicago Social Register. Lake Forest's residents were perhaps a shade wealthier than those of Winnetka, but there were other, more important, differences between the elites of these two communities. They had quite different visions for their towns. In the late 1920s a sociologist contrasted the two suburbs. He described Lake Forest's leading families as being predominantly of an "outdoor, 'society'" group, deeply involved with the activities of high society in Chicago. Winnetka's elite were more civic-minded—concerned with promoting a cohesive, neighborly community. Chicago's social calendar played a less important role in their lives.[3]

Lake Forest did not share Winnetka's "Yankee" reform tradition. Winnetkans, like their New England forbearers, strongly believed in "official community action to promote material and moral progress."[4] Lake Forest, however, represented a more individualistic tradition, and wealthy Lake Foresters were somewhat disdainful of the earnest upper-class reformers of Winnetka. One Lake Forest woman recalls that her friends thought of the women of Winnetka as "blue stockings"—far too involved in intellectual matters. Winnetka's municipally owned electric power plant had no parallel in Lake Forest. More important, Lake Forest had no equivalent of the Winnetka Community House and, as late as 1948, Lake Forest turned down a proposal for a community recreation facility.[5]

It is not that Lake Forest's leading families did not contribute to the general welfare. They were generous supporters of such important Chicago institutions as the University of Chicago, the Art Institute, and the Symphony Orchestra. Their philanthropy, like their businesses, was centered in the city of Chicago. Many wealthy Lake Forest residents viewed their home in the suburb primarily as a place of respite. In contrast to Winnetkans, Lake Foresters were not inspired to make their community into an idealized version of the New England village of an earlier age.[6]

The contrasting ethos of the two communities was reflected in their schools. While Winnetka's public schools were attracting national and even international attention for their innovations, Lake Forest's public schools were unnoticed outside the community. Within the town, they had a reputation for providing a sound education, but they were by no means in the vanguard of educational change.[7] More important, in Lake Forest the schools reflected the division of the town. The children of the families that lived on the estates attended private schools until they were old enough to go east for a prep school education. It was predominantly the children of servants and local tradespeople who attended the public schools.

There was a sharp contrast, too, in the private schools of the two communities. Winnetka's North Shore Country Day School was as well known as the public schools for its progressive ideas. Its headmaster, Perry Dunlap Smith, with Carleton Washburne and Flora Cooke of the Francis Parker School, constituted the faculty of the Winnetka Teachers College. On the other hand, Lake Forest's most prestigious private school, the Bell School, prided itself on its highly traditional curriculum. (Even in Lake Forest, however, change was in the air. In 1928 a group of Lake Foresters committed to progressive education enlisted the advice of Smith and Cooke in establishing a new private school, Lake Forest Country Day School.)[8]

The management of the public schools in the two communities was markedly different. While elections to the school board in Winnetka were under the control of the caucus, in Lake Forest, the schools were even further removed from public control. They were run by a school board that was appointed by the mayor, who, in turn, was chosen by a small group that controlled the nominating caucus. In sharp contrast to Winnetka, Lake Forest board members, for the most part, did not send their own children to the public schools.

At the beginning of the 1930s, Lake Forest schools were under the supervision of a veteran superintendent, John Baggett. When Carleton Washburne came to Winnetka in 1921, Baggett had already been Lake Forest's superintendent for seventeen years. He had come to Lake Forest from nearby Waukegan, where he had been a principal for sixteen years. Unlike Washburne, Baggett trained at a normal school and had not attended college. Unmarried, Baggett devoted his whole life to the schools. His consuming passion was art and beauty. In Waukegan he achieved a national reputation for his efforts to beautify the traditionally drab school rooms and grounds; his room, decorated with reproductions of the great masters, was singled out by *The Ladies Home Journal* as the most beautiful classroom in America. Characteristically, shortly after he came to Lake Forest, he used part of his first paycheck to buy a copy of "Winged Victory" for one of the schools. Gradually he purchased pictures for every classroom.[9]

Baggett's concern for the physical beauty of the schools must have appealed to the leaders of Lake Forest. The town was laid out with great care and its roads wound gracefully through the beautiful lakeside community.[10] Market Square, the town's shopping area, was designed by architect Howard Van Dorn Shaw to resemble a Tudor marketplace. Gorton School was also a noteworthy building; designed by James Gambell Rogers, who had designed the Yale University library, it was enlarged in 1907 under the guidance of Shaw.[11]

Baggett was an impressive-looking man with a clear sense of his educational mission. One of his former Waukegan pupils, Marc Rose, remembered him as "The Most Unforgettable Character I've Met." In a fond portrait, he claimed that no child left Baggett's schools "who could not identify every picture and statue and piece of music." Moreover, Rose was willing to bet, every child who had attended a school supervised by Baggett "could write a good, plain hand and was soundly grounded in arithmetic and spelling."[12]

Under Baggett school buildings were improved, beautifully maintained, and lavishly decorated with pictures and statues. Lake Forest's schools had a kindergarten program for both four- and five-year-olds before these were common elsewhere. During the Baggett years, the schools added a visiting nurse to the staff and instituted a school dental program.[13]

The curriculum, however, was quite traditional. The 1928 fourth-grade "Course of Study" reveals the superintendent's philosophy of education. Baggett believed in close supervision of the teachers. Although the course of study asked teachers to "exercise initiative and individuality," it cautioned them to "Consult with supt., before much omission or much changing is done." Instructions for oral reading lessons were explicit and detailed:

Read orally from the front of the room. Slowly-under-
standingly, good voice, also position of body and book,
clear enunciation. Final syllables and last consonants of
words given their full value; Reading matter of any
subject should always be made a reading lesson.

Silent reading should always be followed by "proper testing" to
determine the "amount and value of work done." Reading and
spelling lessons should be preceded by *"Regular daily* not *spasmodic*
lessons and drills" in phonics. Other subjects in the fourth grade were
language, nature study, history, music, drawing, picture study, physical education, and hygiene. In regard to the latter, teachers were to
cooperate with the school nurse and dentist and to make a "[q]uick
teeth inspection for cleanliness every morning." While teachers
were told to "[t]ake pupils into school yards with notebooks and
pencils" for nature study, there was no mention of field trips.

The superintendent was concerned with more than academic
subjects. He regarded manners and morals as "the largest field for
the teacher to work in. . . . [T]he good results achieved by her
here," he believed, "will just as surely indicate her excellence in
standing as a real teacher as the good results she may get by constant nagging and drilling in arithmetic or other subjects." Teachers were to "[c]ultivate courtesy," "[r]ecognition of authority," and
"real patriotism." As an example of proper behavior, teachers were
told that when the superintendent came into the classroom for the
first time on any day, everyone "should rise as a body and greet
him properly." Teachers were to inculcate a respect for property
and to "stress neatness of desks and floors . . . Never an inkspot on
the floor. Never a scratch on a desk."[14]

The atmosphere in the schools was dominated by the concept of
noblesse oblige. Baggett's goal was to introduce the children of
Lake Forest's servants and tradespeople to the finer things in life.
The schools taught them manners (including "lifting of hats by
boys").[15] Always immaculately dressed, Baggett modeled courtly
behavior and he maintained strict discipline in the schools. Baggett
made it possible for the public school children to see the great art
treasures of the world through the enormous collection of reproductions he accumulated during his summer trips to Europe. He
was famous for sending school children beautiful picture cards for
their birthdays. The schools provided the children with dental and
health care and, at Christmas, gave each child a present. When, in
1933, it was decided to lengthen the school day for first graders,
one of the reasons given was that more teacher guidance was better
for the "children of the masses."[16]

10. Lake Forest's superintendent, John Baggett, was convinced that an important part of the schools' mission was to teach children proper behavior and posture. These seventh graders in Gorton School depicted on a 1925 picture postcard had learned their lessons well. Photographer not known. Courtesy of Gorton Community Center and School District #67, Lake Forest, Illinois.

11. Although he was "Superintendent Emeritus," in 1941 John Baggett was still teaching art appreciation classes. Photograph by Ward H. McMasters. Courtesy of Jean McMasters Grost.

Baggett was well regarded in the community and he continued as superintendent until 1936, when he was gently retired and given the title of superintendent emeritus. By then the courtly old gentleman was clearly a relic of a previous age. His last report to the board of education is revealing. It begins with a hymn of praise to the season: "May has been a wonderful, busy and interesting month for all of us, both pupils and teachers. The month's clear and invigorating air, and awakening beauties of our perennial spring have imbued us all with renewed energy and endeavor." The report continues in a similar vein: "Little God Cupid is again in his work among our Corps of Assistants. Because of this sly little imp Miss Graehling of the Kindergarten will not be back with us next year."[17]

In 1931 the school board, recognizing that Baggett's concept of education was out of date, brought in an assistant superintendent. Leonard E. Loos, who had been a high school principal in southern Illinois, increasingly took over management of the schools. Loos helped modernize the schools, bringing them closer to those of other suburban school districts. Although Lake Forest may not have been ready to accept a junior high school, he created a single "upper school" (a term familiar to Lake Foresters because it was commonly used by private schools) for all seventh and eighth graders.[18]

Loos's most important curricular change was to departmentalize the curriculum in the new upper school. Seventh and eighth graders were now taught social studies, English, mathematics, and science by subject matter specialists. They continued to take home arts, manual training music, art, and physical training, which had been taught by special teachers before the reorganization. The new upper school curriculum was supported by hiring new teachers, who were required to have B.A. degrees, and by the purchase of special equipment.[19]

In the early 1930s the district also hired a special education teacher to work with retarded children and began a comprehensive program of standardized testing. (Previously, the schools' policy for slow or reluctant learners had been to "love them along until they finally get going.") Baggett's description of the eighteen pupils in the special help room reveals, however, that he was neither sophisticated about, nor sympathetic to, the needs of these children: a second grade boy, he says, is "Very weak. Tricky." A fifth grade girl is "very very queer." A seventh grade boy is "Irresponsible" but "Could be made to do."[20]

At a time when most school districts were cutting expenses,

Lake Forest (where the depression had little impact) not only re-sisted this trend, but actually increased its spending for schools. In the early 1930s the board approved a substantial remodeling pro-ject in the upper school, including a new auditorium with a stage and additional classrooms for art and sewing.[21] Although enroll-ments were remarkably stable between 1930 and 1935 (649 pupils in 1930 and 655 five years later), Lake Forest expanded the faculty by almost twenty-five percent. This was especially expensive because it included a significant increase in the number of male teachers (from two to five) at a time when men received salaries as much as fifty percent higher than those of women.[22] While Lake Forest had spent $142.75 per pupil in the 1930–31 school year, five years later it was spending $148.22. In contrast, in the same period Winnetka, like most other districts, cut its school spending, from $191.27 to $160.55 per pupil.[23]

These changes modernized the school program and reflected the fact that Loos accepted some of the principles of progressive edu-cation. By 1936 the schools offered an enriched curriculum that paid greater attention to individual needs and catered more to the interests of the students. Under Loos, the upper school program concerned itself with community life and correlated instruction in several subjects. Yet many of the changes were more in harmony with the efficiency movement in education than with Dewey's child-centered model. The new departmentalized upper school program was "modern," but it was one that put increased emphasis on subject matter. While the schools did undertake some projects, such as having a nature class help do the landscaping at one school, this was clearly a supplement to regular classroom work. Lake For-est did not adopt an activities curriculum, in which the school's program was based on projects.[24]

Baggett remained suspicious of progressive education. He told the board that of the children who transferred into the Lake Forest schools, those who had come from Winnetka were the weakest. A few years later, he complained that "so many extras demand school time of us these days of Progressive Education that it keeps me hustling and wary trying to see that the time of Arithmetic, Gram-mar, Spelling, etc., is not too much curtailed." However, he assured the board, "I insist that proper time and drill be given to these." A year later he complained that "the curricula of public schools is sometimes overly enriched and varied leaving the time for the very necessary drills of the essentials at times almost too short and hur-ried. . . . [W]e have to plan carefully to get enough time for individ-ual attention and the essential drilling that we deem entirely needed and still keep up with the so called Progressive Education procession."[25]

Moreover, despite the changes of the early 1930s, the public schools were still not regarded as the proper place for the education of the children of the elite. Enrollment figures reflected the town's commitment to private education. The number of pupils in the Lake Forest public elementary schools in 1940 was equal to only about half of the town's population under fourteen years of age. This was in sharp contrast to Winnetka where the number of children attending the public schools was equal to about two-thirds of the village's population under fourteen.[26] As one long-time Lake Forest resident recalls, in Lake Forest, there was a "great distinction" between the children whose fathers worked in Lake Forest and those whose fathers took the train to Chicago, between the children who went to private schools and those who attended the public schools.[27] In the 1930s, Lake Forest's public schools had not yet become the community's common school—a place where people from different classes would learn together.

By 1936, however, the board of education was eager to change this.[28] In an unusual step, the board wrote to the mayor and city council and explained that it was "in the process of making certain important changes." The board had "long felt that while our schools are good, they are nevertheless, not of the very high quality to which the community is justly entitled and to which the Board is determined to bring them." But the required changes were "of such a fundamental nature" that it had hesitated until it was "in complete accord." Now, however, the board was ready. It had decided that it was time for Baggett to retire, that the position of assistant superintendent should be eliminated, and that the schools should be directed by a single individual, not Loos, but someone new, who had had no previous connection with the Lake Forest schools.[29]

The new superintendent offered a marked contrast to Baggett. M. G. Davis was a professional school administrator who had done graduate work at Columbia Teachers College and had earned a Ph.D. degree at the University of Iowa. Although he was only forty-two years old when he came to Lake Forest, he had already served as superintendent of schools of Ames, Iowa, for ten years.[30]

Davis quickly took charge. He was critical of the music program. Music books, he said, were old and "in disreputable condition" and music appreciation "had been largely neglected." He was even more concerned about reading instruction, announcing that he would develop a remedial reading program, encourage the study of new teaching methods, and (pointedly) that he would make the ability to teach reading effectively an important criterion in hiring new teachers. Other changes Davis brought to Lake Forest included the establishment of school libraries.[31] Davis recommended establishing a department of "mental hygiene" and adding a "psychologist–visiting teacher" and a part-time psychiatrist to the school staff. Although board members adopted most of the changes that Davis recommended, they resisted this last one, agreeing only to hire a psychologist for four or five days a year.[32]

Davis's and the board's major aim was to broaden the schools' clientele. In pursuit of this goal, the board sent the superintendent to visit a number of the most prestigious eastern prep schools to determine how well the schools were "preparing some of our pupils to meet the entrance requirements of private schools" and to learn firsthand what changes might have to be made in the curriculum "to meet the needs of those pupils who are destined for the private schools." In his report on the trip, Davis defended public education: "the public schools of America are doing as good a job as the private elementary schools" in preparing their pupils for the prestigious private boarding schools. Unfortunately, he noted, this was "contrary to the opinion prevailing in Lake Forest." After his eastern trip, Davis announced significant changes in the curriculum to make the schools more attractive to children whose parents intended to send them to prep schools; students in the upper school would now be able to take Latin as well as additional work in grammar and math.[33]

Introducing Latin into the curriculum was, of course, contrary to the thrust of progressive education. Ancient languages were often cited as examples of traditional subjects that had no relationship to the needs and interests of children and therefore did not belong in the program of a modern school. Yet Davis, unlike Baggett, was not opposed to progressivism. He attended Progressive Education Association meetings and, under his leadership, the schools of Lake Forest described their programs in terms that progressives would approve. For example, a newspaper article about a sixth-grade health and science class' visit to the hospital noted: "In keeping with the modern trend, subject matter becomes a means to the end of more abundant living. The former heavy reliance on textbooks is giving way to a recognition of the valuable learning experiences afforded by excursions . . . and a host of other activities." Under Davis, the schools not only had more frequent field trips but instituted other progressive reforms, such as parent-teacher conferences and a student government in the upper school.[34]

By the eve of World War II, the Lake Forest schools had changed in important ways and the school board began the next step in its program to produce a common school system. It published a lavish illustrated brochure describing the schools and their program and sent a copy to each household in the community. Reflecting the increasing interest in "modern" trends in education, the booklet described the schools in progressive rhetoric. The Lake Forest schools, it proclaimed, paid a great deal of attention to individual differences and the school was concerned not only with learning, but with the development of "the whole child." After pointing out the differences between traditional and progressive education, it claimed that the Lake Forest schools "belong somewhere in the large group of schools which is changing from the traditional to a more progressive set up. Many of the essential elements of progressive education have been accepted here," the pamphlet continued, "but the practical application of these principles has been far less extreme than in many school systems." Textbooks and assignments were still used, but there was "much more teaching and learning

12. A Lake Forest classroom as pictured in the board's 1940 public relations booklet, *Your Schools at Work: The Lake Forest Public Elementary Schools* (Lake Forest: Lake Forest Public Schools, [1940]), p. 19. Just above the picture, the text reads: "The entire program is one of active investigation seeking answers to the constant question, 'Why?' in a laboratory of democratic social living." Photograph by Ward H. McMasters.

based on firsthand experiences of the pupil." Rejecting the philosophy of the project method, which argued that the basic skills could
be acquired incidentally as pupils immersed themselves in a project, the Lake Forest schools continued to believe that drill was an
essential part of learning such skills as arithmetic.[35]

In important ways, the Lake Forest schools echoed the rhetoric
of progressive educators, but their application of these principles
was erratic and sometimes superficial. For example, the schools
responded to the progressives' call for the integration of subject
matter by teaching art almost exclusively in correlation with other
subjects but, on the other hand, the highly departmentalized curriculum in the upper school went directly counter to this philosophy.[36] Similarly, Davis had instituted student government in the
upper school, an application of progressive principles in that it
permitted students to participate in decisions affecting their education and provided a model of the institutions of the larger society.
But the student council was directly controlled by the superintendent, who demanded the right to veto unsuitable candidates for
office, undercutting the meaning and purpose of this progressive
innovation.[37]

In the area of mental health, Lake Forest schools accepted part of
the progressive program by expressing concern with "helping the
pupil to become better adjusted to his present situations."[38] This
was, of course, a far less ambitious aim than the progressive goal of
striving to help pupils to reach their full potential and to live happily as children. But even this limited commitment was undercut
by a failure to hire an adequate psychological staff.

The same year that the schools were mounting their public relations campaign by sending the booklet describing the schools to
Lake Forest households, they invited a local photographer to make
a 16mm film in the schools. Films like this do not capture reality—
this was hardly cinema verité; scenes were obviously posed. Yet the
film is an important document; it gives us the opportunity to look
at the schools the way they probably looked on days when visitors
were expected. At the very least, it shows us how the schools and
the people in them *wanted* to be seen.

"Lake Forest Public Schools on Parade" presents a picture of
cautious progressivism. While the camera shows us parents setting
up a tea and helping children with books and sewing, the narrator
tells us: "It takes parent cooperation to make a good public school."
The film stresses the importance of health care, showing children
being examined by a doctor and a dentist and having their hearing
tested. Then pictures of little children furiously cutting wood ac-

company the narrator's statement: "The kindergarten child learns to adjust to a social group." But, the narrator assures us, "the 3 R's are still the backbone of the curriculum."

Classrooms at the lower level are relatively informal. The children are rather stiff, perhaps because they are aware of the camera. In the upper grades, classes are more formal, yet even here there are projects. An older class is seen looking at maps of South America and making South American costumes and blankets and acting in a play about Latin America. The film then shows student government in action. We see an election with ballots and student officials checking registration and students inspecting lockers: "Pupils learn citizenship through practice." Extracurricular activities are not neglected: "Organized play is educational, healthful, and lots of fun." Students play football in uniforms; a lady in a long gown teaches ballroom dancing. The film's final scene is the spring of 1941. Sixty-two eighth-grade pupils are graduated—two of them are black.[39]

By 1941 the Lake Forest schools could be characterized as modestly progressive. Its administrators spoke in the rhetoric of progressive education and had adopted those progressive practices that could be integrated into a relatively traditional school system. Progressive innovations here, however, were part of a larger effort, the attempt to modernize the public schools and make them attractive to a broader clientele. In the late 1930s, the board of education's major goal was to make the ideal of the common school a reality in this affluent suburb. Progressive ideas could play a role in this effort. Schools that adopted an enriched curriculum and aimed at promoting the development of individuals to their full capacities might well be attractive to parents who might otherwise send their children to private schools.

Lake Forest schools of the 1930s had made only a limited commitment to progressive education, yet they were far in advance of those in Waukegan. Located only a few miles to the north, Waukegan represented a stark contrast to the nearby wealthy North Shore suburbs. In Winnetka and Lake Forest, the lake shore was lined by large mansions and private beaches. While Waukegan, too, had stately homes in a small section on its northern edge, most of its lakefront was occupied by industrial plants and railroad tracks. Lake Forest and Winnetka were the homes of Chicago's social elite, successful businessmen, tradespeople, and servants. Waukegan, for the most part, was the home of blue-collar workers and lower-level managerial employees.

Waukegan schools entered the troubled decade of the 1930s with a traditional academic program and a conservative superintendent of schools, John S. Clark. It had adopted a number of programs consonant with Dewey's contention that schools had to provide services that went beyond pure academic training—physical education, music, art, manual training, and domestic science. Even before the depression, however, these programs were not widely available to Waukegan school children. As late as 1927, a group of citizens petitioned the school board to provide seventh-grade boys with a regular visit by a physical education teacher and asked that manual training and domestic science classes be held at least twice a month.[40]

With the onset of the depression, Waukegan schools were plunged into an extended financial crisis that made the future of every aspect of the curriculum tenuous. Despite the October 1929 stock market crash, conditions were still normal when the schools opened in the fall of 1930. When the children began the new school year, there was a new addition to old North School, and several other buildings were practically new or had had recent additions. A month later, however, the situation began to look ominous; tax receipts were down. By December 1931 it was clear that the schools were in serious trouble. The board of education alerted teachers that unless the state came to the rescue, there would have to be drastic cuts; kindergarten, domestic science, and manual training would probably be eliminated. The board would have to dismiss special teachers for music, art, penmanship, and physical education as well as visiting nurses and truant officers. The *Waukegan News-Sun* warned that this would bring back the bare-bones curriculum that had met "the standards of 20 years ago."[41]

Early in 1932, after the state failed to come to the rescue, the newspaper joined the public demand for reductions in school spending: "The schools must take their medicine with the rest of us. They must cut salaries, eliminate departments, and go easy on purchases and new construction." By February teachers were getting only half their pay in cash with the rest in scrip (a form of promissory notes). In March, in response to the desperate situation and to increasing public pressure, the board cut most teachers' pay by twenty percent and began to release some special teachers. Teachers were further demoralized by the news that they would be on thirty-day contracts. Administrators were not exempt: the superintendent's salary was slashed from $7,000 to $5,000. But even these drastic cuts fell short of the demands of the Waukegan Taxpayers' Association.[42]

When the schools opened in the fall of 1932, there was more bad news. Due to a fifteen-percent reduction in tax valuations, it would be impossible to have an eight-month school year unless there were further cuts. In October, the *News-Sun* announced in a banner headline: "TEACHERS FACE PAYLESS DAYS." The secretary of the board of education urgently begged other agencies to make further cuts in their budgets so that the savings could support education: "Let the schools for our children live!" But the situation continued to deteriorate rapidly. Teachers had been paid in cash only for a few weeks and had not yet been paid for May and June of the previous school year. Local merchants were refusing to accept payment in teachers' scrip. The *News-Sun* reported that many teachers were "in desperate financial straits" and had to find some means of "raising cash in order to continue with their teaching."[43]

Early in 1933 the board cut an additional six weeks from the school year. The shortened school year, combined with salary cuts, meant that Waukegan teachers' pay had been reduced by an average of thirty-six percent and only part of that had been paid in cash. In May, an additional ten percent reduction in salaries was announced. The *News-Sun* noted that "[i]t will be a miracle if such drastic cuts do not lower morale and teaching standards."[44] (Chicago teachers offered an ominous example of what might happen. In the spring of 1934 they invaded downtown banks that had refused to redeem their scrip, splashed ink on the walls, broke windows and partitions, tipped over desks, and fought with the police.)[45]

The depression cut deeply into all aspects of the school program. Special teachers were dismissed, weakening or eliminating programs in instrumental music, penmanship, manual training, domestic science, and physical education. The board stopped requiring teachers to take professional courses in the summer and no longer offered bonuses to those who did. It cut the school supplies budget in half and eliminated eight classroom teacher positions, dramatically increasing average class size. As the schools cut programs, public education was supplemented by private enterprise. To make up for the cut in programs, teachers offered an additional six weeks of instruction in the summer of 1933, for a fee to be paid by parents. Vocal music, which had been cut from the regular program, was also made available to children whose parents were willing to pay.[46]

By the 1935–36 school year, Waukegan, which had spent $75.00 per pupil five years earlier, was spending only $55.00. (Lake Forest was spending three times as much in 1935–36.) Although there had been a six-percent decline in enrollment, the teaching staff had been reduced by over ten percent and salaries had been reduced by over twenty-five percent.[47] Equally important, essential building repairs were postponed until federal funds became available through New Deal programs. For four years the school board did not purchase any textbooks. In the fall of 1934 a representative of the state superintendent of public instruction noted the effects of the austerity budgets: Waukegan schools had too few teachers, classes were too crowded to permit adequate attention to individuals, and there was a shortage of books, maps, and reference materials.[48]

The impact of the fiscal crisis can be seen in the curriculum plans for a fifth-grade history class. Since there was only one copy of the required textbook, the teacher was told to read it to the students; they could supplement this by reading in other books. Although these circumstances could have led to improvisations that moved away from the conventional curriculum, this was not the case. The course was clearly history—not social studies—and its aims were traditional, including a list of names and events that all children were expected to memorize. The 1934 course of study for eighth-grade civics suggested field trips to the county court house and such projects as organizing the class as a local government. But the course guide stressed content and showed no recognition of the fact that the city and the nation were caught in an unprecedented crisis that was straining familiar forms of government to their utmost.[49]

By the late 1930s, the situation was improving. Some of the burden was lifted when federal relief programs began to pay for necessary repairs. By 1939 the board's secretary was able to report that despite new valuations, the schools would operate in the black through June 1940. He cautioned, however, that it might still be necessary to pay teachers in scrip for a short time. The financial situation was still precarious because in ten years property values had dropped by almost one-third, from $24 million to $17 million, while the rate of collection was also dropping, from ninety-eight percent to eighty percent. In keeping with the secretary's concern and caution, in the 1940–41 school year the board's spending per student was still below what it had been at the onset of the depression.[50]

The improved situation allowed some innovations. The board

adopted new textbooks. A new arithmetic program, adopted in 1937, was more in tune with the aims of the progressives. One of the objectives of the new third-grade program was the application of arithmetic to everyday life and eighth-grade teachers were urged to "[s]tress practical applications." Some other progressive ideas had come into play; in 1939 an eighth grade learned about photography after the children had been allowed to vote on what kind of science they wanted to study.[51]

Although some of the worst effects of the depression had been reversed by 1940, for the Waukegan schools survival rather than progressive innovation was the dominant concern of the staff during the 1930s (when progressive education was supposedly at its peak of influence). Unlike the suburban schools of Winnetka and Lake Forest, Waukegan offered a narrow curriculum with little besides the traditional courses. Subject to the careful scrutiny of an active Taxpayers' Association, the schools were under great pressure to prove that the curriculum included no "fads and frills." The schools had no student government, even for older children (there were no separate junior high schools). They offered no counseling program or psychological services, nor was there any sign that the schools' program was based on an understanding of the changing developmental needs of children. Despite the painful effects of the depression, the Waukegan schools were far removed from the radical program of the Social Frontier thinkers who had called on teachers to help construct a new social order.

In 1945 when H. R. McCall came to Waukegan as the new superintendent of schools, he was attracted to the position because "there was a lot of room for improvement."[52] Like M. G. Davis in Lake Forest and Carleton Washburne in Winnetka, McCall would have the opportunity to make significant changes and bring some aspects of the progressive vision of education to these schools. In the period before World War II, however, Dewey's ideas had had little impact on the public schools of Waukegan.

Progressive education had even less impact on the schools of nearby Mundelein. Although the village was only a few miles from Lake Forest and Waukegan, it differed drastically from both of its Lake County neighbors. Much of this small community was still farmland and, even in 1940, the town's population was only 1,100. Unlike the communities along the shore of Lake Michigan, it lacked a clear sense of identity; it had had four names before 1924 when it was renamed in honor of Chicago's Cardinal Mundelein, who had built a seminary in the town.

In the 1920s, Mundelein had enjoyed a brief period of prosperity, fueled by Samuel Insull's grandiose plans to build a rail line linking the town to Evanston. The speculators' real estate boom and the town's short-lived prosperity ended abruptly when Insull's empire disintegrated. Mundelein's economy collapsed in the depression. At one point, the financial situation was so desperate that the street lights had to be turned off.[53]

Even during the relatively prosperous 1920s, the town had had only one school with four teachers who each taught several grades in one of two rooms. While one grade was called to the front of the

13. Lincoln School, Mundelein. Built in 1895, this was the district's only building until the 1950s. Initially, the school had only two rooms, with four grades meeting in each room. By the 1930s the school had indoor plumbing, steam boilers, and several additional classrooms. During the depression, Lincoln School added a WPA-built gymnasium. (See "A Little Red-Brick School Lives On," *Libertyville Independent Register*, May 27, 1976, p. 1b.) Photographer not known. Courtesy of the Historical Society of the Fort-Hill County.

room to recite, the other group was assigned "busy work" at their desks. In the 1924–25 school year, the combined sixth, seventh, and eighth grade class began each day with a ten-minute opening exercise. The curriculum called for separate twenty-five minute arithmetic lessons for each grade, followed by twenty-minute geography lessons, ten minutes of spelling, and a fifteen-minute writing period before lunch. After the lunch hour, there was another opening exercise, twenty minutes of history, a language lesson for the sixth grade, and twenty minutes of grammar for seventh and eighth graders followed by twenty minutes of reading for each grade. The seventh and eighth grade also had fifteen minutes of civics every day during the first six months of the school year, replaced by physiology for the remainder of the year. There was a fifteen-minute recess in the morning and another one in the afternoon. Under this system, teachers were very busy but each child received less than two hours of direct instruction per day.[54]

As in Waukegan, the Mundelein schools had made some limited efforts to enrich the curriculum before the onset of the depression. In 1930 the elementary schools offered music and art for the first time and also began kindergarten classes. But the depression brought real hardship. In the spring of 1932 the board cut teachers' salaries by fifteen percent. A year later, as funds were drying up, the three school directors debated the "best means of carrying on the rest of the school year"; they were forced to close the school after only eight months.[55] In September they eliminated the kindergarten, but more drastic measures were needed. The directors gave teachers a choice: they could get their full pay for three months or half pay for six months. In December teachers were paid with two warrants and told to cash only one and to hold the other until more money was available. The crisis led to increases in class size, with as many as fifty children in a single combined first and second grade class in 1932–33. As in Waukegan, federal relief efforts helped. In 1938, the WPA built a gymnasium for the school.[56] But even during the war years, after the economy recovered, Mundelein's school spending lagged. As late as 1946, the district was spending only $81.18 per pupil per year (less than one-third of the per-pupil expenditures in Lake Forest).[57]

Progressive education was as remote in Mundelein in the 1930s as it was in Waukegan. According to the teachers, the school emphasized rote learning of assigned materials: "we were supposed to cover the material in a year . . . and that didn't leave much time for anything else." Another teacher commented: "It was a structured classroom . . . somewhat similar to what I was brought up with." Although one of the teachers had heard of the Winnetka Plan, she did not consider it relevant to her needs since she had such large classes. Another teacher had neither heard of the Winnetka Plan nor the Progressive Education Association. For the teachers of Mundelein, the activities of the Winnetka schools, only a few miles away, were remote and irrelevant (despite the fact that Washburne's belief in individualized instruction had been the result of his experience of teaching in a similar setting). The major concern of Mundelein teachers was covering the materials the county superintendent assigned.[58]

The history of these quite different school systems offers some clues that can illuminate the factors that influence the adoption of progressive ideas. First, however, a brief look at several other school systems can help to put the experiences of these Chicago area schools in perspective.

Many schools, like those of Waukegan and Mundelein, were unaffected by progressive ideas. For example, in the small town of Hamilton, Massachusetts, in the mid-1930s, classrooms "looked much as they had thirty years earlier," with "bolted-down desks . . . equipped with inkwells." David Tyack, in recalling his education there, describes the teachers as mostly middle-aged women who had trained at Salem Normal School and taught a curriculum in which the subjects were clearly separated. The lower-middle-class children who attended this school all "studied the same things at the same time from the same books." Tyack notes: "The pedagogical and moral order . . . was predictable and secure. Horace Mann would have approved."[59]

Hamilton's school did not claim to be progressive. But, as we have seen, by the 1930s many school administrators had adopted progressive rhetoric in describing the programs of their schools. For example, New York City's public schools of the 1930s was often identified as a system that had thoroughly adopted progressive ideas. While a great deal has been written about the New York City schools, for our purposes, the most valuable is the study of classroom practices by Larry Cuban. In his imaginative study of pupil-centered versus teacher-centered education, Cuban used a large number of diverse sources to establish a scale for rating classrooms to estimate the extent of a school system's commitment to pupil-centered educational practices.[60] In the case of New York, Cuban's study shows how a traditional educational system could function behind a screen of progressive educational rhetoric.

Even though Superintendent Harold Campbell was considered an educational conservative, New York developed its reputation for progressivism in the late 1930s when it began an experimental activities curriculum. Cuban notes, however, that despite "changes in syllabi that incorporated progressives' vocabulary and suggested activities for teachers," the framework within which teachers operated, "classroom architecture, class size, report cards, rules, evaluation process, and supervision," continued to promote the "prevailing teacher-centered practices."[61] Accordingly, despite the highly touted activity curriculum, Cuban estimates that fewer than one out of every four New York City elementary teachers adopted progressive teaching practices.[62]

As a pupil in one of these schools from 1944 to 1946, my own experience in a New York public school that was considered one of the city's best supports Cuban's conclusions. While a few teachers at P.S. 6 did follow a progressive approach, most of them made no effort to enlist our interests. Moreover, the school building itself was old-fashioned, with seats and desks bolted to the floor. The atmosphere was repressive. As Cuban points out, report cards give some indication of what a school thinks is important and my report card (dated June 30, 1946) confirms my memory of a school that had not adopted a pupil-centered approach. While it did include a progressive feature—a place to assess such "desirable traits" as "works and plays well with others"—it devoted much more space to the grades for twelve separate subjects. Moreover, the grades on the "scholarship" side of the card were emphasized by being mostly numerical, worked out to the nearest percentage point. The card provided no place for a teacher to write any comments.[63]

This gap between progressive rhetoric and classroom reality was painful to those who were committed to changing the schools. Samuel Tenenbaum, a New York elementary school teacher in the 1930s and "an early adherent of the project method," recalls the "hope and expectancy" with which he "looked forward to educational changes as the movement gained headway." But, after he "saw what school people were doing in the name of this movement," he was "filled with disillusionment, with shattered hopes and deep disappointment."[64]

In contrast to Waukegan and Mundelein, some school systems deeply affected by the depression did adopt some progressive measures. In New Jersey, both Plainfield and Union Township schools suffered repeated cuts in funding in the 1930s. In Union Township, a blue-collar community, the effects of the depression on the schools was in many ways similar to the story in Waukegan.

Here, too, school budgets were slashed and per-pupil expenditures declined, from $99.69 in the 1929–30 school year to $65.13 five years later.[65] The local newspaper noted the impact of these cuts: "More students are crowding the halls. . . . Classes are being enlarged beyond the point of efficiency. School staffs are being slaughtered. . . . Obsolete equipment isn't being replaced. Manual training, art, music, physical training . . . are being torn out of the school. . . . Salaries, already meager, are being cut again."[66] In addition to having salaries cut, teachers were coerced into making "voluntary" contributions to the schools. A hiring freeze was imposed and the pupil/teacher ratio rose from 31.1 in 1929 to 42.5 five years later. Physical education was eliminated in the first five grades.

Yet in Union Township, unlike Waukegan, the crisis led to some changes that progressives could approve. As an economy move, the schools eliminated a number of teaching positions by developing a "co-ordinate curriculum," which integrated social studies and the related disciplines into a single course of study. In another effort to save money, the schools adopted a program of promoting all students "to move the students through the school system as rapidly as possible." The new policy, despite the pragmatic reasons behind it, was in harmony with the progressive principle of "social promotion." Moreover, under the new policy, "[t]eachers were required to grade each student as a 'total person,' and not merely in scholastic terms."[67]

In nearby Plainfield, too, the depression had a catastrophic effect on the school budget. Per-pupil expenditures declined from $100.63 per pupil in 1930 to $72.91 in 1933. This had serious effects. Teachers who left were not replaced. Maintenance was reduced. Here, too, teachers were forced to contribute part of their salaries. But in Plainfield, as in Union Township, the crisis led to some progressive innovation. The lack of jobs led many children to continue in school beyond the eighth grade. Because of the large increase in the number of students characterized as "dull" or "dull normal" who, in ordinary times, might not have gone to high school, there was a marked shift from the academic program to the vocational and commercial curricula. The depression forced the schools to give "greater attention to individual needs and to intensify efforts to find teaching methods and materials which would be both valuable and appealing." These circumstances led Plainfield to anticipate the post–World War II "Life-Adjustment" curriculum and to heed William Heard Kilpatrick's call for a less academic secondary school curriculum.[68]

Economic stringency was clearly not the only consideration that limited the acceptance of new educational ideas. Another factor that affected the acceptance of Dewey's ideas was opposition by parents and some teachers. Many teachers resisted the implication of progressive ideology that their approach was obsolete. In some cases parents resisted innovation. Moreover, the perceived link between progressive education and political radicalism in the 1930s strengthened the hands of those who resisted the new methods. In addition, professional administrators could defeat the aims of progressive education by adapting it to fit their own agenda.

The story of San Francisco's public schools provides an example of how progressive education became increasingly controversial and how progressive practices could be justified in ways that contrasted sharply with Dewey's ideas.

After 1923, when Edwin Gwinn became superintendent, the San Francisco schools adopted a number of progressive measures. But even in the 1920s, progressive education was controversial. Some parents and teachers resisted change and it is unclear how many teachers actually had child-centered classrooms.[69] But progressivism was frequently an issue in the city's complex school politics. During the 1930s and 1940s, enemies of the superintendent and the board often condemned the administration for instituting a curriculum that slighted the fundamentals. Yet progressive ideas usually prevailed, at least at the central office. As late as 1941, the schools adopted a new social studies curriculum that reflected the progressive philosophy.[70]

During the war years, however, attacks on progressive education mounted. Here, as in many other cities, the Hearst press took the lead in attacking progressive ideas and methods, claiming that the "fundamentals" had been neglected and calling for a return to the 3 R's.[71] The social science textbooks by Harold Rugg served as a lightning rod. Rugg was a member of the Social Frontier group at Teachers College and his social studies books became the focus of attack in many communities in the late 1930s. The books had been used in the San Francisco junior high schools, without opposition, for almost twenty years, but in the early 1940s they became the subject of a fierce controversy. Those who attacked the Rugg books (often without reading them) here, as elsewhere, accused them of being subversive and not sufficiently patriotic. Rugg himself was denounced as a dangerous radical.

The debate over the Rugg books involved more than patriotism; in San Francisco it led to a discussion of the basic principles of progressive education. Critics complained not only about the contents of the books, but they questioned their basic premise—that students should be challenged to think critically about social institutions. Rugg's opponents claimed that children should learn the basic facts of history and civics and that they needed to become imbued with a love of country rather than becoming critics. In an effort to end the controversy, Joseph P. Nourse, the superintendent who had replaced Gwinn in 1936, said that he was willing to remove the textbooks. But this angered the books' defenders. After the debate had died down, however, the board removed the texts. It took no position on the issues that had been raised, claiming instead that it had recently discovered that the books were too difficult for San Francisco's junior high school students.[72]

As his actions in the case of the Rugg texts shows, Nourse had no deep commitment to progressive education. As much as possible, he tried to avoid controversy. His defense of the schools' practices avoided ideological issues. He preferred pragmatic arguments. First, he claimed that "Progressive education methods have not spread any since I became superintendent" and he insisted that "[d]rill in the fundamentals is and always will be a basic part of the San Francisco school systems." But Nourse and his staff also argued that an expanded program was necessary, because parents wanted more than a 3 R's curriculum for their children.

However, they offered another, more important, reason for a less academic curriculum. Nourse conceded that some San Francisco high school graduates did not have a thorough grasp of the fundamentals but, he said, this was not because the schools neglected the 3 R's. Rather, he claimed, it was due to the tremendous increase in the number of children in secondary schools, many of whom, he said, had "poor mental equipment." These children could not be kept in any grade for more than two years and therefore they had to be promoted, even if they were not learning much in school. Therefore, Nourse defended the move from a traditional curriculum as a frank recognition that schools had to adapt to the varying needs and abilities of children as the price for keeping them in school.[73]

The issue that Nourse raised—what should be done to retain children who were not interested in traditional academic programs—would become a major challenge for American education in the postwar period as more and more students stayed in school through the high school years. Increasingly, after World War II, the most important controversies about progressive education would concern the secondary school curriculum.

Nourse's justification for the program of the San Francisco schools—the argument that many students were simply incapable of learning the traditional subjects—would also become more common. This gave an ironic twist to progressive education. It completely reversed Dewey's vision of creating a more equal society through the schools. Nourse and other school people could defend progressive educational practices (such as social promotion and a less intellectual curriculum) for distinctly undemocratic reasons— as a reasonable accommodation to the fact that some children were naturally and inherently incapable of benefitting from a traditional curriculum. In this way, stripped of Dewey's liberal goals, progressivism could be perverted into a defense of the status quo.

The fate of progressive education in the schools of these different communities in the prewar period provides some useful observations for understanding the process of educational innovation. Community wealth was clearly an important factor in the acceptance of new ideas. In the 1930s, the places in which progressive education prospered were typically wealthy suburbs like Winnetka or Bronxville, New York (which had chosen Willard Beatty, a former member of Washburne's staff, as its superintendent of schools). While Pasadena was not a suburb, it had many suburban attributes. The people who were able to control the city were in many ways similar to those who controlled the politics of Winnetka. Progressive education might well appeal to these people because of its emphasis on self-realization and creativity, traits which upper-middle-class people would value for their children. These qualities might have less appeal for the parents of the lower- and lower-middle-class children such as those of Waukegan and Mundelein. In the desperate financial situation of the 1930s, helping children to be creative was probably low on their list of priorities. Many people in these communities regarded schooling as a means for preparing children to get jobs that would bring them economic security; they saw schools as providing the necessary tools.[74]

In addition, there is a direct relationship between innovation in education and finances. During hard times, schools find it difficult to innovate; they emphasize saving as much as they can of their old programs rather than introducing new ones. Lake Forest, which did not suffer from the depression, was able to introduce progressive measures while both Pasadena and Winnetka were working hard to maintain their programs at the predepression level. On the other hand, as was the case in Union Township and Plainfield, New Jersey, some progressive practices, such as social promotion, that made schools more "efficient" might well be encouraged by austerity.

But economic conditions and class are not sufficient to explain the differential acceptance of progressive ideas. The role of community ethos in promoting innovation was crucial, as can be seen in the contrast between Lake Forest and Winnetka. Dewey's ideas were more easily accepted in Winnetka because they were in harmony with the reformist legacy of the village's founders and the ideas of Henry Demarest Lloyd. Lake Forest in the 1930s still followed a path of privatism and noblesse oblige. Yet, Lake Forest was changing and its schools would change too.

Individual leadership is also an important factor in accounting for the acceptance or rejection of new educational ideas and practices. Carleton Washburne's missionary zeal was an important reason for the success of progressive ideas in Winnetka. He could not have succeeded without the support of the teachers and others in the community, but he helped to create and sustain that support. In Pasadena, John A. Sexson demonstrated how a shrewd superintendent could protect a progressive program during hard times.

But the pattern of educational leadership was changing in the 1930s. Professional administrators like M. G. Davis in Lake Forest and Harold Campbell in New York would adapt to the fact that progressive ideas were dominant in educational circles by describing their programs in progressive terms, even when the actual school programs retained many traditional features. As in the case of Joseph Nourse, this pragmatic acceptance of some aspects of progressive education was often quite superficial. As school administration increasingly became a separate profession, its members began to speak to each other in their own language—a language which embraced many of the terms used by progressive educators.

Finally, although progressive education had had an important impact in only a few communities, by the end of the decade progressivism was becoming controversial. San Francisco provides only one example of attacks on progressive education as a soft pedagogy that did not prepare children because it neglected both the "fundamentals" and patriotism. In the 1950s these attacks would blossom as a concentrated assault on progressive education—an attack that mistakenly assumed that a large number of American schools really had implemented the ideas of John Dewey.

5

POSTWAR EDUCATION: THE CHALLENGE

*F*or Americans "V. J. Day"—the end of World War II—was a momentous occasion. It marked the successful conclusion of a long and bloody war and it promised the beginning of a new age. Yet the contours of that new age were by no means clear. The destruction of Hiroshima by an atomic bomb was a pivotal event with consequences that could only be dimly seen. Even as they celebrated, Americans pondered the meaning of the new weapon. "Whatever elation there is in the world today because of final victory in the war is severely tempered by fear," Norman Cousins noted, "a primitive fear . . . of forces man can neither channel nor comprehend."[1] Aware of the tremendous destructive power of the new weapon, many Americans worried that the nation might repeat the mistakes of an earlier generation when it rejected collective security, doomed the League of Nations, and turned its back on Europe. Many also feared the economic impact of rapid demobilization; after World War I demobilization had led to unemployment and a depressed economy. The Great Depression was a fresh memory and the threat of the return of hard times was real and haunting. Yet, this was also a time for hope. The Allied victory was seen as a triumph of America's pragmatic liberalism over totalitarianism, as a dramatic reaffirmation of Jefferson's belief that democratic government was ultimately the strongest as well as the best. Moreover, peace could bring a continuation of the new prosperity and a decision to accept America's role as a leader in world affairs.

The American people were faced with crucial choices. Educational leaders were convinced that the public school system would play an important role in preparing young Americans to help make thoughtful decisions. For many of these leaders, the results of the war gave a sense of direction to their efforts—postwar education would have to prepare youth to become responsible citizens of a new international community in democratic classrooms. The times, they firmly believed, called for the aims and methods of progressive education.

But while education would be crucial in the postwar period, after fifteen years of depression and war American schools faced tremendous problems. It is difficult to draw a comprehensive picture of American schools in this period, but one thing is clear: the most important facts could be expressed in numbers, overwhelming numbers. Americans who had lived through the depression and become accustomed to declining birthrates and teacher surpluses were astounded at what they now saw. More and more children were coming to school every year but, despite desperate efforts by school boards, there were never enough classrooms or enough teachers. Shortly after the war the census bureau warned that within a single decade American schools would have to accommodate almost half again as many pupils as they served in 1947.[2] American communities would need to build half a million new classrooms at a cost of ten to fourteen billion dollars. The leading edge of the population boom would hit in 1953 when schools would face a thirty-four percent increase over the number of first-grade pupils of 1947. The surge in enrollments in the 1950s would prove to be unprecedented, accounting for more than half of the total growth in enrollment in American schools in the fifty years between 1910 and 1960.[3]

After ten years of depression, followed by four and one-half years of total war, American schools were totally unprepared to meet this challenge.

The war itself had had a profound effect on education. Aside from postponing needed school construction, war industries had provided many inducements for teachers to leave the profession.[4] Moreover, while the war had reduced resources, it had also led to new demands on public education. Anticipating a wave of delinquent behavior as war disrupted the family, Americans looked to the schools to provide supervised recreation after normal school hours. The exodus of women into the work force fostered a new interest in day nurseries and early childhood education. At the same time, the draft had revealed that many American youth were neither physically nor psychologically fit; educational leaders recognized that they would have to pay increased attention to health education, physical fitness, and mental health.[5]

Two years after the war the respected *New York Times* education writer, Benjamin Fine, set out to assess American schools. In a comprehensive series of articles (based on a six-month survey), he painted a grim picture. He found little that was good, much that was bad, and some conditions that were disastrous. "Our schools were not bombed as were the European schools. But nearly two years after the end of the war they are being wrecked just as surely as though they had been blasted by heavy bombers." Everywhere he found "schoolhouses in use which violated every principle of democratic education. Old dilapidated, oftentimes built before the Civil War," school buildings were eyesores and "acted as a damper on any enthusiasm that teachers or pupils might have for their schools." They lacked textbooks, paper, pencils, and maps. Books were often outdated; children were learning history from books that did not include World War I. In one school Fine found forty-seven pupils making do with eighteen secondhand readers.[6]

Fine was astounded at the contrasts in American schools. While some schools were doing well, others lacked the most basic supplies. "Some pupils" were "going to school in hovels not fit for cattle." Rural schools were the worst. Thousands of them, in every section of the nation, were "operating on standards that hardly would be acceptable in the most backward nations of the world."[7]

Fine's gloomy views were confirmed by others. A 1951 national survey of school facilities found that nearly one-quarter of the nation's elementary pupils were attending inadequate schools. In nine states, one-third of all school children were enrolled in "unsatisfactory" schools and in three—Maine, New Mexico, and Vermont—the total was over half the school population. A large number of these were one-room schools, many without running water. At the beginning of the first postwar decade, over half of American schools had only outdoor privies.

Black schools in the segregated systems of southern states were abysmal. Anne Moody, who grew up in southwestern Mississippi in the 1950s, remembers her segregated rural school: "a little one-room rotten building," ill-heated, with large cracks in its walls, and a teacher who struck fear into his fifteen pupils. Southern states had not begun their desperate efforts to preserve segregation by improving Negro schools; the average value of property, buildings, and equipment per pupil in the black schools of Alabama in 1945 was $35 (compared to a national average of $441).[8] The results were a dismal mockery of the American ideal of equal opportunity.

His visits to the nation's schools convinced Fine that the crucial problem was "the most acute teacher shortage in the history of

American education." In desperate efforts to make sure that there was a teacher for every class, schools hired "taxi-cab drivers, mechanics, telephone operators, or retired janitors to become teachers." The average teacher now had less training than in 1939—Fine estimated that over half of American teachers had one year of college training or less. "We no longer ask whether an applicant can read or write," a state commissioner of education told Fine. "If she looks as though she is able to stand up we take her." One Wisconsin school hired a busboy to be a teacher. The principal conceded that the man could not "talk coherently" but, he added, "we had to take him. No one else wanted the job." Fine estimated that at least half the children attending rural schools were being taught by incompetent teachers.[9]

Moreover, the situation was getting worse. Teachers were leaving education at the rate of seventy-five thousand a year—a twenty percent turnover rate. (Fine considered ten percent to be normal.) The reasons: low pay, lack of prestige, and the fact that teachers' lives were still circumscribed by archaic rules. They were told which church to attend, how to spend their evenings, even what to wear. In many places, teachers were discharged if they chose to get married. "Never before," Fine concluded, "has the morale of the teaching staff been as low as it is today."[10]

Teachers were not only unhappy about the restrictions on the way they lived, they were increasingly dissatisfied with salaries that failed to keep pace with inflation. Some joined unions and took to the picket line. Minneapolis and Pawtucket, Rhode Island, teachers struck in 1946. A year later a record number of teachers walked out in Buffalo, New York; union truck drivers refused to cross their picket lines and the schools were closed. As strikes became more frequent, it became clear that communities would have to find additional funds to make up for the inflationary erosion of teacher purchasing power.[11]

As the Fine reports made clear, after the war Americans faced the awesome task of virtually rebuilding the public school system. They would have to find an average of 100 thousand new teachers every year for ten years. (In one year alone—*before* the baby boomers reached the first grade—the nation would need 160 thousand new teachers.)[12] At the same time, the nation would have to build thousands of new schools to accommodate the baby boom generation, while renovating or replacing buildings that had been neglected during the depression and the war. In the early 1950s, a new war in Korea exacerbated the situation as schools competed with the military for scarce resources.[13] American education would have to work hard just to stay even and, as Fine had pointed out, staying even was not good enough.

To expand the public schools to meet the crunch of the baby boom while, at the same time, modernizing and rebuilding American schools was an unprecedented challenge, but educators brought to this formidable task a number of strengths. One important asset was a new sense of professionalism that contributed to a new elan among teachers and administrators. Although the teacher shortage meant that many people hired as teachers did not meet professional standards, standards did exist and were increasingly recognized. While educational policies were still controlled by local school boards, teachers and administrators were increasingly sensitive to national professional standards and ideologies. These standards, and the ideologies that reinforced them, were buttressed by well-developed national organizations of teachers and administrators. As recognized experts, school administrators applied national standards to local schools and asked their communities to provide the funds needed to enable local schools to meet these standards.

Teachers' colleges and the education departments of the universities were important in the development of the new sense of professional identity. As we have seen, teachers' colleges had changed a great deal by the 1940s. A significant number of their faculty members had attended Columbia University Teachers College and other universities that had become centers for disseminating progressive ideas. More important, these universities had become crucial institutions for the development of the new professionalism; faculty members came back to local teachers' colleges with a new commitment to education as a profession.

Closely tied to the new professionalism was a common ideology.[14] By now, educational leaders and most teachers shared a view of education that not only defined their aims, but gave them a sense of mission and importance. This ideology provided a special vocabulary that differentiated teachers from laypeople (an important consideration when some school boards were hiring busboys as teachers). In large measure, this ideology was a form of progressivism. Dewey's ideas formed the basis of most professional discussions of educational philosophy, and such progressive shibboleths as teaching the whole child peppered educational writings. For the leaders of the profession, this form of progressivism had become "the conventional wisdom."[15]

Although American educators had adopted many of the tenets of progressive education, the prevailing ideology was not a consistent philosophy. It was a melange of not necessarily compatible principles; progressive ideas resided uneasily in combination with others that could easily undermine them. For example, many educators who saw themselves as progressives also believed in applying the principles of a "science" of education by using standardized tests to place children in classes appropriate for their abilities. This kind of "scientific" classification was popular in the context of the high prestige of science in the postwar period. Moreover, it supported bureaucratic goals and showed how businesslike standards of efficiency could be applied to the schools. But the precise classification of pupils made possible by standardized testing drew its inspiration from Thorndike rather than Dewey.[16] The emphasis on tests, measurement, and efficiency was, as Dewey pointed out, contrary to the egalitarian spirit of progressivism. Testing too often led to classification and labeling for the convenience of administrators rather than for the individualization that progressives promoted.

The emphasis on centralization and school consolidation in the postwar period also reveals the contradictory strains within the prevailing ideology. Replacing one-room schools with larger buildings was a way of promoting the progressive goal of an enriched curriculum for children in small rural communities. At the same time, however, centralization was an important way of promoting an efficiency and standardization that often worked against a central doctrine of Dewey's progressivism—spontaneity and flexibility in the classroom.[17]

Despite its inherent contradictions, however, this ideology served important purposes. It united the profession and provided teachers and administrators with a specialized methodology and language. More important, it gave them a sense of common purpose. The prevailing creed pictured schools as crucial institutions for the communities they served, working to promote prosperity, peace, and democratic harmony. At the same time, it allowed teachers to see themselves as performing a significant role in the lives of the children they taught, going far beyond simply imparting information. Imbued with this faith, teachers and administrators saw themselves as having a vital role in the life of the nation. The prevailing educational ideology, despite its internal inconsistencies, reinforced the new professionalism and unified teachers and administrators, giving them a noble purpose and conferring dignity and prestige.

Progressive education itself changed in the postwar period. Following the lead of William Heard Kilpatrick, progressives began to concentrate on the psychological "adjustment" needs of children while, at the same time, changing the emphasis of their efforts from the elementary to the secondary school.[18] As enrollment in high school became the norm for adolescents, educators worried about serving the needs of the large group of students who, they thought, had neither the talents nor the inclination to benefit from the traditional college preparatory curriculum. Yet these students' needs would not be served by traditional vocational programs. The result was the development of a new secondary school curriculum—education for "life-adjustment." The life adjustment movement was, as Lawrence Cremin has pointed out, the most important of the "postwar refinements of progressive education."[19]

It was based on a number of premises. Most important was the assumption that demobilization could lead to widespread unemployment. Ways had to be found for keeping young people in school and out of the labor market as long as possible. While educators stressed the importance of high school for "*All* American Youth," they recognized that secondary education had a long way to go—less than three-quarters of eligible young people were actually enrolled in high schools. An important reason for this, they argued, was the "failure of too many schools or teachers to provide high-school instruction having sufficient meaning, value, and appeal to the pupils and their parents." Schools would have to change if they were to increase their power to "hold" students. The curriculum would have to be adapted to the needs of children. But the revised curriculum would also have to meet the needs of an increasingly complex society. Proponents of life adjustment education argued that "the vast and complicated responsibilities of adult citizenship in the postwar world" would require "extended civic, vocational, and cultural education."

The goals of the life adjustment movement—to provide an education "which better equips all American youth to live democratically with satisfaction to themselves and profit to society as home members, workers, and citizens"—were well within the progressive canon. Moreover, despite its ill-chosen name, the movement *was* concerned with the development of intellectual skills and it did recognize "active and creative achievements as well as adjustment to existing conditions." It carried forward Dewey's commitment to schools that would serve the needs of all children, regardless of social class. But its basic premiss, that eighty percent of American youth could not benefit from a college preparatory program, had elitist implications and could easily become a self-fulfilling prophecy. Moreover, its unfortunate name, as well as the way the program was implemented, suggested an acceptance of the status quo that violated the basic principle of Dewey's philosophy of education.[20]

Closely associated with life adjustment was the movement for a core curriculum. If more "nonacademic" children were to enroll in secondary schools, then the curriculum needed to reflect their needs and interests. A curriculum based on traditional academic subjects designed to allow students to meet college admission criteria was seen as irrelevant to large numbers of high school and junior high school students in the postwar period. Accordingly, advocates of curricular reform argued that traditional subjects should be replaced by a focus on concerns of young people and the need to prepare them for citizenship. This could best be done by organizing courses around special problems rather than around traditional academic disciplines. For example, just before World War II, one Tulsa, Oklahoma, junior high school merged "all traditional subject matter . . . into a single core period . . . called 'social relations.'" Minneapolis instituted a new "integrated" twelfth-grade social studies course called "Modern Problems."[21] After the war, Minneapolis offered a more ambitious core, the "Common Learnings" program. Organized around "the personal and social problems common to the young people of the school," this two-hour class in junior and senior high school took the place of regular English and social studies classes.[22]

"Adjustment" as an educational goal was evident in a new concern for providing psychological services though the schools. Before the war, progressives had called for the application of "mental hygiene" concepts to all levels of education, but few school systems had actually implemented comprehensive programs. The end of the depression and increased anxiety about juvenile delinquency helped to spark the movement to expand counseling services. After the war, progressive educators devoted more attention to guidance programs, and counseling services became much more prevalent in the schools.

In Ohio, for example, only four percent of school districts employed a school psychologist in 1945, but this had increased to fourteen percent by 1953. More important, in that year nearly half of Ohio's school children were in districts that had school psychologists.[23] In New York State, the pattern was similar. Only 92.5 psychologists and psychiatrists were employed in the schools in 1944–45; ten years later the figure had risen to 353.[24] In one county, near New York City, the increased attention to mental health was even more dramatic. In just three years (from 1952 to 1955), the number of mental health professionals in the Nassau County schools tripled, although the school population had increased by only one-third. While nearly one-third of the county's schools reported that they had no psychological services in 1952, three years later only one school out of fifty offered no mental health services.[25]

In the early 1950s, most professional counselors were in secondary schools; a 1952–53 study reported only 711 elementary school counselors nationally, and most of those were part-time employees. As a contemporary study noted, however, the tendency was to move "gradually but inexorably in the direction of more and more [psychological] services" at all levels of schooling.[26]

But Dewey had envisioned much more than education for adjustment. The whole thrust of his philosophy was that education should play a decisive role in improving society. Social reform was to be an important aspect of the schools' mission. In 1945 progressives did not turn their back on reform. The belief that a better, peaceful world could emerge from the horrors of World War II was a strong theme in the early postwar period. Accordingly, an important part of progressive education's reform agenda after the war was a movement to help prevent future wars by promoting international understanding.

Progressive educators, like other American liberals, believed that the rise of the fascist dictators could have been prevented if the democratic nations had supported the League of Nations and collective security. In the new atomic age, the failure to preserve the hard won peace would bring unprecedented destruction. Those who had accepted the progressives' idea that teachers could play a role in improving society saw a clear mission in the postwar world: educate the next generation for peace and international understanding.

The philosophy of progressive education was easily applied to the promotion of a new internationalism. At its best, progressivism stood for acceptance and even the celebration of individual differences. Progressive schools had long been using units on foreign lands and customs to promote a sympathetic interest in other cultures, and the Progressive Education Association's journal published more articles on intercultural education than any other educational periodical.[27] Dewey's aim of using education to build a better community led quite naturally to the idea of using the schools to promote the ideal of a world community based on harmony and mutual understanding.

Progressive educators, as participants in a broader liberal tradition, believed that misunderstanding played an important role in promoting international conflict. Sharing the tendency of the American liberalism of the time to underestimate and discount self-interest as a cause of conflict and war, progressive educators firmly believed that education could play a crucial role in making the community and the world more peaceful and harmonious.[28] A textbook for elementary school teachers exemplified this belief: "Up to the present, there has been little effort to use education as an instrument for building and maintaining peace." Now, however, "educators are asking, 'Why not ban war and world strife forever by directing education consciously toward that end?'"[29]

The National Education Association took an early lead in promoting international education as a way of assuring a peaceful world. In 1945 it asked a committee on international relations in the schools to study what role "American schools could, and should, play in the maintenance of peace." The relationship between peace and progressive education was firmly established in the 1947 yearbook of the NEA's Association for Supervision and Curriculum Development. "The advent of the Atomic Age," it argued, "has necessitated a new emphasis in education. Teaching the peoples of the world how to live and work together for peace becomes the number one task of the schools." This task "calls for new content, new methods."

But the "new" content and methods were familiar to American educators as progressive education: flexible activity programs in democratic classrooms. The new curriculum would place emphasis on the cultivation of human relationships rather than on the traditional "3 R's." The reorganized elementary school would "recognize as one of its primary purposes the development of a one-world concept on the part of . . . boys and girls."[30]

As late as 1954, Carleton Washburne, one of the leading lights of prewar progressivism, was still promoting progressive education as the best way of securing peace. "Everything we do toward helping individual children and youth to live wholesome, well-adjusted, happy, understanding and co-operative lives will affect the world's future. If one traces the origin of a Hitler, a Mussolini, or a Stalin, one finds that he grew up from a frustrated, insecure, and unsocialized childhood and youth." Progressive education would produce a new generation, dedicated to working for a world that would resolve its problems peacefully.[31]

By the time Washburne was writing, however, the political climate had changed drastically. As Washburne's linking of Stalin with Hitler made clear, Russia was no longer our beleaguered ally, but had become the great enemy. It had become increasingly difficult for teachers to discuss the Soviet Union without incurring suspicion. Both progressive education and internationalism were under a cloud.

In the early 1950s, as America began to think of itself as the embattled leader of the "free world," it increasingly turned inward. In the context of increasingly shrill cries that schools should teach Americanism, a major thrust of the reformist impulse of progressivism became programs to educate for citizenship. Although these programs included materials on promoting an understanding of America's role in the world, the primary emphasis was now on developing loyalty to the American political and economic systems. Yet these programs, too, were described in the language of educational progressivism.

The Citizenship Education Project, developed by Columbia University Teachers College, was the most important example of this new movement. Generously funded by the Carnegie Corporation, the project had impressive backers. General George C. Marshall, a member of the Carnegie board, played an important role in alerting the corporation to the need for improving citizenship education. Marshall's message was reinforced by Columbia's president, Dwight Eisenhower. William Russell, president of Teachers College, was responsible for the initial design of the project.[32]

From its very beginning, the project was tied to Cold War issues. In 1948, in his first report as president of the Carnegie Corporation, Charles Dollard had complained that American schools, in their desire to avoid propaganda, "have tended to become exhibit halls in which the American value system is displayed with all others as one of a great variety of equally workable systems." Although the corporation was unwilling to offer any single solution or to "underwrite emotional appeals to Chauvinism," Dollard announced that it would "welcome any carefully conceived plan which is designed to give young Americans a fuller understanding of the American tradition. . . . Such an understanding," he argued, "might be our best defense in the hard years ahead."[33]

Russell, a dedicated anticommunist, was sympathetic to Dollard's views. The president of Teachers College had an apocalyptic view of America's future. He saw the western world as "engaged in a worldwide struggle with the forces of tyranny represented by the Soviet Union. This struggle for the survival and growth of freedom would be won or lost . . . in the minds and hearts of mankind.

Thus education and the schools became the main and final battle-ground." The nation "would go socialist" unless the schools taught the "understandings and insights to enable every citizen to participate with intelligence in voting and political activity."[34]

Although the Cold War rhetoric and the attack on relativism resonated with themes associated with attacks on progressivism, there were, nonetheless, important links between citizenship education and progressive education. The laboratory experiences developed as vehicles for teaching the essential components of good citizenship were based on Dewey's principle of learning by doing. As Richard Streb's history of the project points out, "[t]he rationale for the development and use of lab practices . . . was right out of Dewey's, *Democracy and Education.*"[35]

Another example of how educators could enlist in the Cold War without abandoning their commitment to a version of progressive education was provided by a 1951 conference on "The Schools and National Security." After an introduction that bristled with Cold War rhetoric, its report on how the nation's schools should respond to the threats posed by the USSR offered few surprises. Despite the crisis, schools "should continue to develop class instruction in accord with modern conceptions of organizing curricular materials into comprehensive units of work." This would allow children to develop the skills they would need to cope with the Cold War crisis. The required "competencies," it turned out, were firmly based on progressive precepts. Listed first was the "[a]bility to work with groups of one's peers"; second, the ability to participate "in planning objectives and activities through group processes"; and, third, to develop individual capacities "while at the same time contributing to the thinking and welfare of the group." The message was clear: the best way for American schools to contribute to national security would be to follow progressive practices in the classroom.[36]

The record of progressive education in the 1950s demonstrated that its rhetoric could be adapted to the changing political climate. The principles that had supported Harold Rugg's pro-New Deal social science texts were now used to promote an emphasis on national security in the face of a series of international threats. But the alliance of educational progressivism with anticommunism proved to be no defense against the increasing attacks on Dewey's educational ideas in the early 1950s. Critics refused to accept the new version of progressive education as a substantial improvement.[37] As Arthur Bestor noted in his caustic critique of *The Schools and*

National Security, "[b]ecause the theme is 'national security,' some of the old ideas are dressed in new costumes, just as the chorus of a Broadway revue sometimes does a number with muskets and a flag to remind the audience that a war is on."[38] It was clear that despite its altered political agenda, progressive education would face substantial challenges in the 1950s.

6

PROGRESSIVE EDUCATION
UNDER FIRE

*I*n the summer of 1948 when Willard Goslin arrived in Pasadena, California, as the new superintendent of a widely admired progressive school system, the news was only of local interest. Two and one-half years later, when Goslin was forced to resign, the events in Pasadena provided headline copy all over the nation. What happened in Pasadena became a symbol of the turmoil in American education in the postwar period.

Goslin, a tall, lanky man who had been a principal when he was only twenty-two, brought with him to Pasadena a solid reputation as a proven administrator. He had served as superintendent of schools in an upper-class suburb of St. Louis and then in Minneapolis; he was the newly elected president of the American Association of School Administrators. The Pasadena school board chose him because it wanted a leader who would help the community maintain its reputation for educational leadership. Pasadena welcomed its new superintendent with a great deal of enthusiasm.

Goslin was no radical; his approach to education was well within the mainstream. Therefore, when he was forced to resign in the wake of vicious attacks on progressive education, the struggle could be seen as an attack on the broad consensus that informed American educational thought in the early 1950s. But the Pasadena story was more than a struggle over progressive education, it revealed in microcosm many of the problems of American education in the postwar period.[1]

Soon after his arrival, Goslin recognized that he had inherited a number of problems. The community was changing rapidly. An influx of war workers had strained school facilities. Although new buildings were needed, many community leaders were reluctant to

pay for new schools at a time when building costs seemed astro-
nomically high.

The school building issue was further complicated by the fact
that the war had brought more members of minority groups to
Pasadena.[2] Initially, this had little effect on school politics; white
families living near blacks and Mexicans in so-called "neutral
zones" had the option of enrolling their children in predominantly
white schools. Now, as part of his building program, Goslin proposed new school attendance zones. Goslin, a liberal on racial issues, believed that the new district lines should be based on geography, not race; white parents in the "neutral zones" would no
longer be able to enroll their children in predominantly white
schools. This early effort at school desegregation proved to be an
emotional issue in Pasadena and was a crucial factor in the organization of a group opposed to the new superintendent and his policies.[3]

Goslin also had to deal with a crisis in morale. The school system
was torn by conflict. In his final years, the previous superintendent, John A. Sexson, had not been effective. After a serious auto-
mobile accident, he was in constant pain and he had become less
and less tolerant of dissent. Pasadena's teachers had additional
grievances. The previous administration had been slow to restore
depression era salary cuts. Teachers were also unhappy because
they thought that the Sexson administration had shown favoritism
in promotions. While school board elections were usually uncon-
tested, in an unprecedented move, the teachers had put up two
candidates in the last election and had helped to defeat two incumbents.

Thus Goslin faced what proved to be an explosive mixture: a
discontented staff, parents opposed to sending their children to
predominantly minority schools, and taxpayers concerned about
the expense of a school construction program.

Although Goslin brought to his new position a great deal of
experience, his administrative style proved a liability. It was very
different from that of his predecessor. Before his accident, John
Sexson had been a consummate politician. He had taken great
pains to work with the leaders of the business community, lunch-
ing with them several times a week at the University Club and
maintaining an open door policy.[4] Goslin, on the other hand, was
efficient but remote. As one observer noted, Goslin's "philosophy
was wonderful, but he didn't seem interested in selling his program to people who count." A National Education Association
committee that investigated Goslin's dismissal concluded that

while Goslin "showed a warm-hearted open-minded attitude toward the minority groups and the underprivileged, he seemed to be more or less on the defensive with influential people in the community."[5]

While Goslin was not identified as a leader of educational progressivism, like many professional educators, he supported a mild version of its principles.[6] Goslin could see that the Pasadena schools had already adopted a progressive program and during his short tenure in Pasadena he instigated no major curricular changes. (He did invite William Heard Kilpatrick to address teachers at a summer training institute, a move that later proved to be highly controversial.)

Even though Goslin did not change the curriculum, the school system came under sharp attack soon after he arrived, and progressive education became a leading issue in the campaign to oust the new superintendent. Goslin's opponents first began to organize to defeat an increase in school taxes. After its victory in that campaign, the group gained strength as Goslin became the focus of accumulated grievances and discontent with the schools. Finally, it was able to pressure the board to demand Goslin's resignation.

Goslin's opponents charged that the schools were too expensive, that the "frills" of progressive education cost too much, and that they had led to the neglect of traditional school subjects. They identified Goslin with the most radical progressives, the social reconstructionists, who, they claimed, wanted to use the schools to promote socialism. Locked into a Cold War mentality, they feared that the schools were promoting internationalism rather than old-fashioned patriotism. More fundamentally, they believed that progressive education, based on Dewey's philosophical relativism, undermined traditional values. The attack on Goslin was, for some of his opponents, a religious crusade.[7]

Goslin's opponents, united in an organization called the School Development Council, were supported by a number of nationally organized right-wing organizations, including American Patriots (an organization founded by the unsavory Allen M. Zoll, who had links to various anti-Semitic movements) and the Pasadena chapter of Pro-America.[8] Goslin's cause also attracted attention from groups outside the community. The circumstances under which the school board asked for Goslin's resignation indicated the national significance of the case: its telegram reached Goslin in New York, where he was attending a meeting of the National Citizens Commission for the Public Schools. Supporters of "modern" public education were convinced that much more was at stake than the superintendency of Pasadena. For them the Pasadena situation was a "'test tube' for attacks on public schools." The events in Pasadena became a national news story in 1950 and 1951. Many believed the significance of the "Pasadena story" was that it was the first skirmish in a protracted struggle for control of public education.[9]

What happened in Pasadena was important, not just because it was an illustration of the ways in which progressive education was challenged in the postwar period, but because Pasadena illustrated in microcosm many of the problems facing American schools in the 1950s. The underlying issues here, as in many other communities, were the need for new buildings, the relationship of educational administrators and the public, teacher morale, and the segregation of minorities. The struggle over progressive education in Pasadena (and in the nation) in 1950 was a debate about what public schools should be accomplishing and what resources they needed to do the job.

While attacks on progressive education were already an important factor in public debates on education on the eve of World War II, now the assault on its "soft" pedagogy escalated rapidly. The war and the increasingly technological society that emerged pointed to the need for a more rigorous curriculum to prepare highly trained graduates, while widespread fears of a dramatic increase in juvenile delinquency led to a new focus on discipline in the schools.

Worries about discipline were part of a larger issue. The defeat of Germany and Japan was followed by a frightening new struggle with our former ally—a struggle that seemed all-consuming. Many Americans of the Cold War era were convinced that the United States not only had to contain the threat of Soviet military expansion, but as Elaine Tyler May points out, they were equally concerned with a "domestic containment"—focusing on internal subversion and dangerous social forces that could destroy the American character and the ability to resist external enemies.

Progressive education was closely linked to several of the feared new social forces—secularism, bureaucratic collectivism, and cosmopolitan urban culture. Progressivism became an easily identifiable symbol for the forces that were seen as undermining the ability of Americans to resist the onslaughts of communism.[10] The passions aroused in the battle over the Pasadena schools reflected the beginning of a struggle, not just over the schools, but over the souls of Americans.

As the Cold War became more intense, critics increasingly accused the schools of being soft on communism. A survey of news-paper articles critical of the schools found that almost half of these dealt with the fear that teachers were spreading subversive ideas.[11] By 1952, *The New York Times* found evidence of a "concerted cam-paign . . . [all] over the country to censor school and college text-books." Groups were "being formed in nearly every state to screen books for 'subversive' or un-American statements."[12]

The 1950 National Education Association convention recognized "a general attack . . . on public education." Its Academic Freedom Committee reported "a sharp increase in censorship in the schools." During the Korean War, the situation rapidly grew worse. The NEA's Commission for the Defense of Democracy Through Education reported to the 1952 convention that the "number, vari-ety and violence of attacks on public education has substantially increased during the past year." Delegates were told that "the situ-ation was more serious than at any time since the public schools were founded more than one hundred years ago."[13]

The progressives' internationalist agenda was a specific target: "Teachers are accused of being 'subversive' in some communities because they introduce material dealing with the United Nations or UNESCO." In Chicago, a new civics course earned the praise of the *Chicago Tribune* for eliminating "a section devoted to outright propaganda for the United Nations and world government." The new course guide, the *Tribune* happily noted, did not "even men-tion the United Nations or 'social problems' in America."[14]

The NEA found itself in a difficult position—for several years it had sponsored seminars and workshops to "prepare teachers to take an active part in developing an international point of view among the nation's youth . . . Now some communities find that the United Nations or UNESCO material is being challenged as 'sub-versive.'" Teachers came under suspicion merely for using UN ma-terials in the classroom.[15] The NEA itself was under assault. The American Legion (previously considered a friend), attacked the or-ganization's leadership as "one of the strongest forces today in propagandizing for a socialistic America."[16]

In the fall of 1952 the federal government joined the offensive; the Senate Internal Security Subcommittee began investigating "subversive influences" in the nation's schools. Few educators re-sisted. Benjamin Fine, education editor of the *New York Times,* spoke for many professional educators of the McCarthy era when he ob-served that the investigation might well prove to be good for the profession since it would demonstrate how limited the number of subversives really were and prove that "the profession in general is almost unanimously loyal." The *American School Board Journal* also defended the congressional investigation, pointing out that subversives should have been eliminated by local authorities, "but in a period of democratic innocence we were all a little too unconcerned." Although members of the Association of School Board Administrators were disturbed about the congressional investigations, virtually everyone who attended the 1953 annual meeting agreed "that any person who was a Communist or subversive in any other way should not be permitted to teach."[17] Despite the obvious threat to academic freedom, educators refused to take a clear stand against the congressional investigations, which increasingly turned into witch-hunts.

Although the anticommunist hysteria diminished by the middle of the decade, the hopes that teachers could foster progressive education's social reform agenda by using their classrooms to promote peace and international understanding had faded. Most teachers now had accepted and internalized the constraints. The 1954 NEA Convention (devoted to the theme of academic freedom) reported that "[b]ecause of Congressional investigations of education and current attacks on the public schools, a type of self-censorship has developed among teachers . . . No one actually says 'don't talk about controversial subjects,' but the teachers are afraid."[18] Many teachers went further and endorsed the rhetoric of the Cold War. A statement of beliefs developed by Evanston, Illinois, High School social studies teachers listed as its *first* tenet: "Opposition to Communist and other totalitarian doctrines should be a concern of every American citizens."[19]

As in Pasadena, the attack on the schools often combined criticism of the curriculum for fostering internationalism and sympathy for communism with attacks on progressive education. For example, in accounting for the causes of the widespread public suspicions about education, the editor of the *Denver Post* reported that the schools were under "a cloud of fear," accused not only of "teaching communism" and advocating "loyalty to an international organization rather than to the United States of America," but neglecting the fundamentals and emphasizing "extra and useless activities."[20] Increasingly, attacks on the schools linked progressive education with treason and subversion.

In postwar America, a vocal group saw progressive education as subversive because it did not prepare children for the coming battles. As progressive methods moved into secondary education, critics were more and more alarmed. A series of acerbic but popular books led a sustained attack on progressive education and the professional educators who had accepted a version of Dewey's ideas. In 1949, Mortimer Smith's stinging critique, *And Madly Teach*, charged that progressivism—a faulty "theoretical and philosophical basis" for education—had been foisted on the schools. Public education had been "taken over by a coterie of experts who have erected it into an esoteric 'science' where every prospect pleases and only the amateur is vile." These experts, "with a clearly formulated set of dogmas and doctrines," were "perpetuating the faith by seeing to it . . . that only those teachers and administrators are certified who have been trained in correct dogma."[21]

Nineteen fifty-three marked the high tide of the attacks. Albert Lynd's *Quackery in the Public Schools* blamed progressive education for the follies of professional educators and attacked its intellectual foundations, the thought of John Dewey. He argued that Dewey's instrumentalism "excludes God, the soul, and all the props of traditional religion" as well as "the possibility of immutable truth" or "permanent moral principles." Dewey's vision of a democratic society, while firmly anticommunist, was "unmistakably socialist." Far worse than Dewey were his disciples, especially Kilpatrick, the "Grand Master of the cult," whose ideas could be described as "elementary Deweyism heavily adjectivized." Lynd's major argument was that despite their talk of "democracy," professional educators were foisting a curriculum based on Dewey's principles on people who, if properly informed, would find these ideas totally repugnant: "You know your neighbors. How many of them would vote for Deweyism if they understood the philosophical ballot?"[22]

The same year that Lynd accused the schools of quackery, one of the most intelligent of the critics of progressivism, Arthur Bestor, described America's public schools as *Educational Wastelands*. Unlike Smith, Lynd, and most other critics, Bestor, a professor of history at the University of Illinois, was not unsympathetic to some aspects of progressivism. He was, in fact, an acknowledged product of a progressive school. In the 1920s, he had attended that well-known exemplar of progressivism, Lincoln School of Columbia University Teachers College. While Smith and Lynd excoriated Dewey, Bestor quoted him respectfully to bolster his thesis that professional "educationists" (an unholy alliance of professors of education, school administrators, and members of state educational bureaucracies) had "repudiated the original principles of progressive education."

Educationists had confused the technology of education—pedagogy—with its purpose. "Genuine progressive education" linked pupil interests "to the traditional program of intellectual training."

It had been replaced by "regressive education" when educationists became preoccupied "with the learning process" and "lost sight of ultimate educational purposes." These professional educators enthusiastically endorsed Dewey's principle that to promote real learning it was important to use children's interest in classroom activities, but what they failed to understand was that *what* was taught should not be dictated by what was thought to be intrinsically interesting to children.

Taking issue with Kilpatrick and his followers, he charged that educationists failed to recognize that the methods of education suited to the lower grades were not appropriate for higher levels: "progressive education became regressive education when it projected these methods upward into higher levels of the school system." Although Bestor did not mention him by name, *Wastelands* was, in fact, a sustained attack on Kilpatrick's version of progressive education. Bestor pointed out the anti-intellectual premises of this educational thinking, and he called for a traditional curriculum, based on the academic disciplines of the liberal arts that could not be reduced to the educationists' "subject matter."[23]

The furor raised by these widely publicized criticisms put professional educators on the defensive. They found themselves engaged in an extended debate, defending "modern" education at the same time that they were desperately seeking more money to meet the enrollment crisis. For the most part, they allowed their opponents to define the terms of the debate. When it became clear that the term "progressive education" was capable of arousing strong emotional opposition, administrators avoided those words and began to speak of "modern" education.[24] They argued that modern schools were not subversive and that they did not neglect reading, writing, and arithmetic; that they were, in fact, more effective than traditional schools in teaching basic skills.[25] The Progressive Education Association changed its name to the New Education Fellowship and then, in 1955, quietly disbanded.[26]

But abandoning the words "progressive education" was not enough. As Bestor made clear, the problem involved more than competing philosophies of education. Fueling the controversy was the increasing separation between educational administrators on the one hand and parents and citizens on the other. The new style of administrators offered inviting targets for critics.

Like the members of other incipient professions, educators had attempted to define themselves by emphasizing the ways in which they differed from those who were not initiates. They had sought to insulate their new field from the influence of laypeople who, they believed, were not knowledgeable about the science of education. Increasingly, educators had developed their own language and addressed each other through specialized journals. While the new professionalism provided support at a time when education was under fire, its excesses offered critics a broad target. Administrators found that they had cut themselves off from the public whose support they desperately needed. Rebuilding American education would require dramatic increases in financial support at the district and state level and, many educators believed, probably some form of federal aid. Superintendents and school boards would need the support of a broad coalition to get the required funds. Administrators began to recognize that many of their critics were genuinely concerned about public education and were potential allies instead of enemies.[27] They saw that the schools would have to engage in an extended effort to re-establish their ties with the community. The price of continued isolation would be high; an important lesson of the Pasadena story was that public relations would have to become a priority for everyone connected with public education.[28]

Ironically, the organization Goslin was meeting with at the time he got the school board's demand for his resignation, was hard at work building public support for the schools. A direct response to the educational crises of the postwar period, the National Citizens Commission for the Public Schools was established in 1949. The new organization recognized a crisis brought on by rapidly increasing enrollments, inadequate facilities, too few teachers, and inadequate levels of revenue in a time of inflation. On the other hand, it also saw public support threatened by the increasing attacks on the public schools. Without dramatically increased public support, American schools could not meet these threats.

The commission's chairman, Roy Larsen, knew a lot about mobilizing public opinion. He was president of Time, Inc., and had worked on all of its magazines; he was responsible for the popular March of Time films and radio programs. According to Larsen, the new organization could help people not directly connected with the schools to join in support of public education in communities all over the nation. The commission would work with professionals and with existing organizations, but it would avoid being identified with any single group—it would accept as members only people "not professionally identified with education, religion, or politics." The most important principle behind the new movement was expressed in the words of the Connecticut school study commission: "education and citizens *do* mix. And when they mix better schools result."[29]

Fred Hechinger, a prominent educational journalist, saw the new public interest in improving schools as a genuine grass-roots movement, without a "central source of power or of funds"; it was only after the movement had begun at the local level that the National Citizens Commission was organized.[30] The commission served as an information exchange, coordinating and publicizing the school improvement movement with the aim of arousing "in each community the intelligence and will to improve our public schools." To promote local efforts at school improvement, it published and circulated a large number of free pamphlets answering such questions as "How Can We Help Get Better Schools?" "How Do We Pay for Our Schools?" and "How Can We Advertise School Needs?" The commission avoided taking positions on controversial issues but endorsed an expanded curriculum and the goal of paying more attention to the curricular needs of those high school students who were not college bound.

The work of the local citizens' committees was crucial in awakening the public to the needs of the public schools; voters were much more likely to support a referendum for school bonds in communities that had citizens' committees. Although the commission was careful to avoid becoming a lobby for school administrators, it did urge local groups to cooperate as much as possible with school authorities; the goal was "to help school boards and administrators create good schools, not to replace them."[31]

The commission held a number of regional conferences to encourage the formation of local citizens' committees. It enlisted the cooperation of the Advertising Council in preparing public service messages urging support for the schools. The Commission's message, "Better Schools Make Better Communities" could be seen on license plates, bread wrappers, and matchbooks.[32]

Larsen's Time/Life Films devoted two "March of Time" films to spreading the message. One focused on school improvement efforts in Arlington, Virginia, where a determined citizens' group wrested control of the schools from local politicians, instituted an elected school board, and then got voters' approval for a desperately needed bond issue to finance school expansion. The second showed how citizens had worked to consolidate rural Illinois schools, eliminating a number of one-room schoolhouses that had offered very limited educational opportunities.[33]

Between 1949 and 1955, school study committees were organ-

ized in thousands of communities across the nation; by 1953 there
were over eight thousand. Although these committees were committed to improving schools, they often had to overcome the resistance of educational bureaucrats. In Albany, New York, for example, a "Know Your Schools Committee" had been organized by six
local women's organizations in 1948, before the national commission's formation. It began by documenting the desperate need for
new facilities. After a year's study, it found that Albany's school
buildings were generally "outmoded," no new schools had been
built since 1925, and some buildings were over seventy-five years
old. In many schools the "lighting as well as the paint in the corri-
dors" were "dismal," making them "cheerless and uninviting."
Schools lacked playgrounds and gymnasiums. Sanitary facilities
were very poor: "Many of the toilet rooms were dark and dirty, and
most had no facilities for washing in them." The committee reported that textbooks were recent and in good condition; it did not
examine the curriculum.[34]

Despite the report's focus on facilities, not personnel or educational programs, school officials were suspicious and uncooperative. It took several years before a new, broadly based, citizens'
committee established a good working relationship with the board
and school officials.[35]

Although the reports of the national commission invariably
sounded an optimistic note, the movement met considerable resistance. As in Albany, professional educators sometimes opposed the
efforts of "lay" people to investigate the schools. Teachers, aware of
the tenuous nature of the new professionalism, resisted attempts
by outsiders to influence the curriculum. The American Federation
of Teachers' Washington representative denounced such efforts as
"exceedingly dangerous" and warned that they could lead to totalitarianism. On the other hand, public apathy and resistance to raising taxes were also problems. In Norfolk, Virginia, for example, a
black newspaper editor reported that although the rapid increase
in both the white and the black population had "created a crisis in the
Norfolk public-school system," its citizens were still "apathetic."[36]

But, increasingly, professional educators found that working
with citizens' committees was a good way to get the resources they
needed. They found that informed citizens could be valuable allies.
For example, in 1953, when academic freedom was threatened by a
congressional investigation of communism in the schools, it was a
member of the National Citizens Commission who made one of the
most scathing attacks on the committee.[37]

Even when citizens' committees did take the potentially controversial step of examining the curriculum, administrators found they had little to fear. In Connecticut, for example, the eighty-five committees that examined the schools' programs in their communities did not find themselves in significant disagreement with the views of professionals. School people learned that "parents and other taxpayers . . . have no desire to throw out the window the body of system and method that professional educators have worked over the years to create." While almost half the committees did stress the need for more emphasis on the fundamentals, almost all of them also recognized that this was not enough. They endorsed important parts of the progressive agenda, calling on schools to do more than merely teach the 3 R's; they wanted citizenship education, more art and music, more field trips in social studies, and more guidance counselors.[38] Educators, despite some reservations, were increasingly willing to work with these groups. The Association of School Administrators issued a cautious endorsement, pointing out that cooperation with citizens' school committees could "build a broad road for school public relations." (A little gun-shy, it did warn that the road could still suddenly turn "bumpy and hard to travel.")[39]

It turned out that despite their bitterness, the attacks on the progressivism of the schools had less support than educators had feared. Despite the heat of highly publicized controversies, such as in Pasadena, most Americans were not dissatisfied with their community's schools. In 1950, early in the period of intense criticism, fewer than seventeen percent of those who responded to a Roper poll were dissatisfied with the schools. Moreover, two-thirds of the respondents thought that what was now being taught was more worthwhile than the curriculum of twenty years earlier.[40] Two years later, a survey of parents of school children in five Illinois cities confirmed these results—sixty-two to eighty-three percent of the parents said that they were "satisfied with the school their children attended" and only two to ten percent were dissatisfied. Moreover, many parents thought that the schools should devote *more* attention to such progressive aspects of their programs as teaching children to get along with others.[41]

The attacks on progressivism and subversion subsided markedly in only a few years. By 1955, when President Eisenhower launched a series of conferences on education, culminating in a widely publicized White House Conference, there were few echoes of the controversy. "[O]ne of the milder surprises" at the preliminary Illinois conference "was the absence of any great degree of criticism of what the schools are now doing." Instead of criticizing the expanded curriculum, a Chicago reporter noted, "delegates spoke out for an even greater scope for the schools." While the Florida conference was in "unanimous agreement" that the schools should teach the "basic skills," over three-quarters of the delegates wanted "to include not only the traditional ones but also certain other skills 'essential' to satisfactory living today." The expanded list was permeated with such progressive goals as getting along with others and training in tolerance for other people and ideas.[42]

By the time of the culminating White House Conference, educators saw that their views of the purposes and methods of schooling had widespread public support. For the most part, delegates endorsed the mild progressivism that educational leaders had been promoting. To be sure, some delegates did ask the schools to devote more attention to science and math and to support moral education, but the conference reports revealed a broad consensus on American education and its aims.[43]

To a large extent, the breach between professional educators and the broader public had been healed. The vicious attacks on progressivism and the fears of subversion in the schools subsided. While the Cold War was far from over, the battles on the domestic front had quieted down. President Eisenhower had denounced "book burners"; the Senate censured Senator McCarthy.[44] While problems of inadequate facilities and too few teachers persisted, there were real grounds for optimism. As Fred Hechinger put it, the "frantic, screaming, argumentative postwar phase that cried out for immediate solutions and left no stone unturned to look for scapegoats under it—that hectic, panicky, unsafe" period was over. By 1955, people were "arguing about ways of getting more and better schools rather than whether certain labels and theories were subversive."[45]

Yet the period of calm proved brief. For several years Admiral Hyman Rickover had been arguing that the nation's schools had been misled by progressive educators. They had emphasized "adjustment" instead of rigorous instruction in the sciences and mathematics, making the United States vulnerable in a world increasingly dominated by technology and sophisticated weapon systems. In 1957, when the Soviet Union launched Sputnik, the world's first space satellite, Rickover could claim to have been vindicated: America had fallen behind because its schools had mistakenly adopted the soft pedagogy of John Dewey.[46]

In the wake of Sputnik, a comprehensive review of the curriculum led to new attention to science, mathematics, and foreign languages. University-based scientists and mathematicians developed new courses of study (with little or no participation by local teachers). While the new curricula did follow Dewey's principle of enlisting the interests of students, they paid little attention to the school as a learning community and gave teachers few opportunities for creativity and spontaneity. They emphasized subject matter rather than the needs of the individual pupil. Progressive education, it was now argued, had played an important role in undermining the nation's military and industrial strength. Now, however, professional educators offered little resistance; most accepted the demands for more rigorous programs in science and mathematics—providing they could get funds to hire new teachers and buy new equipment.

By this time, American schools were much stronger than at the beginning of the decade. Educators and their allies in the National Citizens Commission for the Public Schools had had considerable success in persuading Americans to give increased support for education. More new schools were built in 1954–55 than in any previous year. The proportion of the gross national product devoted to education had begun a remarkable rise. In 1945, Americans had spent an equivalent of only two percent of the GNP for education; by 1957 that figure had risen to nearly five percent—the highest figure since before the depression.[47] This increase was not merely a function of increased enrollments; between the 1949–50 and the 1955–56 school years, expenditure per pupil in average daily attendance (measured in constant dollars) increased by nearly one-third.[48]

There was remarkable progress in other areas. School consolidation proceeded at a rapid pace, eliminating many one-teacher schools. More and more rural children were now attending larger schools with more varied curricula and the kinds of specialized teaching and services that had become the norm in urban schools.[49] Increasingly, communities provided public kindergartens (a progressive feature that many schools had lacked).[50] More schools had begun to employ school psychologists and counselors. Elementary guidance programs were becoming the norm.[51] Benjamin Fine, whose gloomy reports had helped alert the nation to the postwar crisis, told his readers in the fall of 1955: "As parents visit the schools this week, they can be reassured that despite any shortcomings, the public schools today are better than they have ever been before."[52]

Teachers now had more training. In Illinois, for example, in 1944–45 only thirty-seven percent of the elementary teachers had had college degrees. Ten years later, this figure had risen to sixty-two percent.[53] Teachers were more satisfied with their jobs than they had been at the beginning of the postwar period. Although they still believed that they needed better facilities, two-thirds of the elementary school teachers reported that the materials and equipment provided were "more satisfactory than not." (But only half of the teachers thought that their own classrooms were in this category). Two-thirds of the teachers now said that school boards and administrators placed no restrictions on their personal lives. Significantly, over three-fourths of the elementary school teachers said that, given the choice, they would "probably" or "certainly" become teachers again.[54]

In the decade since the attack on Willard Goslin seemed to signal the beginning of a comprehensive attack on American educators, they had succeeded in re-establishing links with their communities and, for the most part, they had gotten the funds required to meet each year's larger enrollments. Progressive education, however, had not fared well. Increased pressure to deal with high school students who were not thought able to benefit from a college-preparatory course did lead to important changes in the high school curriculum. While they no longer talked of "life adjustment," high school administrators did establish special programs for students who, it was thought, could not benefit from the college preparatory curriculum. At the elementary level, teachers were urged to pay attention to the needs of "the whole child" and guidance programs, designed to foster adjustment, were now common. Virtually all new school buildings had portable desks that could facilitate a progressive program. But part of the price that educators had paid for increased community support had been to abandon much of the progressive impetus. Dewey's central concepts—that the schools should enlist the interests of pupils and, more important, that the schools should foster the birth of a better, more lovely, community, were not part of the new national consensus.

7
POSTWAR EDUCATION IN
THE SUBURBS

*I*n 1958, progressive education was, once again, on the defensive. *Time* found a "New Mood" in American schools, an emphasis on "not the social but the intellectual in education." The nation was now "pretty well fed up with the philosophy of education" that had "dominated the public schools for the last three decades." Even teachers recognized that "progressive education has failed the American public."[1]

Like other attacks on progressive education, the *Time* report had about it an air of unreality; it assumed that Dewey's ideas had had a major impact on American classrooms. Accounts of the undermining of America by permissive schools that neglected the teaching of basic skills and traditional values made a powerfully attractive story. At a time when Americans lived in the shadow of nuclear war, many people resonated to these attacks on a visible source of subversion, one that was close to home and one that might be subject to their control. But while newspapers, popular magazines, and countless books were arguing as if Dewey's ideas were the dominant philosophy of American schools, it is by no means clear that these ideas had had much effect on typical American classrooms. The strident attacks on progressive education in the 1950s were ultimately much more revealing of the mentality of Cold War America than they were reflections of what was actually happening in American schools.

Contemporary studies give little support to the popular notion that Dewey's ideas had transformed American schools. Even Albert Lynd (author of the polemical *Quackery in the Public Schools*) admitted that "[t]he new education has touched the curriculum in our town only lightly." A reviewer pointed out that if Lynd had visited other schools he would have found a similar picture because "fundamentally education has changed but little in the last half century."[2]

A number of school surveys support this view. In 1949 Allison Davis, a University of Chicago social anthropologist, reported on a five-year study that had taken him to five hundred classrooms. According to Davis, schools paid little attention to Dewey's principle that the curriculum should enlist pupils' natural curiosity. "Most teachers, facing a curriculum which cannot hold the interest of their pupils . . . have made 'discipline' their chief concern." As a result, "the majority of children do not understand the work supposedly 'learned' in school." Teachers' disciplinary efforts included whipping, locking children in rooms, and threatening them, as well as such "self-administered" punishments as "compelling second grade pupils to place their heads on their desks when visitors entered a room."[3]

These findings were echoed by others. Ralph Tyler, who had served as research director of the Progressive Education Association's famed Eight-Year Study and who had participated in many of the University of Chicago's school surveys, maintained that "school practices fail to take emotional learning into account. The program of the school," he charged, "is primarily concentrated upon the acquisition of facts through repeated recitations, and the development of certain skills and habits through continued practice."[4] An angry parent's polemic, *The Public School Scandal*, agreed. Earl Conrad castigated the schools for their failure to adopt the principles of progressivism. American schools, he charged, were routinized, mechanical, and run like factories. Primarily concerned with academic subjects, they did not individualize and made no efforts to meet the emotional needs of children.[5]

In 1953, when the attack on progressivism was at its peak, the American Association of School Administrators reported that of the four basic patterns of curriculum organization, the most traditional—the "subject curriculum"—was still "the most widely used" in American schools. On the other hand, the most radical pattern, the experience or "activity curriculum," based "solely on the basis of pupils' needs and interests," was "more of a theoretical pattern of organization than an actual one . . . more talked about than practiced."[6]

Classrooms remained quite traditional even when schools created conditions in which progressive practices could flourish. Although most schools now had moveable desks, a study of school seating in Texas reported that teachers often arranged them in

straight rows and "spent much time in maintaining exact place-
ment." Moreover, far from embracing opportunities for transforming their classrooms into Dewey's cooperative learning communities, teachers complained that portable desks "made it more
difficult to keep pupils seated quietly" and that they "encouraged
pupils to work together." The study concluded that "[t]eachers in
general have not learned how to use the freedom made possible by
flexible furniture and improved classrooms."[7]

When a school system made a commitment to a progressive curriculum, this, too, did not necessarily change classroom practices.
In a study of curricular reform in the Minneapolis public schools,
Barry Franklin found that although the schools adopted features of
the "core curriculum," this had only a limited impact. An integrated "Modern Problems" course, introduced just before World
War II, differed little from previous social studies courses. A more
ambitious "Common Learnings" program, begun in 1945 (when
Willard Goslin was superintendent), was never implemented in all
of the system's secondary schools. Moreover, the social studies and
English teachers who did teach in the program received little special instruction or guidance. Accordingly, teachers in Common
Learnings classrooms followed a variety of practices, some related
to students' interests and needs and some that were quite traditional. Two of the teachers in the program confided that they
taught the same college-preparatory curriculum in their Common
Learnings courses as in their regular classes. The program had
aroused strong opposition, but in most of the classrooms that participated, it changed the traditional college-preparatory curriculum
only slightly.[8]

The attacks on progressive education in the 1950s, like the rhetoric of the progressives in the 1930s, gave the impression that
Dewey's philosophy had triumphed. But accounts of what was
happening in American classrooms presented a decidedly different
view. Once again the rhetoric of educational advocacy muddied the
waters. Accordingly, the real impact of progressive ideas can only
be seen by looking at individual communities and their schools.
Local studies can afford important insights into the role of the ideology of progressive education in day-to-day decisions by school
boards, administrators, and teachers. The story of schooling in
Winnetka, Lake Forest, Waukegan, and Mundelein after World War
II, therefore, provides a useful perspective on the meaning of a
turbulent and troubled era. How were these communities affected
by the debate on progressivism and subversion? Did the strident
attacks on Dewey's educational philosophy lead to controversies in

their schools? This chapter tells the story of postwar education in suburban Winnetka and Lake Forest; the next deals with the schools of Waukegan and Mundelein.

Lake Forest and Winnetka commuters, riding the Northwestern train to their city offices, undoubtedly read the *Chicago Tribune*'s articles and editorials that heatedly denounced progressive education and socialist teachers. But these accounts did not reflect what was happening in their own schools. During the postwar period, both school systems changed a great deal, but not in ways that would have been anticipated by simply reading newspaper and magazine stories about the national crises in education.[9] In each case, the ways in which the schools changed was a product of their own histories, developments within each community, and the personalities and goals of their superintendents.

The national reaction against progressive education had its most direct effect in Winnetka. Although the town had had a national reputation for its innovative school system, by the 1950s Winnetka's experiment in progressive education was floundering. The man who had molded the Winnetka program, Carleton Washburne, had been gone for a dozen years. Since his departure, the schools had seen four superintendents come and go.[10] The Graduate Teachers College had disappeared, the counseling program had been curtailed and Winnetka had stopped publishing its own instructional materials. By the early 1950s, the Winnetka schools were no longer in the forefront of educational innovation; they were drifting. While the schools had kept many progressive features from earlier years, these had become diluted by other, contradictory practices. For example, the 1952–53 board of education report showed fourth graders at Crow Island School in an activity program using the school's museum to study "the formation of the world" and third graders preparing to spend some time living as the early settlers did in the "Pioneer Room" in the school's basement. It also showed some very traditional practices: second graders "enjoying their phonics drill" and a third grade "drilling with flash cards." A picture of a third-grade reading period at Crow Island showed all the specially designed, portable desks neatly facing the front of the room.[11]

Washburne was gone but not forgotten. Sidney P. Marland, Jr., who became Winnetka's superintendent in 1956, remembers with amazement that his secretary occasionally promised to put callers through to Dr. Washburne—"This, after thirteen years!" Marland knew that the long shadow cast by Washburne was one reason for the rapid turnover of superintendents, and he saw his major task as moving away from the Washburne legacy, redefining the schools and their mission.[12]

Marland recognized that the times were different and that the role of the school superintendent had changed significantly. Washburne had been an innovator, a man who enjoyed trying out new ideas and who inspired others. Like John Baggett of Lake Forest and John Sexson of Pasadena, however, Washburne, despite his genuine love of democracy, was clearly the commander in the school hierarchy. His model of leadership was distinctly paternal. While he encouraged free discussion and collaboration among the members of "his" staff, it was always clear where the real power (amply clothed in charm!) really lay.[13] Sidney Marland, like Willard Goslin in Pasadena, represented a new type of school superintendent. Marland depicted Washburne as "an intellectual giant . . . an indefatigable writer of very important educational works," but he described himself as "a garden variety working superintendent." His kind of instructional leadership, he said, leaned "heavily upon the creativity of others," and his writing was largely confined to communicating with the board of education, the faculty, and the community. This reflected national trends. As the times had changed, so had the role of educational administrators. By the 1950s, in the midst of a nationwide teacher shortage, teachers had achieved a greater sense of their own dignity and power, and school superintendents no longer could count on the kind of deference from the staff that allowed young Carleton Washburne to impose his vision of a new educational program. The new leader of the Winnetka school system defined his role in a revealing way. He saw himself as "superintendent of educational enterprises" rather than as "superintendent of instruction"—charismatic leadership had given way to the "Organization Man."[14]

The town of Winnetka, too, had changed since the day when a brash young Carleton Washburne could aspire to rebuild the schools and make them into a showcase for progressive education. Most of these changes had taken place long before Marland arrived. Unlike other suburban communities in the era of the baby boom, the pace of growth in Winnetka had slowed. While the community had grown rapidly in the 1920s, after World War II, there were few vacant building sites and existing homes were usually out of the price range of the young parents of baby boomers. During the 1950s, while the populations of some Chicago area suburbs were increasing by factors of four, five, or even six, Winnetka's population increased by a sedate ten percent. Moreover, Winnetka's population now was significantly older than that of other suburbs. The community did not face the seemingly insatiable demand for new school buildings and ever more teachers.[15]

In choosing Marland, Winnetka made clear that it was looking for a new kind of superintendent. Marland was a decorated veteran of the Pacific campaigns of World War II who had become an "outstanding" high school English teacher before becoming superintendent in another wealthy suburb—Darien, Connecticut. The new superintendent (who would later serve as President Nixon's Commissioner of Education) was not a progressive. Significantly, several members of the Winnetka school board were upset by Marland's decision to meet with Washburne before taking up his new duties. They pointedly told the new superintendent: "We invited you here because you were different from Mr. Washburne. We trust we were not in error in this judgement."[16]

Marland recognized that by the mid-1950s many Winnetkans were no longer happy to have their schools identified as exemplars of progressive education. As one parent had observed a few years before Marland's arrival, there was now "a great deal of new interest in what is being taught in the schools"; people wanted to "know how the goals in modern education can be measured against the old subject matter goals and whether the schools are on the right track. They wonder if the schools and the community can agree on an American heritage which should be taught."[17] Many were convinced that the schools were "preoccupied with non-intellectual activity, and that academic discipline was out of vogue." The board of education's message to Marland was clear; it wanted the new superintendent to make "a major re-evaluation of the curriculum toward giving a much larger emphasis to scholarship and standards." This mandate did not bother him. He believed that "Progressive Education had had its day"; it had made important changes in the schools, but now it was time to move on. It was time to re-emphasize "what we once disparaged as subject matter and academic discipline."[18]

Within the schools, too, there was a sense that something was wrong. The heart of problem, as Marland saw it, was that although the schools were still following many of the practices inspired by Washburne, they had not sustained the spirit of innovation and creativity that had been Washburne's most significant contribution to the Winnetka public schools in the 1920s and 1930s. Teachers were using materials developed twenty-five years earlier, a curriculum which a new generation of teachers had had no hand in creating. As Marland put it, "those of us who were 'new to Winnetka' found ourselves coloring in the line drawings created by other artists."[19]

Marland recognized that he had to move the schools in a new direction to solve two major problems—the community's suspicions that the curriculum lacked rigor and the teachers' sense of drift. He told the Winnetka teachers and staff that it was time to move beyond labels such as "Deweyism or . . . Progressivism," time to move beyond pedagogical ideologies. "Progressive Education . . . was no longer a meaningful term." Without discarding concern for meeting the needs of "the whole child," teachers would have to recognize that the primary role of the school was to "stretch the mental resources of every child to his greatest fulfillment . . . [I]n our fervor to serve the whole child," he noted, educators have given so much emphasis to the "emotional, social and physical parts that our lay audience believes we have omitted the part about which we are most competent and concerned, . . . [the] intellect. In this we have done ourselves, as teachers, and education in general, a disservice."[20]

To make changes, Marland knew he would have to win the allegiance of the teachers, some of whom, "bemused with Winnetka's past," regarded change as heresy. Marland noted that the traditionalists were entrenched in the Winnetka Teachers' Council and he saw the power of the council as a threat to his leadership. "I had not come to Winnetka," he recalled, "to be a ballot counter for the teachers' association." The new superintendent had a strong aversion to teachers' unions. He saw them as threats to his authority and as incompatible with professionalism. He challenged Winnetka's teachers to reject "the unbecoming posture of coal miners or teamsters huddled in collective security."[21]

Marland moved quickly to outflank the council, creating a new organization composed of teachers and administrators—the Planning and Advisory Committee. This new organization quietly "absorbed the deliberative function that was once felt to be the full faculty's prerogative in the teachers' association."[22]

The most important task of the planning committee was curriculum reform. Marland was convinced that "the intellectual fare" offered by the Winnetka schools was "thin" and his major goal was increasing academic rigor. He called for a new curriculum that would retain many aspects of Washburne's approach but which would set higher goals for each grade and each subject. Under Marland's guidance, the committee began a revision process that involved virtually the whole faculty. They developed a new curriculum that was still highly individualized, but emphasized (in direct opposition to Washburne's ideas) moving topics to earlier grades. The revised program paid more attention to meeting the needs of "gifted" children and markedly changed the group and creative activities. These were now much more closely tied to academic topics for, Marland thought, he could not "justify today the pupil time and teacher energies called forth for an activity that had no relevance to the [academic] curriculum."[23]

Yet, despite this marked change in emphasis, Winnetka retained the framework of individualized self-instruction, using locally developed materials, with individually paced progression through the subjects. Marland also followed Washburne's example in ask-

14. "Social Studies Project" at Skokie Junior High School in the 1950s. Although Carleton Washburne and Raeford Logan had left, Winnetka retained many of the progressive features they had brought to the junior high school program. Photograph by Marshall Berman, Jr. Courtesy of the Carleton Washburne Memorial Library, Winnetka Historical Museum.

15. Children working at their desks at Greeley School, Winnetka, in the 1950s. Note that the desks, though not bolted to the floor, are neatly arranged in rows. The children, however, are apparently working independently and the teacher is not at the front of the class. Photographer not known. Courtesy of the Carleton Washburne Memorial Library, Winnetka Historical Museum.

ing classroom teachers to participate in developing the new program. This gave them a renewed sense of commitment; they were no longer merely carrying out plans drafted long ago by others. Like the teachers who had worked with Washburne in the 1920s, they believed that they were engaged in an important process that would affect American education beyond the boundaries of Winnetka. As Marland put it, the process of revising the curriculum reaffirmed "Winnetka's role as experimenter, innovator and contributor to education at large."[24]

Increasing the academic emphasis met some of the criticism that had been leveled at the schools, but Marland knew that it would take more to win the community's support. Like the founders of the National Citizens Commission for the Public Schools, he recognized not only the importance of re-establishing the public's faith in the schools but the reasons behind the public discontent. For too long, he charged, "the schools of this nation held themselves apart from the people." It was time to recognize that "[w]e cannot succeed without their understanding and support."[25]

The mid-1950s, when Marland came to Winnetka, was the height of the wave of popular criticism of American schools and attacks on educational progressivism. Recognizing that many people in the community were unhappy with the schools, the new superintendent moved rapidly to deal with public relations. In a bold move to capture the initiative, Marland called a large public meeting and asked for public comments about the schools (in writing rather than in speeches—thereby avoiding a forum that could exacerbate dissatisfaction). After reviewing the comments, he appointed nine study groups, made up mostly of laypeople, but led by faculty members. In most cases, their recommendations were implemented. As a result of these efforts, "the administration gained a spirit of general warmth and affirmation in the community." Rejecting the idea that only professional educators should be involved in establishing curricular policy, Marland used these lay-professional committees to discuss such potentially controversial issues as teaching about communism. In addition, Marland used monthly meetings of the Central PTA board and the principals as "a continuing lay-professional advisory body on broad policy matters." His efforts were remarkably successful; by 1961, when an outside agency surveyed community attitudes, ninety-five percent of the respondents reported that they were satisfied with the schools.[26]

Yet Marland had not won community acceptance by making Winnetka into a conventional school system. As he put it: "amid the ashes of Progressive Education" Washburne's ideas (with the exception of postponing learning) were "as vital today in Winnetka . . . as they were 40 years ago." The schools still emphasized individualization of instruction with a goal of 100 percent mastery of each goal (and therefore no conventional grading).[27] But there were real differences. Washburne's decision to postpone learning was based on an important principle. He believed that education should be based on Dewey's axiom of enlisting the child's interest, and his conviction that efforts to teach children subjects before they were ready would "permanently blight" their desire to learn: "After all, what is the hurry?"[28] Marland, on the other hand, was concerned with insuring that each child learned as much as possible at every grade level. While in their 1961 statement of "Beliefs and Objectives" the Winnetka schools still included the progressive goal: "Consider the Child as a Total Human Being," it had now become the third objective, coming after "Give Primary and Unremitting Devotion to Intellectual Growth" and "Teach the Basic Skills Thoroughly." Furthermore, the most progressive features of the Winnetka schools in the 1930s—the group and creative activities—were now considerably less important (although there was still a student-run co-op store and a student insurance company that paid for broken dishes in the lunchroom).

By the early 1960s, the schools saw themselves once again as "on the cutting edge of educational advance." But while keeping much of Washburne's emphasis on the scientific study of education and the promotion of efficient learning, they had jettisoned much of the other—the progressive aspects—of Washburne's program.[29] The schools were still receiving national attention, but they were no longer offered as examples of Dewey's principles in action.

Although World War II would lead to a radical transformation of American suburbs, in 1945 Lake Forest was still a small, upper-class enclave. Its lakefront was still dominated by elegant estates, the homes of many of the members of Chicago's social elite. In other parts of the town were the homes of servants, former servants, and tradespeople. The town was run by and for the interest of the elite. The line between public and private services was blurred. Residents of the estates on Lake, Sheridan, and Green Bay roads often hired uniformed off-duty members of the town's police force to guide traffic for their large parties. Political decisions were made by a small, self-perpetuating caucus dominated by the members of the exclusive Onwentsia Country Club. The public schools were governed by an appointed school board composed of people who, for the most part, did not send their own children to these schools.

Yet it was clear that change was coming. Unlike Winnetka, Lake Forest had a great deal of vacant land and the owners of large estates were increasingly willing to divide their property and sell off building lots. Population increased rapidly in the 1950s—from 7,819 to 10,687 (an increase of thirty-seven percent). By 1960, almost half the houses in town had been built in the last decade. As more and more members of the middle class moved in, the town would have to change.[30]

These changes, in turn, would have a profound effect on the schools. When the war ended, Lake Forest's schools still reflected the class divisions within the town. Despite the school board's efforts to broaden the appeal of the public schools, they still served primarily the children of the town's servants and tradespeople. The families that lived in the estates continued to send their children to the private elementary schools in town or, as they got older, to eastern prep schools. The ideal of the common school—a place where people from different classes would learn together—was still unachieved in 1945. But as new residents moved into town, the schools would have to adapt. Middle-class parents would not be satisfied with a system that asked them to pay taxes to support one school system while they paid tuition for their children in other schools; nor would they want their children to attend schools regarded as unsuitable for the children of the elite.

Within a few years the pressure of increasing enrollments was noticeable. Right after the war, the public schools had thirty-five teachers and 618 pupils. In 1956, enrollment totaled 987, and the next year the number jumped to 1,145. By 1961, eighty-two teachers taught 1,346 pupils in the Lake Forest Public Schools.[31]

The board of education had begun to prepare for change in the late 1930s. Superintendent John Baggett had been eased out and a new "modern" superintendent had begun the transformation of the schools. Under M. G. Davis, Lake Forest had adopted a number of contemporary reforms. By the eve of World War II, the schools had changed in important ways and the board of education described its schools in progressive rhetoric. But many of the "progressive" changes Davis had brought to the schools were relatively superficial. The real task of changing and selling the schools would fall to Davis's successor, Frederick Quinlan.[32]

Quinlan arrived in Lake Forest in 1944. (Davis had moved on to a superintendency in a larger system.)[33] Within a few weeks he began implementing one of his major goals: reshaping the community's relationship with its schools. Public relations would be a major emphasis of the Quinlan administration. Accordingly, a careful reader of the local newspaper would conclude that Quinlan was everywhere in the community, visiting and joining organizations. Almost every week the newspaper reported on the new superintendent's activities in Lake Forest or his participation in state and national educational activities. His energy and his commitment to community involvement in the schools were soon clear to everyone.

At the end of his first year Quinlan prepared a report (published in the newspaper) which frankly stated his goals. Foremost among these was "selling" the idea that the public schools should be the schools of the whole community. "[T]he schools' relation to the community," he said was of "paramount importance." The PTAs could play a crucial role in this—they offered many opportunities "to interpret the [schools'] program to the community"—especially to members of its elite. The PTAs, he pointedly noted, made a "serious effort . . . to interest *intelligent, discriminating* people in what really takes place in the schools of Lake Forest." An encouraging sign of the community's increasing interest was the willingness of nineteen prominent members of the community to accept his invitation to visit the schools. While promoting public education, Quinlan was careful not to antagonize the private schools: "the several schools may flourish side by side and continue, each in its way, to contribute to the educational program of the community." When Quinlan invited prominent Lake Foresters to the schools, he shrewdly included the headmaster of the town's most prestigious private elementary school.

Quinlan recognized that "the quality of the teaching staff" was essential to his goal of enhancing the community's acceptance of public school education; well-qualified teachers who had attended eastern colleges would help improve the image of the schools. Accordingly, the board authorized him to "seek qualified teachers not only in the Middle West but in the East or in any section of the country from which satisfactory teacher applications may come."[34] The new superintendent's program to sell the schools to the community received the enthusiastic support of the board; it hailed the beginnings of Quinlan's term as a "golden year."[35]

The board and the administration's emphasis on public relations, the product of the unique place of the public schools in the community, put them in a good position to weather the storms of national educational controversies. The stress on building public support for the schools anticipated the work of the National Citizens Commission for the Public Schools, and Lake Forest was well prepared to allay the wave of public suspicion of the schools that marked the early 1950s. For example, when, early in the days of the Cold War, critics were charging that "unsavory indoctrination" was infecting the nation's schools, Quinlan merely reiterated his usual invitation to the public to visit the schools and to examine the course of study and textbooks to see for themselves what was happening in the town's classrooms.[36] This approach was effective and there is no evidence that charges of subversion were leveled at the Lake Forest schools or teachers.

Quinlan was an easy man to talk to and he welcomed public discussion of educational policies. He avoided the mistake of some professional administrators of the 1950s who locked the schools behind walls of educational "scientific" expertise and educational jargon. The superintendent encouraged citizens to study the curriculum (which in other school systems was often jealously guarded from tampering by "lay" people) and was willing to listen to their suggestions. In 1948, for example, at Quinlan's behest, a fathers' study group discussed methods of grading and reporting student progress as well as ways of bringing new teachers to the schools and retaining them.[37] A year later, working closely with the teachers, Quinlan produced "A Statement of the Curriculum" to promote "an intelligent understanding of the much discussed but rarely documented public school curriculum." The report, distributed to parents, served as the basis for discussions by several curriculum study groups sponsored by the PTAs.[38] Rather than imposing change from the superintendent's office, Quinlan consulted teachers and parents, holding special meetings with parent groups before making any substantial alteration in the schools' programs. Significantly, the local newspaper published its account of a parents' meeting that discussed a new policy under the headline: "Parents Approve School Changes."[39]

Constantly aware of the need to build community support for the public schools, Quinlan, used the newspapers, a "Home-School Relationship Committee," the board itself, and especially the PTAs to publicize the activities of the schools.[40] His relationship with the PTAs was exemplary; Quinlan shared his experience with a national audience, addressing a joint session of the American Association of School Administrators and the National Congress of Parents and Teachers on "The Superintendent and the PTA."[41]

Like the legendary Carleton Washburne, Quinlan was a charismatic figure, popular with teachers and throughout the town. A tall man, with a distinguished mustache, he "looked like a bank president," and friends remember him as "very impressive" and highly personable. Commenting on the visibility of class divisions within the town, Quinlan recalled that when he first came to Lake Forest "the gardeners and the chauffeurs would all tip their hats to him," but "he broke them of that in a hurry by tipping his hat back to them!"[42] Not willing to be confined to an office, he was seen everywhere and he was eager to talk to everyone. A parent recalls that he had friends in all of the political and economic groups, including the elite. "He touched base with a wide group of people and was at home with all."[43]

He also emulated Washburne in giving teachers a sense that they played an important role in determining the direction the schools would take and that he valued their contributions to planning and innovation. One teacher remembers Quinlan as "just terrific. He encouraged his teachers [and] he got the best out of them."[44] In

1946 he began a series of faculty meetings during school hours focused on the curriculum. (Holding these meetings during the school day was a significant innovation and merited an article in the *American School Board Journal*.)[45] Within a few months Quinlan reported to the board that the program demonstrated the teachers' ability "to organize and carry out an effective program of curriculum improvement."[46] A year later, Quinlan began the school year with a special three days of seminars for teachers. These pre-school meetings soon became a regular part of the schools' calendar. Sometimes they concluded with an invitation to the staff to have tea at the Quinlans'.[47] As part of his emphasis on faculty development, Quinlan got funds from the board to encourage teachers to attend professional meetings and to visit other schools. Most important, when he reported on new programs to the board, he enthusiastically praised the teachers who had helped develop them.[48]

Quinlan recognized that in order to succeed at his major task—improving the image of the public schools so that they would become the schools of the whole community—he needed to establish a reputation in national educational circles. Accordingly, at the same time that he cultivated the people of Lake Forest, Quinlan was active in a host of national educational organizations. He maintained close ties with Columbia University Teachers College and he was one of the founding members of the Association of Public School Systems (APSS), based at Teachers College.

Although APSS was affiliated with Teachers College, it reflected the research and efficiency movements in American education rather than the philosophy of John Dewey and William Heard Kilpatrick. The inspiration for the organization was Professor Paul Mort, whose research focused on new methods to improve the process of diffusing educational innovations—his emphasis was on administrative efficiency.[49] Quinlan also brought Lake Forest into another national program administered by Teachers College—the Citizen Education Project (CEP), which carried with it the prestige of its head, Dwight Eisenhower.[50]

Lake Forest's membership in APSS and the CEP made it clear that the community's public schools were among the most modern in the nation and could serve as a model for other, less favored, towns. They learned, for example, that the eighth-grade program at Gorton School had been commended in the "nationally circulated" CEP newsletter for implementing a program originally devised for the high school level.[51] At the same time, Lake Foresters noted that their superintendent of schools (who was elected national president of APSS in 1950) was recognized outside of the community as an educational leader.[52]

The educational program of the schools, however, underwent few dramatic changes during the Quinlan years. The new superintendent's first reports to the board on the curriculum reflected an educational philosophy that combined some progressive principles with traditional educational goals. He spoke like a progressive when he stressed the importance of the "interest factor in the teaching of reading" and the importance of recognizing "the individual's rate of progress." But he echoed more traditional attitudes when he referred to the "transfer value" of arithmetic teaching and the importance of drill. He built on the policies begun by one of his predecessors, Leonard Loos, grouping children by age, putting all of the lower grades in a single building and adding the fifth- and sixth-grade program to the upper school.[53] Later, when rapid growth called for new buildings, Quinlan and his staff developed a system that housed the lower grades in neighborhood schools and the upper grades in a new, modern, centrally located facility, Deer

16. Students working together in the Gorton School library, 1946–47 show the way that the informal learning advocated by progressives had entered the Lake Forest schools. Photograph by Ward H. McMasters. Courtesy of Jean McMasters Grost.

Path School. These policies reflected the recognition of children's differing developmental needs as well as a concern for administrative efficiency.

The curriculum continued to feature some progressive aspects— a junior kindergarten, frequent field trips, projects, and participation in student government at the elementary level.[54] For example, pupils in a history class at the upper school enriched their study of the colonial period of American history by creating their own "colonial documents" written from the viewpoint of contemporaries in the language of the period.[55] Children at Everett School made a project out of organizing a country fair. According to an enthusiastic newspaper account, this served important educational purposes; the children learned a great deal through the practical application of arithmetic, writing, art, music, and bookkeeping. Echoing the principles of Kilpatrick, the paper concluded that "[n]o amount of reading or recitation could be as convincing as first hand experience."[56] In a similar vein, report cards for elementary students disappeared and teachers gave parents a written report and held individual conferences. (The schools had not, however, given up on grading—despite the elimination of report cards, records of student progress were kept on file at the school.)[57]

Yet Quinlan (like Washburne) knew that the schools would be judged by student success in mastering the traditional curriculum, and the most prominent feature of the curriculum in the Quinlan era was ability grouping. Beginning in the 1946–47 school year, the schools combined two or more classes and then divided them into reading groups on the basis of the children's reading levels. In the upper school, fifth and sixth graders shared reading groups. While ability grouping could be seen as an attempt to adjust the curriculum to the needs of the individual child (a progressive principle), school officials stressed instead that the major advantage of this program was that the plan "tends to eliminate waste . . . and makes for a greater degree of efficiency."[58]

Ability grouping soon became the most significant distinguishing feature of the Lake Forest Public Schools. By the mid-1950s, when the national debate about education focused on the "softness" of the curriculum and on providing special encouragement to gifted children, the junior high school could point to an elaborate homogeneous grouping program (based on performance on standardized tests and on teacher evaluations) in English, science, mathematics, and social studies.[59] Quinlan argued that grouping was an effective way of encouraging gifted children, and the administration was proud of this program. Ability grouping was described in two out of the three articles about the schools published in educational journals. In a rousing conclusion to one of them, the principal of the new Deer Path Junior High School declared: "Yes, we group homogeneously, and we recommend it to all who are seriously interested in taking children to their highest capabilities."[60]

The Lake Forest schools' reliance on ability grouping can serve as an index to their commitment to progressive principles. While ability grouping did recognize the progressives' premise that children matured and learned at differing rates, grouping readily lent itself to stigmatizing children in the lower groups and could easily lead to self-fulfilling prophecies. Therefore, despite rhetorical obeisance to the doctrine of the "whole child," schools that adopted ability grouping usually paid scant attention to the social and emotional needs of children. The fact that ability grouping was not in harmony with many of Dewey's ideas did not bother Quinlan. According to his friend, Professor Ned Reichert, chairman of the education department at Lake Forest College, Quinlan's educational philosophy was "very conservative"—"He'd been at Teachers College, but I don't think he absorbed much of what he heard there."[61]

In sharp contrast to Winnetka's emphasis on the schools' role in promoting mental health, Lake Forest made no provision for psychological counseling within the schools. At various times during the 1950s, physicians and nurses were listed as part of the school staff, but there was no school social worker nor psychologist. In 1947, at Quinlan's suggestion, the board eliminated the "Special Room" for "backward" students and its teacher was reclassified as a "remedial" teacher.[62] But this did not lead to any new emphasis on mental health. After studying the possibility of providing psychological services in cooperation with the family service agency of a neighboring community, the board decided, instead, that when a child was deemed to need "individual professional diagnosis and therapy," parents would be notified. If, because the parents could not afford it, "desirable treatment" was impossible, the superintendent was authorized to pay "a reasonable amount" for the required therapy. (At the same time as the board elected not to play a role in psychological services, it was providing free dental examinations for all school children, twice a year.) In Lake Forest, providing psychological services through the schools was still a controversial question.[63]

During Quinlan's years at Lake Forest, the schools were in harmony with the ideas of this conservative suburb. But the relationship between the public schools and the community changed. By 1957, when he resigned, Quinlan had established close links between the schools and the town. He had led the way in establishing a new kind of public school system for Lake Forest—a system that was respected by the whole town.[64]

The postwar period had brought important changes to the schools of both Winnetka and Lake Forest, but neither of these suburban communities experienced the kind of controversies about progressive education and subversive influences in the schools described in contemporary newspapers and magazines. Winnetka did reflect national trends in its decision to hire Marland and then to step back quietly from its earlier progressivism. Lake Forest schools, on the other hand, did not make major changes in the thrust of their curriculum. While these schools changed in significant ways during this period of expansion and affluence, Lake Forest did not adopt the kinds of child-centered, socially transforming schools that John Dewey had called for at the beginning of the century. The real issue in Lake Forest school politics in the postwar period was not progressive education. The central question that Quinlan faced was modernizing the public schools and bringing them to a respected position in the eyes of the community's elite. In both suburbs public relations—not progressive education—was the crucial issue for their school superintendents. For Winnetka, progressive education was a movement whose day had passed; in Lake Forest, its day had never come.

8

POSTWAR EDUCATION IN MIDDLE AMERICA

*B*efore World War II progressive education had had little impact on the schools of the industrial city of Waukegan or the rural village of Mundelein. Although the children of these communities attended schools that were only a few miles from Lake Forest and Winnetka, they sat in classrooms of a different era, with fixed desks, old textbooks, and teachers with little training. Their schools (which were probably typical of many nonsuburban schools) were far more traditional than even those of Lake Forest. These communities had been deeply damaged by the depression; new programs had been out of the question for almost ten years and, in fact, the schools had repeatedly eliminated "nonessential" courses. Some residents of Waukegan and Mundelein, however, saw the end of the war as the beginning of a new and hopeful future. The economy was now expanding and both towns were caught up in the postwar housing boom that brought thousands of new residents to the housing developments that were hastily constructed on farmlands. Enrollments grew rapidly and the schools soon faced a desperate need to expand facilities.

The need for new schools and new teachers brought many opportunities for change in the schools' programs. New buildings could facilitate new programs, and new teachers, most of them recent graduates of teachers' colleges, could bring new ideas. Moreover, the residents in the new subdivisions would want schools that were as up-to-date as their new homes. But the rapid expansion of the schools also afforded opportunities for resistance to innovation. The need for new funds would force the schools to repeatedly ask for new revenue. In this context, school officials had many incentives to be cautious in introducing new programs; they knew that some citizens, suspicious of any effort to raise their tax bills, would be looking for evidence that the schools were wasting money on "fads and frills." Therefore, as Waukegan and Mundelein grew at an unprecedented rate, the schools became the arena for serious conflict; school politics provided a forum in which people could debate their different hopes for the future of the community.

By the early 1940s Waukegan had emerged from the depression. As America's factories were recruited for the war against Germany and Japan, plants in the Waukegan area rehired old workers and brought in new employees. In the postwar period, the area's industries continued to thrive and unemployment was low. The city expanded rapidly; new subdivisions rapidly emerged and hundreds of families seized the opportunity to become homeowners. In the early 1950s, more and more of these families were ready to send their children to school each year.

After the war a crucial question faced the citizens of Waukegan: how could the public schools, which had survived the depression only by drastic cuts in spending and in programs, be prepared to meet the needs of the explosive increase in the number of school children? This was part of a larger question—what kind of community would Waukegan become in the postwar period? Would it be the kind of city that offered the quality of public services that would attract businessmen and middle-class professionals?

Even during the war some residents had begun to prepare for their vision of a new future for the city. Both the grade school and the high school superintendents had been in office for over twenty years. Neither man had the imagination or the energy to revitalize the schools and both school boards, independently, forced their superintendents to retire. In both schools new superintendents accepted the mandate to modernize the schools. With new leaders, new teachers, new buildings, and more resources, progressive ideas might well have gained a foothold in Waukegan.

The opportunity for rebuilding Waukegan's schools led to a number of important questions: what kinds of schools should be built and, perhaps more important, where should they be located? These were political questions, and in Waukegan political issues were hard fought. Although the grade school board was not elected, it was deeply involved in politics. The board was appointed by the mayor with the approval of the city council; in practice, this meant that the mayor named the board's president while aldermen chose the representatives from their wards. Accordingly, in 1941 a newly elected reform-minded Democrat appointed a new board president, Wallace Green.[1]

The new president, a well-established member of the city's elite, was a "dynamic personality with lots of ideas." Soon after Green took charge, the board found it could not run an acceptable program with the available funds. Faced with the possibility of further cuts in programs, parents demanded that taxes be raised. The board agreed and mounted a hard-fought campaign to win additional funds. With the cooperation of teachers, the PTAs, organized labor, and civic groups, board members relentlessly publicized the desperate needs of the schools. They argued that "the standards of the school system are declining because of the starvation basis on which it is operated."

The issues were crystal clear in the debate that ensued. Predictably, the real estate board opposed the tax increase. More significantly, the leader of the opposition was none other than Green's predecessor as president of the board. Reflecting the traditional attitude of the board, he argued that parents should be satisfied with what the schools offered—they should not "hope for any improvement in educational standards." Waukegan, after all, was not Winnetka.

Despite this powerful opponent, the referendum won by a two-to-one margin, but Green recognized the need for caution; he pledged that the board would "keep in mind . . . that Waukegan citizens demand economy and an educational program that will meet the demands of our country without unnecessary frills."[2] Even with new funds, however, the possibilities for real change were limited by the presence on the board of a powerful advocate for the status quo, John E. Reardon. Having served on the board since 1903, Reardon was the board's perennial secretary. His long tenure had given him a great deal of power, which he used to resist efforts to increase spending. For three years he fought Green on every issue.[3]

Finally, Reardon and two other holdover board members resigned, and the board launched its effort to improve Waukegan's grade schools. Although superintendent John S. Clark (who had been superintendent since 1918) was still nominally in charge, under Green's leadership, board members moved ahead independently. They engaged consultants from Northwestern University and, completely bypassing Clark, instituted a new in-service training program for teachers. At the same time, the board adopted new rules which would force Clark's retirement.[4]

The board looked outside the Waukegan school system for his replacement, someone who could build a school system worthy of a progressive community in the postwar world. The man they chose was Dr. H. R. McCall, professor of education at the University of Missouri and former superintendent of schools in Chillicothe, Missouri. McCall was an ideal candidate. An energetic and ambitious young man whose doctorate gave him status and whose close contact with modern thinking about schools would be an important asset in the modernization of Waukegan's schools. At the same time, he represented traditional American small-town values. In Chillicothe he had been highly active in community affairs. As an inveterate joiner, he would fit in well in his new community.[5]

From his first visit to Waukegan, McCall recognized that the city's schools were in trouble. Clark had made few changes in the curriculum; "there was a lot of room for improvement," he recalls. For an ambitious man, the Waukegan schools offered an opportunity to rebuild a system that was in dire straits. School buildings were old and dilapidated, some had been built before the Spanish-American War.[6] In the words of a University of Chicago survey, these "sub-standard" nineteenth-century school buildings were not only dangerous, but they would impede efforts to implement "modern programs of education." Nearly half of Waukegan's school buildings were relics of "horse-and-buggy-days," yet they would have to house a curriculum that would "prepare young people for living in an atomic age."[7] Textbooks were antiquated, the staff included teachers without college degrees; salaries had not recovered from the drastic cuts of the depression era.[8] McCall came to his new position with high hopes, yet he must have recognized that he faced immense problems; he would have to revitalize an ailing school system and help the city rebuild an old and collapsing school plant.

McCall, who arrived in Waukegan just as World War II was ending, got to work right away. Within a few weeks, he prepared a superintendent's manual that set a new and relatively progressive tone. It told principals and teachers that the new superintendent expected schools to be organized and administered democratically and that the democratic spirit should infuse the classrooms. By achieving good relations with their pupils, teachers could eliminate much of the need for punishment. Promotion or failure should be based on "child development." Parents should be encouraged to come to school to talk about their child's progress and behavior. A later edition of the manual spells out McCall's modestly progressive philosophy: "We are not interested in the 'fads and frills' in this school system . . . but, we do not believe that school work needs to be dull and uninteresting. We believe every child has something he can do well. We should help him discover his strengths and build on them."[9]

Working with the teachers, McCall introduced new, progressive, report cards that replaced the old forms that had called for little more than subject matter grades. In keeping with the progressives' emphasis on socialization and the developmental needs of children, the new forms devoted a great deal of attention to "social habits" and "work habits." Moreover, as McCall pointed out in a letter to parents, even the marks for subjects were not given on a "comparative or competitive basis. Each pupil is rated as if he were the only one in the room."[10]

Coping with the dramatic increases in population proved to be the major issue that the new superintendent would face. Within a year of his arrival, McCall and the board were forced to ask for additional revenue. Among the highest priorities were additional teachers, new classrooms, and new equipment, including moveable desks. McCall recognized that to change the schools he would have to help teachers develop new skills and new attitudes. He proposed, therefore, to use some of the new revenue to put teachers on a twelve-month basis, so that they could spend the summer either taking classes or working on badly needed curriculum revision. New funds would also allow the schools to develop new services by hiring specialists in reading, testing, and guidance and to extend existing programs. With only two shop teachers for ten schools, for example, instruction in shop was restricted to seventh and eighth graders for a single period each week.[11] McCall warned that without money for increased salaries, teachers would leave for better-paying jobs elsewhere, and replacements would be impossible to find because of Waukegan's low salary scale and the increasingly desperate national teacher shortage.[12]

The school board's success in the May 1946 referendum was only a first step.[13] Less than a year later, as prices began to rise rapidly, teachers demanded higher pay. The inadequacy of the old school buildings was obvious and, as the new school year began in the fall of 1947, Green told board members that it was time to prepare for the expected "influx of children." A few months later, McCall and the board warned the community that it was "faced with a building program of vast proportions in the immediate future."[14]

For Waukegan, the like so many other American communities, the baby boom and the migration from rural areas to cities meant an unprecedented increase in population. The 1940 census had listed

34,241 residents; by 1960, the population was 55,719. Waukegan's population increased by 43 percent during the 1950s. Moreover, the number of elementary school pupils increased even more rapidly. In a single five-year period, from 1950 to 1955, while the population increased 20 percent, the number of elementary school pupils increased by 60 percent.[15] Therefore, at the same time that the community needed to revive its ailing school system, it had to deal with a rapidly expanding population that needed new school facilities and filled them almost as rapidly as they could be built.

To launch the desperately needed building program, the board had to enlist the support of a highly diverse community. Waukegan was still primarily a working-class town. While the northern sections of the city had stately homes, occupied by business people and professionals, the city was the home of many blue-collar workers, lower-level managerial employees, and people who owned or managed small businesses. Many of the townspeople worked for the nearby naval base, and others worked in one of a number of factories in the city and the surrounding area.[16]

Not only was Waukegan's population diverse in occupations and income but, even more important, it represented a high level of diversity in ethnicity and race. Washington Street divided Waukegan's predominantly ethnic, Democratic, south side from the predominantly nonethnic, Republican, north side. Finns, Lithuanians, and Slovenes were the predominant older ethnic groups. Increasingly, however, the south side had a significant Spanish-speaking population that totaled an estimated six thousand Puerto Ricans and three thousand Mexicans by 1960. Increasingly, too, Waukegan was attracting African-American residents. In 1950, the population was 5.9 percent black. During the decade, the black population almost doubled, and by 1960 Waukegan was 8.5 percent black. African Americans were concentrated in two neighborhoods. The south side, the home of the poorest black families, was almost one-third black in 1950. A second area, just west of the central business district, was a bit more prosperous. Segregated housing, combined with a system of neighborhood schools, would create an increasingly segregated school system that would lead to sharp racial divisions.[17]

Rapid increases in school enrollments forced McCall and the board repeatedly to appeal to voters for funds for new buildings. While Waukegan's postwar prosperity was an important asset in this rebuilding process, there were real limits on the program the city could support. McCall soon learned that Waukegan was, in some ways, "an industrial city without industry"; many of the companies that employed Waukegan workers were located "just outside the city limits" and were not part of the city's tax base.[18] Each new attempt to build required a tremendous public relations effort, and McCall and the board became highly adept at involving community groups in these extensive campaigns for voter approval, realizing that in the absence of new construction, children would be left without classrooms. A total of twelve new school buildings were erected during McCall's twenty-year tenure.[19]

While McCall and the board focused on bricks and mortar, they recognized that there was a direct relationship between the kinds of schools they chose to build and the educational program. In 1947, in a sharp break with the tradition of neighborhood schools, McCall and the board developed a building program that would establish separate intermediate schools for seventh and eighth graders.[20] To help them develop their plans (and to get support from a recognized authority), the board asked Professor William C. Reavis, of the University of Chicago, to survey the schools' building needs. Reavis, who represented the prevailing philosophy of schools of education—a mild progressivism made up of a blend of child-development and efficiency concerns—was a strong advocate for junior high schools.[21] Separate facilities for pupils in the later years of elementary school, he believed, helped overcome difficulties in making the transition to high school. Junior high schools not only served the developmental needs of seventh and eighth graders, but they allowed fifth and sixth graders to assume leadership roles within their schools. In addition, centralized junior high schools (rather than neighborhood schools) would make possible "broader educational offerings in special fields."[22]

Reavis predicted that advocates of neighborhood schools might oppose this program. He was right. The intermediate school proposal (perhaps for public relations reasons the administration preferred calling the separate seventh and eighth grade buildings intermediate schools instead of junior high schools) was to become the single most important issue for the Waukegan elementary schools in the early postwar period.

Reavis's endorsement of the basic idea of separate, centralized intermediate schools spurred a majority of the board to move ahead with a bold building plan designed to meet the community's needs for the next ten years. The plan faced immediate opposition from those who were appalled by its cost. Within a few months of Reavis's report, a sharply divided board decided to ask voters for funds for an ambitious building program that included two intermediate schools (one on the south side and one on the north side) at a total cost of well over $3 million.[23] A vocal minority on the board thought the plan was too expensive, and the city council (whose approval was needed) opposed the building program as "unnecessary."[24] The council's opposition forced the board to postpone a scheduled referendum and to reconsider its plans.[25] Green and McCall continued to support separate schools for seventh and eighth graders, pointing out that this pattern was "widely used" and that it would allow the schools to relieve overcrowding and to provide an enriched program, including music, art, and applied arts.[26] Several months later, the board adopted a compromise plan that called for a single, central, thirty-room junior high school. While the revised proposal marked an even sharper break with the idea of the neighborhood school, it had the advantage of costing much less than the original proposal.[27]

Strong opposition to the new plan soon emerged. Parents of children in the already overcrowded Washington school (in the western part of the city) spearheaded a campaign to defeat the proposal. They argued that even the compromise proposal was too expensive, but the central issue for them was that it would require their children to travel too far; they wanted the board to provide new rooms for existing schools.[28] While the board argued that the new intermediate school would relieve overcrowding in neighborhood schools, opponents held that the building program was too extensive, that Waukegan did not need thirty additional classrooms.[29] The superintendent and the board defended the intermediate school plan as a "modern answer to modern problems of education." A separate intermediate school would make it possible to have facilities and teachers for subjects that could not be taught in each of the elementary schools. The junior high would be organized on a departmental basis and teachers would be specialized. Since enrollments were increasing every year, the board argued, a centralized intermediate school would be an efficient way of dealing with overcrowding in the other buildings. In its effort to overcome opposition to the proposal, the board tended to emphasize cost rather than educational issues; the centralized intermediate school, they claimed, was the "cheapest possible answer" to the enrollment crunch.[30]

The fight over the intermediate school did not immediately become a fight about educational innovation; it was a struggle between people from different neighborhoods. Sectional hostilities were clearly evident in a pervasive rumor that parents of a wealthier north side neighborhood would not be required to send their children to the central intermediate school. McCall vigorously denied that the board had ever considered special treatment for the north side children, but the rumor had done its damage.[31] Despite a hard-fought publicity campaign, few voters turned out and its opponents succeeded in narrowly defeating the referendum. Heaviest opposition came from the Washington school area, but the poorer ethnic areas on the south side also voted against the plan.[32]

McCall and board members were deeply discouraged and confused by the defeat of the compromise proposal. They knew that without new buildings the continuing enrollment pressures would force major cuts in programs. Kindergartens and special classes for the handicapped might have to be eliminated.

Before embarking on a third effort to develop a building plan, McCall and the board called an open meeting to explain the schools' needs and to ask the people of Waukegan for a sense of what kind of a building program they might support. McCall recommended resubmitting the narrowly defeated proposal. An intermediate school would "eliminate [the] necessity of assigning teachers to subjects in which they have no preparation; provide equalization of class sizes, and provide one good science room, library, physical education program, workshop, and household arts classroom rather than 10 mediocre ones." Most of the people at the meeting, however, favored going back to the first proposal—two intermediate schools in the northern and southern parts of the city.[33] Now the board found itself badly split once more, unable to agree on any plan.[34]

The impasse was broken late in the spring of 1949 when the new mayor, Republican Robert E. Coulson, ousted Wallace Green as board president. As the new president, Coulson chose a retired Johns Manville Corporation vice-president in the hopes that a man of his considerable administrative experience would be able to unite the board in support of a building plan.[35]

Like the new mayor, who counseled against coddling juvenile delinquents, the new board president, John P. Kottcamp, was an educational conservative. He told the board that its major function was assisting "the teachers and the school officials in instilling in the children of the elementary schools the basic moral principles of integrity, hard work and unselfishness to prepare them for their lives beyond school." Its second responsibility was to be sure that the taxpayers "get a full dollar's worth . . . for every dollar they pay in taxes."[36] With its new president, the board avoided the troublesome issue of centralized schools and opted for a referendum to allow it to buy several sites, leaving the kinds of buildings to be erected on these sites for a later time. Now, for the first time since 1946, voters approved a referendum that would allow the board to deal with enrollment pressures.[37]

Two years later, however, McCall warned again that overcrowding was becoming acute; this might be a good time to revive the idea of centralized intermediate schools.[38] Accordingly, early in 1953 the board reopened the debate on intermediate schools. After months of deliberation and a poll of parents, the board proposed once more the two intermediate school plan and scheduled a referendum.[39]

By 1953, however, there was a new context for the debate about intermediate schools. The Cold War had become a hot war in Korea, and McCarthyism was at its height. With the publication of *Educational Wastelands* and other books attacking progressive education, the nation's schools were on the defensive. While opponents continued to focus primarily on the cost of the program, some now argued that the new plan represented "frills" rather than sound educational practice. As one critic put it, "the educational program offered (For which the two new intermediate schools are being specifically built) will have only one half of each day devoted to the 'Three R's.' . . . I cannot see that we are improving our community by dedicating half the time children spend in school to training their bodies rather than their minds." Another critic argued that putting seventh and eighth graders together in separate junior high schools was undesirable because this would "accelerate a more sophisticated life."[40]

Proponents appealed to civic pride, arguing that far from being a radical idea, intermediate schools had been adopted by most of the nation: "Only 25 per cent of the pupils in this country still attend the type of grade school system we now have in Waukegan, and almost all of them live in rural areas or in cities of less than 10,000 population." The new intermediate schools would have better facilities, but no "frills" in their curricula. Moreover, the intermediate school plan offered "by far the cheapest solution" to the enrollment crisis, which had forced the use of auditoriums, gymnasiums, and malodorous basements as classrooms.

The board worked hard to win public support and secured the endorsement of the mayor, the city council, and virtually every civic group as well as the local newspaper, The *Waukegan News-Sun*, which was always leery of tax increases.[41] Six years after McCall had proposed the idea, voters finally approved the plan by a wide margin. The board president saw the surprisingly large vote as part of the city's "miracle of growth," fully in accord with "the Lord's plan."[42]

As the adoption of the intermediate school plan indicates, the need for new buildings provided opportunities for changes in school programs. But, as the six-year struggle over the issue demonstrated, change did not come readily to the Waukegan schools. The new intermediate schools had a richer curriculum than had been available before because these buildings had separate classrooms for shop, science, physical education, and home economics. The new school organization allowed for more specialized programs to suit the needs of individual students—one of the goals of

17. A classroom in Waukegan's Daniel Webster Junior High School, shortly after the school opened in January 1957. Webster was the first of three junior high schools that resulted from the long and hard-fought battle for separate "intermediate" schools. The others were named for Thomas Jefferson and for one of the city's favorite sons, the comedian Jack Benny. In these schools, special rooms for science, shop, and home arts permitted an enriched program for seventh and eighth grade students. Note, however, in this "typical classroom" all the chairs are in neat rows, facing the front of the room. H. R. McCall, "Daniel Webster Junior High School," *American School Board Journal* 136 (January 1958): 19. Photographer not known. Courtesy of *American School Board Journal*.

progressive education. Yet the thrust of the program in these schools, with their departmentalized curriculum, was contrary to the Dewey's concern for a curriculum that did not break up human knowledge into arbitrary subject areas. Moreover, the excruciatingly slow pace of this change was testimony to the conservatism of the community.

At the same time as the schools were devising the intermediate school plan, they embarked on a policy that was in harmony with the postwar goals of the progressive education movement—a new emphasis on guidance and psychological counseling. Beginning in 1945, the elementary schools cooperated with the high school in establishing a comprehensive guidance program.[43] The schools used state funds to hire a special teacher for the "socially maladjusted" and the mentally retarded and set up a special ungraded room for educable mentally handicapped students. In 1955, Waukegan hired its first school social worker (called a "visiting counselor.") By 1957, special education had become a major component of the schools' program, with separate classes for children with special needs. The schools now offered classes for physically handicapped children, a sight saving class, a class for blind children, and a class for children who were hard of hearing. The schools' staff included three speech correctionists, two school social workers to work with "maladjusted children," and a specialist responsible for IQ testing.[44]

The primary impetus, however, for increased attention to the psychological needs of students came from outside the community. Increasingly, in the postwar period, the professional staff in the state superintendent's office developed legislation designed to "both entice and pressure local school districts . . . that had traditionally neglected auxiliary programs in social work, counseling, health, and personality adjustment." In Waukegan, these efforts met little resistance. Unlike other innovations, these programs made few demands on local taxpayers and could be instituted without widespread public discussion. Chronically short of funds, Waukegan school officials viewed the state programs as providing a painless way to bring in new staff and services.[45]

Aside from the belated and reluctant adoption of the intermediate school proposal and an increased attention to guidance, how far did progressive ideas affect the school program? A series of articles, by the superintendent and the school staff, provide an unusual opportunity to evaluate the educational ideas of a large sample of teachers and administrators. Beginning in late January 1952 and continuing though early June, the *News-Sun* published almost one hundred articles by more than sixty members of the school staff. Although this was part of an attempt to promote public support for the schools, and especially the intermediate school plan, it provides an unusual perspective on the educational views of a large number of teachers and administrators.[46]

Ten of the articles were written by McCall. They show that the progressive tone that McCall had sounded in his superintendent's manual had all but disappeared. In his first article, McCall sets a conservative tone. Summing up in a single sentence the goals of the schools, he says "we try to develop those qualities that make good American citizens." What does that consist of? Most important, "the good American citizen needs to be able to read, write and figure with a degree of skill in keeping with his ability." Accordingly, "there is no trend in the schools of Waukegan to place less importance on the development of these skills." Beyond "the basic skills of the three R's," the schools have a relatively traditional curriculum: "spelling, oral and written expression, history, geography [*not* social studies], science, shop, household arts, art, music, health, and physical education." In addition to these subjects, the schools carry out a progressive goal: "we try to help children learn to work and play together in a spirit of peace and harmony." They also strive to instill the traditional virtues, teaching children to "distinguish right from wrong. . . . We try to help them to be honest; to assume responsibility; to respect authority . . .; to develop good work habits; to believe in the principle of working and earning a living; to understand our democratic form of government; to develop a strong loyalty to our government; to encourage spiritual development."[47]

Ten days later, McCall takes up "the most common criticisms that we hear"—that the schools "contain too many fads and frills." But which subjects are "frills" that should be discarded? Should the schools abandon music, art, shop, household arts, supervised play, health and physical education? While McCall recognizes that "it would be possible to place too much emphasis" on these, "[w]e try very hard to keep that from happening. . . . We, too, are opposed to fads and frills."[48]

A few weeks later, McCall takes up the troublesome issue of discipline. He advocates a middle-of-the-road approach: "we do not believe in the extremes of permitting pupils to do as they please or of allowing them no freedom at all." Rather, the Waukegan schools try "to train these children in such a way that they will be good citizens in a democracy." McCall agrees with Dewey on an important point, recognizing that democratic citizenship can only be learned through practice. "Therefore, we try to make our schools' children get the actual experience of democratic living," and this means that "[w]e believe in permitting them to have as much freedom as they know how to use or are willing to use wisely." At the same time, however, the children must learn that "for each and every right and privilege there is also a duty or responsibility. We try in every way . . . to develop in pupils a sense of obligation to accept these duties and responsibilities." Moreover, "[w]e expect pupils to respect the rights of others and to respect proper authority wherever they find it." An orderly classroom is important and all teachers are expected "to maintain at all times a teaching-learning situation. Teachers know what this means and they know when they have it. The good teacher . . . will use whatever disciplinary measures are necessary as she works with children along these lines."[49] Waukegan's teachers knew that a quiet, orderly classroom was a high priority.

Near the end of the series, McCall returns to an issue he raised in his first article—one that is obviously deeply felt—his conviction that the schools must play an important role in inculcating traditional moral values. "The public schools," he says, "have a responsibility for teaching spiritual and moral values." While he recognizes that public schools are prohibited from inculcating any specific religion, there is much they can do. First, teachers must set a good example. "I believe that teachers should have religious interests, and that they should be of good moral character." Second, "there is no reason why a teacher should not discuss with pupils . . . the importance of a spiritual environment, and of becoming affiliated with and participating in the activities of a church." This can be done "without any attempt, directly or indirectly, to sell her own particular brand of religion." Finally, he argues that "it is the responsibility of every school system" to foster character development and, in Waukegan, "we are using every method at our command to teach such values as honesty, fair play, truthfulness, temperance, self-control, respect for the rights of others, an interest in the welfare of others, an appreciation for things spiritual, and all the other qualities that come under the classification of moral and spiritual values."[50]

Despite both McCall's endorsement of traditional values and the increasing attacks on progressive education nationally, many of the other articles in the series have a progressive tone. While the phrase "progressive education" is never used, many of them celebrate "modern" educational practices and point to their superiority over old-fashioned ways. "Learning," we are told, "is no longer limited to the memorization of facts, recited to the teacher in 'parrot-like' fashion." Instead, "[m]odern education is more concerned in training children in the ability to think and to solve problems that have been set up by teachers and pupils planning large units of work together."[51]

As might be expected, those who teach the early grades put more emphasis on progressive ideas. In kindergarten, "[p]lay is the natural way to learn"; "[p]lay to the young child is his work."[52] In the first grade, too, the emotional needs of children are seen as very important: "One of the first grade teacher's greatest privileges and obligations is to keep the child happy. A happy mind is a receptive mind . . . The cardinal rule for happiness is a sense of security."[53] Teaching is based on evoking interest in the children: "One of the most important functions of the first grade teacher is to help the children in her class realize that reading is fun." Therefore, "[t]he old-time word drill is gone and in its place we find word games which show better results."[54] A principal, writing with an understanding of child development, endorses the "whole child" approach to learning: "The child grows in many ways," he points out, "and academic work is only one of them. The child is a physical being . . . He is an emotional being . . . He is a social being."[55]

Science teachers recognize Dewey's principle that schools should use children's natural interests to promote learning: "Science in the elementary grades develops from . . . [children's] curiosity and makes use of [that] . . . curiosity to help the child better understand his world and prepare him to live within it."[56] One teacher describes the science curriculum as "exceptionally flexible" in all the grades: "A bird's egg, an unusual butterfly, a hamster, an electric eye, or even a wasp's nest . . . may direct class interest for a day, week, or even longer."[57] Field trips are an important part of the school program. They are "more conducive to learning" than just reading about interesting places."[58]

Teachers vary in the degree to which they endorse progressive principles. A teacher at Whittier School writes about the importance of teaching first-grade children arithmetic based on an understanding of numbers. "Drill, when it means having the children do the same thing over and over, cannot develop meanings. Instead we try to provide practice in using numbers, so that the child will learn that numbers have a definite use."[59] A teacher at North School, however, suggests that children who find arithmetic difficult need not only "sympathetic understanding," but also "firm discipline" and drill.[60]

Art and music readily lent themselves to progressive methods.

"In Waukegan, as in most of the schools of the United States today, the aim of art education is to help the child to become a thoughtful, creative, sympathetic person and citizen." Art adds to the traditional curriculum "through the three 'E's': Experience, Explore, and Express." Music carries out the progressive agenda of tying different subjects together; it is "correlated with all the subjects in which the primary child is engaged."[61]

As might be expected, child-centered educational ideas are less prevalent in the upper grades. There are, we are told, three ways of organizing the curriculum for the junior high school years. (There are, as yet, no separate intermediate schools.) The traditional approach uses specialized teachers for each subject. A more radical approach attempts "to eliminate all subject lines and work out a unified program of things children should learn from all subject areas." Although there is some variation between the programs in different schools, "they will all be found somewhere between the two extremes of organization." Generally, subject areas are divided into groups, making it possible for "two or more teachers to work together on projects and activities, using some of the same materials and subject matter."[62]

Despite the recognition of the principles of child development, the emotional needs of children, and the importance of using the child's natural curiosity, Waukegan administrators and teachers do not endorse an activity curriculum like those developed in some of the progressive private schools twenty years earlier. The school day is divided into clearly distinguishable periods. In the first two grades, two hours a day are usually devoted to reading and forty minutes for recess and play period, leaving about two hours for a "sharing period," art, music, science, social studies, spelling, writing, and numbers. As one teacher put it, "We have little time for art work . . . because we must drill and drill on learning how to read."[63]

Except for McCall's low-key response to questions about fads and frills, these articles, written in a period of concentrated attack on progressive education, give no sense that Waukegan's teachers were defending a philosophy of education that was under attack. Equally remarkable is that although the Cold War was at its height, the articles are strikingly free of jingoism. No one claims that the schools are in the front line of the fight against communism. While articles elsewhere in the newspaper bristle with anticommunist rhetoric, this language does not find a place in the articles written by the school staff. A view of the national educational scene would lead a reader to expect to find teachers embattled by attacks on their loyalty and their progressive ideas, yet the tone of these articles is remarkably undefensive. Although the newspaper often spoke of the threat of subversion in other communities, it cast no suspicions on the Waukegan elementary schools.[64]

It is difficult to determine how far teachers went in implementing the progressive ideas they espoused in these articles. However, the Waukegan schools allowed individual teachers and principals considerable latitude, and some classrooms and even schools were certainly more progressive than others. For example, as the result of work with parent groups to change grading practices, some of the schools moved further away from using traditional report cards, relying instead on parent conferences and narrative reports.[65] Similarly, when, in the aftermath of the Sputnik crisis, schools began to emphasize programs for the gifted, Waukegan used different approaches in different neighborhoods. As one administrator put it, "[i]n a larger school system in which various socioeconomic groups reside and in which school buildings vary in size . . . an eclectic philosophy has been the policy with reference to the education of the gifted."[66]

By adapting their programs to Waukegan's different neighborhoods and by always paying a great deal of attention to instruction in the basic subjects, the Waukegan elementary schools avoided the attacks on progressive education that afflicted other communities.

But while the neighborhood schools allowed considerable variation, they also fostered racial segregation. As new schools opened in the mid-1950s, the board drew new attendance boundaries in a way that led the Whittier School, which was adjacent to the west side black community and had been twenty percent black in 1953, to become nearly all black. By the end of the decade, the predominantly black Whittier and McAllister Schools (in the heart of the south side ghetto) were inferior in almost every way to the more modern, nearly all-white, schools that had been built in the newer areas of the city. Progressive principles that recognized individual differences and that respected the interests children brought to school were much less likely to be applied in these schools than in the new schools in other parts of the city. A 1968 survey of Waukegan schools reported that classrooms in the black areas of the city "seemed less 'happy'" and "more barren"; a large number of teachers in these schools taught "in a discouraged, routine, often dictatorial manner."[67]

While the modest progressivism of some of the elementary schools aroused little controversy, progressive education emerged as a major issue at Waukegan Township High School. Although

Waukeganites were willing to support progressive approaches for younger children, they were much more suspicious of a major effort to transform the high school.

At about the same time that the elementary school board forced superintendent Clark to retire, the high school board was maneuvering to oust Superintendent John W. Thalman, who had been in office for twenty years. Unlike the elementary schools, the high school was governed by an elected board and, in the spring of 1944, a "new order" slate of candidates, committed to ousting the superintendent, won a decisive victory.[68] The reformers picked as the new superintendent Dr. J. Lloyd Trump, an energetic and imaginative young University of Chicago Ph.D. strongly committed to a new vision of high school education.[69]

Trump recognized (as did the founders of the life adjustment program) that the postwar high school had to serve the needs of a new clientele. Increasingly, American high schools, which had seen their primary role as preparing students for college, were attracting students who were not college bound. Trump believed that Waukegan Township High School (which served North Chicago as well as Waukegan) needed to change in order to serve the needs of the forty percent of the student body who would drop out before graduation, either because they found the curriculum irrelevant or because they were unable to do the required work. Trump was deeply committed to democratizing high school education.[70]

The revitalized high school program, as developed by Trump, included a night school for adults, a summer program that would allow students to make up credits, a new health and guidance plan, and an "expanded athletic program" that would involve more students and would increase community support for the school.[71] The most radical of Trump's innovations was a required sequence for all freshmen entitled "Self-Appraisal and Orientation," a life adjustment program designed to orient incoming students to the school "and into the lives they will lead after they leave school." The new course included a hodgepodge of subjects: "food, clothing, electricity, handicrafts, personal relations . . . and fine arts courses." At the same time, under Trump's leadership, the board abandoned the invidious distinction between college preparatory and "industrial" diplomas.[72]

It soon became clear to Trump that, if the high school were to serve the needs of all of its students, individual courses would also require drastic changes. For example, since half of the entering students were reading below the ninth-grade level, the school desperately needed a new English program. Accordingly, Trump encouraged a group of teachers to develop a series of courses, General English, for students who were one or two years behind in reading. The focus of these courses was on "the relationship between English and every day living."[73]

The new sequence followed the principles of William Heard Kilpatrick: "Philosophically, it is assumed that the student himself is of first importance; subject matter, secondary. Without regard for the former inflexible standard, the teacher of General English is expected to take the pupil from where he is in his life-adjustment and his communication skills to whatever point of development he can reach." The aim was to "develop well-adjusted citizens for a democratic society." Instead of the classics of English literature, teachers selected material that would appeal to reluctant readers; texts were chosen for their "social utility," as well as the "development of appreciations." Topics covered ranged from the important and controversial (Civil Rights) to the inane (Manners for Moderns—"What is the best way to ask a girl for a date?"). Suggested reading ranged from *Johnny King, Quarterback* to selections from Benjamin Franklin's *Autobiography*.[74]

These changes in traditional courses encountered little opposition outside of the school (although there was some resistance from teachers who preferred teaching the customary curriculum to college-bound students).[75] Nor was there resistance to the night and summer programs. The new emphasis on guidance and the athletic program aroused a great deal of enthusiasm. The new freshman program, however, proved to be highly controversial. Unlike the General English courses, the Self-Appraisal and Orientation course (contemptuously dubbed "South American Oysters" by students) was required for everyone, directly affecting students who saw themselves as college bound. Some of their parents angrily protested that the course repeated work their children had already done in grade school and, most important, that it was not an acceptable course for college entry. Trump assured parents that students would be adequately prepared for college, but he pointed out that the high school had to pay attention to the needs of the forty percent of its students who were dropping out before graduation.[76] The opposition probably was not mollified, but the issue did not play a role in the April 1946 school board elections; unlike the previous year, there was no organized campaigning.[77]

In June, however, the defeat of a high school referendum offered an opportunity for the city's newspaper to begin a sustained attack

18. Dr. J. Lloyd Trump, whose brief term as superintendent brought many innovations to Waukegan High School. The 1946 high school yearbook called the superintendent "A Friendly, Progressive Educator." It noted that "Dr. Trump has introduced many new and desirable changes in the school program," and it praised his
"democratic administration" for creating "a feeling of unity among the student
body." *The Annual W, 1946* (Waukegan, IL: Waukegan Township High School), p. 19.

on the new program. One reason for the referendum's defeat, the
editor surmised, was "the apparent lack of confidence in the administration at the high school." Waukegan "has always been po-
litically conservative." In the wake of the New Deal's victories,
"residents of Waukegan watched helplessly as liberalism, so-called
progressivism and downright radicalism moved in to local institutions." The editorial went on to charge that "[t]he practice of the
high school administration in labelling everything in the past as
wrong" had alienated people. The editor castigated the "Ultra-lib-
erals on the high school board" and then got to the main point: "the
changed curriculum . . . was rapidly leading to the establishment
of an exclusively industrial school."[78] Two days later, the newspaper resumed its attack, publishing a front-page article attacking
progressivism. Relying largely on material drawn from a Los Angeles newspaper, it argued that teachers were increasingly dissatisfied with progressive education. "Teachers themselves admit that
they are powerless to stop the swift curve to the left that the public

schools are making." Even in Waukegan, the article ominously noted, a "retiring teacher . . . sounded a warning note against the folly that in many cases masquerades under the name 'progressive education.'"[79]

The newspaper's attack on Trump and his progressive reforms had little immediate effect. The board went on to win a referendum in February 1947 and, in April, the board election was again marked by no outstanding issues and no real campaigning. The one challenger who talked about improving the academic reputation of the high school (which could be taken as a covert attack on Trump) came in last.[80]

The *News-Sun* continued its attack on Trump's policies, citing the president of Ripon College, who, during a visit to Waukegan, attacked "liberal-progressive" education and said that the high school's "so-called orientation course" was "worse than nothing" because it encouraged students to loaf.[81]

While Trump was eager to change Waukegan Township High School, he was no ideologue—he was willing to make changes in the program to accommodate criticisms—but he remained committed to democratizing the high school and to the idea of a common freshman course. Despite the fulminations of the *News-Sun*, it was clear that he was succeeding in transforming the school. In its first two years, the new administration reduced failures by forty-six percent and the reorganized athletic program was fielding championship teams that drew enthusiastic crowds.[82] It turned out, however, that the spring of 1947 marked the high point of progressive reform at Waukegan Township High School. In August, quite unexpectedly, Trump offered his resignation. Although he regretted leaving when there was still "so much left undone," he found it impossible to turn down an invitation to join the faculty of the University of Illinois. "There are still too many students failing, too many young people dropping out of school, too many adults who don't think deeply enough on the issues of society. There is so much left to do," he ruefully noted in an emotional farewell speech.[83]

After Trump left, the board never recovered the reform impetus. Since Trump resigned late in the summer, the board had little choice in picking a replacement. It appointed an acting superintendent, the high school principal, a man who had spent thirty years in the Waukegan school. The choice of C. E. Prichard was hailed by the *News-Sun*. While changes would take some time, the editor promised that now the school would place "emphasis on accepted educational standards." He assured parents that with Prichard in

charge, graduates of the high school would have "acceptable credits" and would "be prepared to enter any trade or profession with
a sound background of normal secondary school training."[84] Although Prichard was later denied the permanent position, the man
ultimately chosen, Clarence Lee Jordan, was "a good gray compromise" candidate whose appointment would cause no "trouble or
unrest."[85] Waukegan's brief period of spirited educational innovation was over.

Like Lake Forest and Waukegan, Mundelein began the postwar period with a new superintendent. Unlike these other communities,
however, Mundelein chose a local candidate, Albert Kroll. The new
principal-superintendent had been a star high school football
player in the neighboring community of Libertyville. He went on
to play varsity football at nearby Lake Forest College until an in-
jury forced the amputation of his right leg below the knee. After
graduation, he became a coach and a teacher in several schools in
the area before coming to Mundelein.[86] This one-building school
district could not afford a full-time administrator; in addition to his
administrative duties, Kroll was a full-time teacher, directed the
boys' physical education program, and did part of the janitorial
work for the school.[87]

In 1945, when Kroll began his new job, Mundelein was facing an
even greater rate of growth than Waukegan, changing from the
"sleepy, pastoral village" of 1940, with a population of just over
1,300, into a suburban center that would have a population of over
10,500 by 1960. Located only thirty-two miles from Chicago's Loop,
the town became a major focus for the postwar housing boom.
Soon after the war ended, bulldozers began clearing farmland to
meet the pent-up demand for houses. New subdivisions opened
each year, and by 1950 the population had increased 140 percent
since the last census. The housing boom continued well into the
next decade. In the 1950s, Mundelein's population increased more
than 230 percent.[88] Enrollment in the town's single school ex-
ploded. Lincoln School, which had served 118 pupils in the 1939
school year, was bursting at the seams ten years later with 274
pupils.[89]

Although Kroll now sees himself as having been suspicious of
progressive education, he brought a number of new, innovative
programs to the Mundelein school. Only a few weeks after he arrived, he spoke to the PTA on "Progressive Education and the
Grading System," explaining that now teachers in the primary

grades would use a "pamphlet" form of report card and that conventional letter grades would only be used in the upper grades.
Another Kroll innovation was a student council that not only organized paper drives but played some role in running the school.
Kroll gave the council the job of writing a "code of conduct" for
students and of developing rules for bicycles. Although he did not
believe in an "activity curriculum," he was quite willing to assign
his students a real-life project; he asked his eighth-grade social
studies class to conduct a community census which could serve as
the basis for estimating future enrollment patterns. Other changes
in the early postwar years included restoring the district's kindergarten program and instituting a weekly class for sight and hearing
impaired students.[90]

Kroll enjoyed teaching and had a good relationship with students. He often came to Lincoln School on Sundays to catch up on
his work and he would open up the gym so that kids could come in
and shoot baskets. As one parent put it, her children believed that
"[n]ext to their daddy, Mr. Kroll is just tops."[91]

The 1949–50 school year proved to be a crucial one in Kroll's
efforts to improve the Mundelein school. He was busier than ever
that year. Besides his extraordinarily heavy duties as superinten-
dent-principal, he was mayor of Libertyville.[92] In addition to that,
he was completing a master's degree in educational administration
at Northwestern University. For his final project in that program,
Kroll (with the help of his thesis director and some fellow graduate
students) conducted a survey of his own school and prepared a
plan for the future of the rapidly growing school district. Although
the report was in some sense, of course, addressed to his thesis
committee, its primary audience was the community of Mundelein
and especially the school board—the first chapter was entitled, significantly, "Pertinent Facts About *Your* School."[93]

Most of pertinent facts were grim. Lincoln School offered a sharp
contrast to the schools that Kroll was studying in his courses at
Northwestern. First, the school was incredibly crowded; accommo-
dations had "reached a saturation point" and every nook and
cranny was used as a classroom. The kindergarten met on the
school stage and the fourth grade met in a temporary room in the
school's dank basement. The superintendent's office was a parti-
tioned corner of the sixth-grade classroom; forty-four pupils in a
combined seventh and eighth grade class met in a single classroom.
The building, which had been opened in 1894, was poorly maintained and quite unattractive. It was not properly fire-resistant,
had no ventilation system, and was inadequately lit and heated.

The stairway to the basement twisted treacherously. Classroom seats were old-fashioned and uncomfortable, and the rooms lacked the kinds of equipment that were common in the classrooms of Lake Forest and Winnetka.[94] The school offered a bare-bones program. It had no industrial art courses, no counselors, school physicians, or regular school nurses. There was no school library, no lunchroom, and no health room where a sick child could lie down. Mundelein's school had no art or music programs (apart from the singing led by regular classroom teachers, who desperately needed a decent piano).[95]

Kroll recognized that many of the school's problems could be attributed to the district's poverty. Although the residents of the new subdivisions were changing the town, Mundelein remained relatively poor with a low tax base. In 1957, for example, per capita property valuations were one-third lower than those of Waukegan and two-thirds lower than those of Lake Forest. Moreover, the town had a great deal of difficulty in collecting its taxes; tax revenue was usually less than eighty percent of what was levied. The situation was further complicated by the fact that the town's resources were used inefficiently. Although Mundelein was still very small, some of its children were assigned to either of two other small school districts, resulting in wasteful duplication. Another limiting factor was that almost one-third of the district's elementary school-aged children would attend a new Catholic parochial school. Parents of these children (whose parish dues reflected this expense) might well resist the new taxes needed to improve the public school.[96]

The central point of Kroll's thesis, however, was that, despite these constraints, Mundelein could do much more for its children—"the Mundelein school system does not represent the best that Mundelein residents should and could have." The board's most important role, as Kroll saw it, was to educate the community. "Any long range educational program for improving the educational opportunities for the Mundelein school children must be supplemented by a sound program of citizen education and good public relations." Once that was done, the most important goal was a new building, which, Kroll suggested, should be located in the southern part of town, close to the district's new population center. This building would not replace the old school—that could become the district's junior high school. Reflecting what he was learning at Northwestern, Kroll pointed out that "[t]he separation of the primary grades from the upper grades is not a new practice. . . . It is highly recommended by school authorities." Kroll's other major recommendation was that the district seek a merger with the other two districts that served portions of the town.[97]

In addition to these major plans, Kroll suggested a long list of improvements. To allow the district to recruit and retain good teachers, the board should reduce class size so that no teacher would teach more than thirty pupils. It should bring the salary schedule up to the level of other schools in Lake County. The board should also encourage teachers to take on "professional growth activities." The district should hire a music supervisor. New facilities and programs recommended by Kroll included a cafeteria that could serve hot lunches, a school library, and industrial arts courses. In addition, he recommended instituting a regular schedule for cleaning and painting the old building; landscaping the grounds; bringing toilets, lavatories, and staircases up to minimum state standards; and providing a health room.[98]

At first it seemed that Kroll's suggestions would become a blueprint for a new, modern school system. After reading his report, board members told him they "thought it was great." In August 1949 (the same month that Kroll was awarded his graduate degree), the board, which had been discussing expansion for several years, scheduled a referendum for a new school building. Kroll had laid the groundwork for this a year earlier, distributing a pamphlet to all parents that described the school's "dire need" for new facilities. He supplied the local newspaper with the statistics that supported the theme of his thesis: Lincoln School, built to house 130, could not cope with the educational needs of the 300 pupils expected in September. Voters approved the referendum and the board drew plans for a new kindergarten through fourth grade building.[99]

Under the surface, however, trouble was brewing. It is difficult to sort out exactly what happened, but it probably began in April 1949 as the result of an unusually bitter and hard-fought school board election. Thomas R. Doran, who had been president of the board for only one year, was defeated. Another board member, Julia Annable, who had served as the board's secretary (and kept the board's records at her house) had chosen not to run again. While the new board was beginning to implement Kroll's plan, these two worked with the new members to try to get Kroll to resign. Doran enlisted the help of the executive director of the Lake County Civic League, a group devoted to the careful scrutiny of public expenditures, to look at the district's financial records. The board held secret meetings, to which Kroll pointedly was not invited. In April 1950, a group of residents petitioned the board for

Kroll's dismissal. The board readily agreed and, by a vote of four to two, asked Kroll to resign. If he agreed to go quietly, he was told, he would get a fine letter of recommendation. Kroll, who felt that his reputation had been besmirched, chose to fight.

Since Kroll was a teacher, protected by Illinois's tenure law, the board was put in the difficult position of providing specific charges to support its decision. This task was complicated by the fact that it had given him a raise each year and had given him an unusually large raise in his last contract—a reward for his new graduate degree. Moreover, the board had never told the overworked superintendent that it was dissatisfied with his performance. The board's position was weakened by the fact that it had no written statement of rules and procedures by which it could measure its superintendent. After citing a number of minor incidents, the board could only say that firing Kroll was justified by the fact that he had "lost the confidence" of the majority of the board. The specific charges it eventually brought forward were incredibly petty. For example, Kroll had not responded quickly enough when one parent wanted her oversized son moved into the first grade from kindergarten; he had not enforced his own rule that boys should put their bicycles in the bicycle rack; he had authorized the repair of a broken sidewalk without prior permission from the board (he had seen a village crew repairing sidewalks and he had simply asked them to fix the school's walk too).[100]

Kroll appealed the board's decision but, after a heated debate at an open meeting, the board reaffirmed its decision. Kroll, buoyed by the solid support of the teachers and many parents, hired a lawyer and took his case to the county superintendent of schools, who appointed a special board to rule on the case. After reviewing the record and listening to attorneys representing the two sides, the board overturned Kroll's dismissal. But the case was not over. The school board instituted a suit to reverse that decision. While that case was still pending, a group of Kroll's supporters fielded an opposition slate for the school board that handily defeated the incumbents. Feeling vindicated, Kroll took his lawyer's advice and accepted a settlement that gave him a year's pay. By then he was "just disgusted" and he temporarily left teaching.[101]

The Kroll case is puzzling because there was certainly something behind the petty reasons the board cited when it was forced to justify its decision. Clearly, there were personal agendas. Doran, the former school board president, was upset by his failure to be re-elected. Kroll's attorney, William Behanna, speculated that Julia

Annable, who he saw as the moving force behind the effort to oust Kroll, simply wanted the position herself. (She had a graduate degree and had taught in a Texas teachers' college—she may well have thought she was more qualified than Kroll to run an expanding school district.) Kroll, however, while he agrees that Annable was the leader of the group that wanted to dismiss him, discounts the theory that she simply wanted his job. He saw financial concerns as a major motive for many of his opponents; in his view, the community simply did not want to raise taxes in order to improve the school.

The hearing before the county superintendent's board reveals several other underlying issues. Neither Kroll nor the board was good about keeping records. Recognizing that Kroll was too busy to undertake any additional duties, a board member had agreed to keep the district's financial records in order, but he had not done so. In the absence of any formal procedures, the board communicated with the superintendent largely through informal conversations. Because Kroll's office (carved out of a classroom) had no storage space, the board's records were incomplete and difficult to locate. In short, the rapidly growing Mundelein school was being administered as if it was still a rural one-room school. Once the board decided to build a new school, it became clear that that would have to change. Kroll, although he was not the cause of the problem became, for some, a symbol of the administrative chaos of the district. Dismissing him could be seen as a way of getting a fresh start.

More directly, Kroll's efforts to build public support for school improvement aroused resentment among some board members. They resented his public relations efforts, which they saw as attempts to undercut the board. During the hearings, the board's attorney repeatedly depicted Kroll as devoted to "building up a personal prestige for himself in the community" instead of taking care of "what might be regarded as the drudgery of school administration. . . . These routine things, they weren't important. Writing reports to the community with reflections on the school board, signed always 'Albert Kroll, Superintendent' on the front page . . . That is the sort of thing Kroll was interested in." Board members resented Kroll's public recommendations that the board should improve the landscaping and the playground and "spend liberally" for a school library without, they thought, adequate recognition of the fact that the district was strapped for funds. According to the board's attorney, Kroll was trying "to undermine confidence in the school board by the reports which he sends out by 'Albert Kroll, Superintendent.'"[102]

Fundamental to the controversy was the fact that the community was undergoing rapid and painful changes. As the old town center was being surrounded by housing developments and as more and more commuters moved into town, the school became a focus for community tensions. As one parent, a strong supporter of the beleaguered superintendent, put it, "since Mundelein has started to grow so has trouble. New people with city ideas are coming in and trying to change over the town, school and church. Old-timers are making the mistake of giving in to them."[103] Another Kroll supporter, a parent who had been president of the PTA, also pointed to the changes in the community, but he saw the "old-timers" as the villains. Many of the new residents who had come into the town were college-educated younger people, who "had a completely new and more progressive philosophy with respect to the type of education their children were to receive from the schools they were maintaining by their tax contributions." The school board, dominated by old-timers had "paid little heed to the changes in trend and the progressive requirements of the new citizenry." For years, school boards had been reluctant to propose a needed bond referendum to expand the school because that would increase taxes. The boards had asked the superintendent and faculty to do a crucial task with inadequate "boys['] play tools."[104]

While Kroll, through his survey and long-range plan for the Mundelein school had begun the reform process, he had aroused resentments and become entangled in a struggle between old and new residents who were trying to define the future of the community.

Yet none of Kroll's reforms were radical. By 1945, a student council for junior high school students was not a new idea. His attempts to expand the school's program to include music, a hot lunch program, industrial arts, and providing the services of a school nurse were in harmony with Dewey's concern for the "whole child," but these changes had come to other schools, such as those of Winnetka, Lake Forest, and even Waukegan, much earlier. Kroll did not want to move much beyond this program (which would not have been regarded as radical in the 1920s). He believed that the primary task of the school was to teach the "basics—reading, writing, arithmetic" and that children need not necessarily enjoy the process. "I never believed that if they felt like dancing they should dance . . . And I think the board felt the same way." The major area of disagreement between Kroll and the board was not about the content of the curriculum but about the kinds of programs that the community could afford.[105]

After Kroll left, the district appointed as superintendent an older, more experienced administrator from southern Illinois. Unlike his predecessor, the new superintendent, Clyde Travelstead, kept a low profile. Under his aegis some of the changes Kroll had urged were quietly instituted, including a hot lunch program and the hiring of two music teachers. The efficiency of the administration was undoubtedly increased by making the superintendent's position full time and hiring a clerk.[106] During the 1950s, the district periodically explored merger with Diamond Lake School, one of the other districts that served Mundelein, but the districts remained separate.[107] With Travelstead in charge, the board won several tax referendums and constructed a third building.[108] But neither Travelstead nor the community was much interested in making changes in the curriculum or ways of teaching, and there is no evidence that educational innovation was an issue in Mundelein after Kroll's departure.[109]

The early postwar period brought rapid growth to both Waukegan and Mundelein, and in both communities the influx of young children meant that new schools were built, more funds were appropriated, and new teachers were hired. In a context of early postwar idealism, these conditions afforded many opportunities for potentially controversial innovations. Although the schools of Waukegan and Mundelein did become involved in controversies in the years after World War II, progressive education was not usually the major issue.

In Mundelein, the fight over the dismissal of Superintendent Kroll was a clear sign that the community was reluctant to accept rapid changes in its schools. Although some changes came as new schools were built and new teachers were hired, Kroll's successor did not make any major efforts to change the ways in which the children of Mundelein were taught. Both Mundelein and Waukegan got portable desks in their classrooms and, in Waukegan, the schools paid considerably more attention to guidance and psychological counseling. In Waukegan, the struggle for a junior high school program and Trump's innovations at Waukegan Township High School did, to some degree, echo national debates about progressive education. Yet the degree of change in the elementary schools was not impressive. While some of Dewey's ideas were accepted by many teachers in Waukegan, their implementation was generally limited to the new, middle-class, sections of the city.

In both communities, the superintendents saw the grade schools primarily as places in which children learned the basic subjects of reading, writing, and arithmetic. Classrooms might be organized in a less authoritarian manner and the fundamentals might be supplemented by art, music, and industrial arts, but they were wary lest these innovations distract from the schools' primary mission. Neither the superintendents nor the communities they served were interested in promoting Dewey's vision of schools that would point the way toward a new and happier way of living.

9

PROGRESSIVE EDUCATION AND THE PROCESS OF REFORM

*I*n the early 1950s, as he neared the end of a long and prolific career, John Dewey reflected on the fate of the movement he had inspired fifty years earlier. His tone was melancholic. The Cold War and McCarthyism reflected a national mood that was inimical to every ideal he had fought for. In this atmosphere, he knew that education, as "part of the common life," would suffer: "When repressive and reactionary forces are increasing in strength in all our other institutions . . . it would be folly to expect the school to get off free." Even more depressing, however, was what had happened to his ideas in the years before the Cold War. While Dewey recognized that schools had changed in the last fifty years, he saw that much of this change had been superficial. The "older gross manifestations of the method of education by fear and repression" had, for the most part, disappeared, but the basic attitudes behind those methods endured. "The fundamental authoritarianism of the old education persists in various modified forms." While there was "a great deal of talk" about progressive principles, even in "progressive" schools this was usually "more a theme of discourse" than an accurate description. The reason? Changing "long-established habits" was exceedingly difficult. Institutions—"social habits organized in the structure of common life"—were even harder to change. They "drive to assimilate and distort the new into conformity with themselves." This is what happened to the "ideas and principles of the educational philosophy I had a share in developing." In teachers' colleges these ideas had been "converted into fixed subject matter or ready-made rules, to be taught and memorized." This "perversion" led to the ridiculous assumption that anyone who could recite the ideas of the movement was "*ipso facto* a 'progressive' teacher."[1] Progressive education, a movement based on a philosophy of change, had become a fixed series of educational methods to be learned by aspiring teachers.

The story of American schools during the depression decade and the Cold War supports Dewey's assessment. Measured by the high hopes and lofty ideals of progressive education, American schools had failed. The ultimate failure was that so much of progressivism's apparent success was rhetorical. While some schools and individual teachers had heeded Dewey's call for a more child-centered school, most had given only lip service to these ideas while continuing older practices.

One explanation for this is, of course, that circumstances were unpropitious. The depression years devastated American schools and, as in the case of Mundelein and Waukegan, made it difficult to maintain even a bare-bones curriculum. Moreover, because of the falling birthrate and the fact that few teachers voluntarily left the profession, there was little room for new teachers with new ideas. While the tremendous expansion of schools during the baby boom years of the 1950s could have provided many opportunities for innovation, the Cold War atmosphere of conformity discouraged experimentation.

Yet circumstances alone do not provide a sufficient explanation for the failure of progressive education to transform American schools. While many schools responded to the depression by ruthlessly cutting "frills," the schools of the blue-collar community of Union Township, New Jersey, adopted progressive ideas as a way of coping with the crisis. These schools developed a coordinate curriculum that integrated social studies with material from other subjects into a single course. The schools also began promoting all students to move them through the system more rapidly. This policy, despite the pragmatic reasons behind it, was in harmony with the progressive principle of "social promotion." Moreover, teachers were now urged to assess each student as a "total person" and not to base grades simply on academic performance.[2]

Similarly the impact of the Cold War was not uniform. The Pasadena story showed that progressive education could be linked to Cold War issues; by depicting progressive practices as unpatriotic, critics stifled reform. But in most of the communities we have examined, the Cold War had little direct effect. In Lake Forest, for example, superintendent Frederick Quinlan regularly attended meetings of the Progressive Education Association without incurring any criticism. Waukegan's newspaper did publish several columns attacking progressive education as subversive, but these were about schools in other parts of the country. Lloyd Trump's attempt to bring progressive innovations to Waukegan Township High School in the late 1940s aroused strong opposition, but the main issue was the adequacy of the new curriculum for college-bound students, not whether it was subversive. Cold War issues played only a minor role in Waukegan's debates about education.

In less direct ways, however, the effects of the Cold War were pervasive. Increasingly, critics blamed progressive practices for the nation's disgraceful lag in producing scientists. After Sputnik, demands for a more rigorous curriculum in science, math, and foreign languages, coupled with attacks on progressive principles, became the new educational dogma.[3] By 1960, even the Dean of Columbia University Teachers College rejected the doctrine of teaching "the whole child" and argued that schools should emphasize "intellectual competence" instead of assuming responsibility "for all of the services the child needs in his development."[4]

But while the depression and the Cold War had impeded progressive reform, a more important reason for the limited impact of progressive education was, as Dewey recognized, that its implementation would require real change and would have to overcome resistance to changing "long-established habits." Schools that were to become child-centered, that were to address the "whole child," would be radically different from the traditional schools that most adults had attended. They would provide new services; they would require different kinds of facilities and new teachers. This would be costly and would require a strong public commitment. In towns like Lake Forest and Winnetka, where cost was not a major issue, this was possible; but in other places, like Mundelein and Waukegan, every effort to build new facilities met with great suspicion. As the effort to build junior high schools in Waukegan demonstrated, educators were immediately put on the defensive when innovations required additional funds.

The junior high school controversy in Waukegan also demonstrated how the process of change could be frustrated by the power of strong, emotional attachment to traditional schooling patterns. The powerful grip of the idea of the neighborhood school made it difficult to establish centralized junior high schools even when it could be demonstrated that this innovation would not only make possible an enriched program but that it would be more economical in the long run. Educational reform of any type is easily frustrated by the fact that the people who ultimately must vote for school board members and funding need to be convinced that the traditional patterns they are familiar with need to be altered, that what was "good enough for me" is no longer adequate. In Lake Forest and Winnetka, where a good financial base meant repeated tax referendums were not needed, school superintendents like Washburne and Frederick Quinlan had much more latitude for innovation than H. R. McCall in Waukegan or Albert Kroll in Mundelein.

In most communities reform was limited by the need for public support. And, as Robert and Helen Lynd found in Muncie, Indiana, in 1935, the educational program that called for "education for individual differences" was "no more consonant with certain dominant elements in Middletown . . . than was the philosophy of Socrates with that of the Athens of his day."[5] The ideals of progressive education were anomalous in a society that stressed competition more than cooperation and that placed an inordinate value on economic success, valuing it as an honorable reward for effort.

In many ways, professional educators contributed to the indifference of their communities to progressive reform. By the late 1930s, superintendents who had not had specific training in school administration, like Lake Forest's John Baggett and Waukegan's John S. Clark, were seen as anachronistic; their replacements, M. G. Davis and H. R. McCall were seasoned professional administrators. Shortly after World War II, a teacher-coach could still serve as superintendent of the tiny Mundelein school district, but when the district was ready to build a second school, the board replaced Albert Kroll with a professional administrator. These new administrators were tempted to turn inward and to look to other members of their profession for support. The new profession increasingly saw its members as specialists with their own language who could not easily communicate with laypeople. As more and more teachers graduated from four-year teacher preparation programs, they brought to the schools a new outlook, one which made them more independent of the communities they served, but one that also distanced them from parents and other voters.

For example, Waukegan parents must have been dismayed to read articles, written by teachers for the local newspaper, that argued that parents might actually harm their children if they tried to teach them reading or number skills. "Teaching a child the ABC's, writing his name or counting up to 100 has very little value as preparation for learning to read or do numbers work. Sometimes it interferes with learning . . . Real harm can be done by forcing some children to undertake a task that cannot be accomplished successfully."[6] As Lawrence Cremin has pointed out, the new professionalism which increased the distance between school personnel and the general public, turned out to be "a supreme political blunder" because it led to the erosion of lay support that became so evident in the 1950s.[7]

Yet professionalization of teachers and superintendents did not irrevocably cut them off from lay support. The campaigns of the National Citizens Commission for the Public Schools helped to bridge the gap and showed that administrators, teachers, and laypeople could cooperate for common purposes. While the fate of Willard Goslin in Pasadena illustrated the danger in allowing professionalism to isolate the schools, both Sidney Marland in Winnetka and Quinlan in Lake Forest demonstrated how the new kind of administrators could self-consciously make public relations a primary concern.

Some critics of American education have pointed to the increasing bureaucratization of schools as an important factor in explaining their unresponsiveness to reform efforts. As the result of the efforts of the reformers who David Tyack has called "administrative progressives," American schools had become more and more to be governed by professional administrators and subject to objective and even rigid patterns of rules and regulations. Educational bureaucracies are often conservative, dedicated to preserving power and privileges and suspicious of innovations that might undermine traditional power relationships. Increased bureaucracy undoubtedly played a role in blunting the spontaneity that lay at the heart of progressive education. As Dewey had pointed out, progressive teachers would have to be exquisitely sensitive to their pupils' varied needs and even their moods. A curriculum built upon the interests of children had to be highly flexible. Bureaucracies, on the other hand, developed to assure that all are treated alike, rely on set procedures that are known in advance. This discourages innovation and flexibility by those who provide the services that the bureaucracy is designed to support.

Bel Kaufman, who taught in New York City Public Schools for fifteen years, drew an indelible picture of an urban school bureaucracy in the years after World War II. Sylvia Barrett, the teacher in this autobiographical novel, had been trained to follow Dewey's philosophy of education. She had been told that she should teach "not the subject but the whole child." When she begins teaching at an urban high school, however, she finds herself in a building without adequate supplies and students who cannot read beyond the fifth-grade level. When, despite these overwhelming handicaps, she is able to arouse the interest of her class by debating the meaning of a Browning poem or by playing a recording of John Geilgud reading Shakespeare, she gets into trouble because her class becomes too excited. Her enemy, the bureaucracy, is personified in the administrative assistant ("Admiral Ass"). He chastises her because her students are talking as they leave her classroom: "The cardinal sin, strange as it may seem in an institution of learning, is talking."[8]

But, as James Q. Wilson has argued, bureaucracies are not all alike. Many bureaucrats are as rigid as Kaufman's "Admiral Ass," but others can be remarkably flexible and innovative. Bureaucracies respond to incentives within the larger context in which they operate. Therefore, if the incentives change, bureaucracies can be enlisted on the side of reform.[9] In Lake Forest and Waukegan, the shift to a more professional superintendent did not retard reform but led, in fact, to innovation.

More important in accounting for the failures of progressive education than the problems of the depression and Cold War was, as Dewey argued, that real reform had been undermined because schools adopted progressive rhetoric much more readily than they implemented progressive practices. Teacher training played a crucial role in disseminating the progressive ideas that were the basis for that rhetoric. By 1960, most teachers had had at least four years of professional training. Moreover, most teachers' college faculty members held advanced degrees; many of them had gone to Columbia University Teachers College, where they had taken courses with mentors like William Heard Kilpatrick, or even Dewey himself. Yet these professors brought back to the teachers' colleges other influences too. Even Teachers College—in many ways the center for the dissemination of progressive ideas—provided other nonprogressive influences. Paramount among these was an emphasis on the "science" of education with its concerns for measuring, testing, and efficiency. This arcane science, which reinforced the new professionalism of faculty members at teacher training colleges, served to undermine progressive ideas. Moreover, the impact of even this diluted form of progressivism was muted by the separation of educational leaders (Arthur Bestor's "educationists") not only from laypeople, but even from classroom teachers.

By the end of World War II, teacher-training institutions promoted a progressive approach to teaching with an emphasis on individualization, student-initiated learning, and democratic classroom management. Yet, even while faculty members stressed these progressive goals, their own teaching often consisted of formal lectures and short-answer examinations, contradicting the principles they espoused. And, as Seymour Sarason has pointed out, the most important influence on the ways in which teachers teach is the ways in which they have been taught.[10] Although the rhetoric of progressivism had permeated educational discourse, classroom teachers, like their instructors in normal schools and teachers' colleges, often revealed through their teaching practices that there was a large gap between a theoretical progressivism and their activities in the classroom. When teachers (like Bel Kaufman's Sylvia Barrett) entered the "real world" and faced the problems of managing a classroom in communities that demanded order and tangible results, they had many incentives to discard a child-centered theoretical framework and adopt older methods. Therefore, despite the fact that many teachers claimed to accept the principles of progressivism, these often had little effect on the way they taught.[11] Consequently, as in the case of Lake Forest's booklet of 1940, progressive rhetoric frequently masked relatively traditional procedures.

Moreover, Dewey's principles, which left room for varying interpretations, were often distorted even by educators who saw themselves as loyal disciples. For example, adjustment was an important theme for Dewey, who argued that for humans, as part of nature, adaptation is the price of survival. Learning is an essential part of the adaptation process. The individual encounters new situations and copes with them by learning new behaviors. But, for Dewey, adaptation is not merely adjusting to an accepted environment. "Adjustment is . . . a continuing process, an active process in which we attempt to reshape our environment so as to eliminate ills and evils, and secure the reasonable goods and values that we want to achieve."[12] For too many of those who emphasized the role of the school in promoting adjustment, however, this meant little more than fitting children into established patterns of schools and society.

Dewey's disciple, William Heard Kilpatrick, despite his role in the Social Frontier group and his commitment to social change, played an important role in changing the meaning of adjustment through his emphasis on the school's role in providing psychological guidance. The guidance movement, which became so important in the 1950s, provided important services to troubled children, but it took on an important aspect of the ethos of the decade. As part of what Elaine Tyler May has called a domestic version of containment, the "therapeutic approach . . . was geared toward helping people feel better about their place in the world, rather than changing it."[13] The ideology of the guidance movement implied that children needed help in adjusting to existing situations and that a child's failure to follow accepted procedures was the problem of the individual child, not the school or the larger society. Thus

Dewey's concept of adjustment—an idea with radical implications—became a tool for promoting acceptance of the status quo.

Similarly, Dewey's principle that education should be adapted
to the needs of individual children was often distorted into a justification for establishing separate tracks for children who, because
of their race or class, were considered unsuitable for rigorous
academic programs. Although tracking was already a common
practice in the 1930s, in the postwar period, as schools faced
tremendous growth and as more and more children remained in
school longer, tracking became the norm. In Lake Forest, for example, tracking was regarded as a major innovation. In Waukegan's
high school, the antiprogressive aspect of tracking was seen in the
reaction to Trump's efforts to democratize the curriculum by
lowering the barriers between the college-preparatory and other
tracks. Some parents of college-bound children objected to these
changes, which they saw as diluting the quality of the college-preparatory program. Lake Forest school officials repeatedly assured
the community that there were plenty of opportunities for children
to move from one track to another, but too often tracking became a
self-fulfilling prophecy; once a child was put into a lower track it
became very difficult to move out.

Moreover, the increasing attention to tracking diluted the
schools' academic focus and led to decidedly antidemocratic conclusions. By the 1950s, educators were ready to accept as a fact that
many children simply could not benefit from the traditional aspects of the curriculum. Increasingly, the doctrine of the "whole
child" was used to disparage academic concerns. Significantly,
when a United States Office of Education pamphlet listed the purposes of elementary schools, it put first "[t]he attainment of physical, emotional, and mental health"—well ahead of helping each
child "become effective in the use of the tools of learning."[14] By the
1950s, a principal could argue in a national professional journal
that the junior high school curriculum should be "improved" by
devoting less attention to reading, writing, and mathematics because "not every child has to read, figure, write and spell" and
"many of them either cannot or will not master these chores."[15] The
antidemocratic nature of this self-fulfilling prophecy directly con-
tradicted Dewey's emphasis on education as a vehicle for attaining
a more egalitarian society.[16]

Especially after World War II, many educators followed the lead
of Kilpatrick and applied Dewey's focus on a child-centered as
opposed to a subject-centered curriculum to high schools. This,
too, was a distortion of Dewey's ideas. He had argued that while

"the organized subject-matter of the adult" could not "provide the starting point," it still represented "the goal towards which education should continuously move." While education should be based on experience, in order to be educative experiences "must lead out into an expanding world of subject-matter . . . of facts or information and of ideas." Education had to be adapted to the needs of "individuals of various degrees of maturity" and this could not be "the same for a person six years old as they are for one twelve or eighteen years old."[17] By the time children reached secondary school, they could understand the long range goals of education, and the curriculum should be less concerned with their immediate interests and more and more directed toward mastery of subject matter. The watered-down curriculum of the Life Adjustment movement was, therefore, a caricature of Dewey's vision.

Dewey firmly believed that the only constant in life was change, and he was careful not to set ultimate goals and proclaim ultimate values. For Dewey, values emerge from intelligent deliberation with the aim of forwarding the growth of the community. Because of the vagueness of this concept, it was possible for his followers to enlist in a variety of political movements. Thus in the 1930s the Social Frontier group sought to use the schools as a way of producing a more just economic system and an egalitarian society. In the 1950s, however, educators could invoke Dewey's principles when they argued that the schools should use progressive techniques to make schools more effective in preparing children for the Cold War.[18]

Dewey, of course, recognized that what was called progressive education was often a sad perversion of his ideals. Yet the failure of progressivism cannot be understood as simply a perversion of Dewey's principles. As radical critics of American education have pointed out, this argument may miss a crucial point: an important reason for the failure of progressive education may have been that the ideal itself was flawed. There were significant reasons for the failure of progressive education that stemmed from the philosophical underpinnings of the movement itself.

It must be recognized that Dewey's prescriptions for humane schooling easily led to an unattractive reliance on manipulation. Although progressive teachers were to begin with the interests of the children, they had to have a clear sense of where they would end. That is, although a class project might begin with the pupils' interest in newspapers and then lead through that to a consideration of making paper, printing, journalism, and the business of selling the finished product, the teacher's role would be to guide that interest toward worthwhile subject matter. From the very beginning of the project the teacher knew that by the third or fourth week the class would be learning, for example, simple multiplication by figuring out newspaper sales. While seemingly spontaneous, much of what went on in a progressive classroom was, in fact, determined well ahead of time. A major difference between the progressive classroom and a conventional classroom was, therefore, that in the former the guidance was hidden. This could leave children with a vague feeling that although they were supposedly making their own choices, they were not really doing what they wanted to do. The hand of authority was there but so disguised that it could not be readily recognized.

Moreover, in Dewey's vision of the reformed community that was the ultimate goal of his philosophy of education, the need for coercion would be reduced because individuals would be taught to want to act for the common good. In these communities constraints would not be eliminated but they would be replaced by a hidden form of social control. Over time we have come to recognize how dangerous this can be. As Henry May has pointed out, "[o]nly by painful experience have we learned to fear, even more than the old-fashioned visible tyrant, the pressures against which it is unthinkable to rebel."[19]

Equally important, Dewey had inspired teachers with his vision of a society transformed through education but, as many public school teachers learned painfully during the Cold War, the idea that progressive teachers should prepare the way for a "more lovely" society could arouse a great deal of hostility. During the crisis of the depression, George Counts could challenge teachers to dare to build a new social order, but even in the 1930s this aroused a storm of opposition from those who did not want the schools to become advocates for social change. As Carleton Washburne ruefully noted, the new social reform agenda that Counts presented to the Progressive Education Association created great difficulties for the public school members of the organization; it is difficult to imagine that any of the communities we have examined would have hired (or retained) teachers who advocated a serious restructuring of American society.[20]

A flaw in Dewey's social reform agenda was its neglect of power relationships. Robert Westbrook, a Dewey scholar who admires his subject a great deal, admits that the philosopher of democracy "did not really have much of a strategy for making American schools into institutions working on behalf of radical democracy."[21] His idea that teachers, many of whom were still subject to the authoritarian rule of school boards that, during the 1930s, still told them where to live and what churches to attend, could lead a major social revolution, was unrealistic.

Radical critics of American education have pointed out that any program of social reform through education ignores the fact that schools necessarily reflect basic patterns of social organization and that schools are designed to reproduce, not change, social patterns. These critics see American education as a vast "sorting machine," designed to confirm existing class relationships. Educational reform, therefore, they argue, can only be the product, not the cause, of fundamental social change.

The radicals are correct in recognizing that schools necessarily have an intimate relationship to the community in which they operate; parents choose a community (at least in part) because of how they perceive the schools. Winnetka in the early days of Carleton Washburne was a village that prided itself on a sense of community, where residents supported "progressive" social reform. Sympathetic to the strain of progressive thought that hailed the scientific expert in civic government, most Winnetkans endorsed Washburne's blend of scientific education and progressive educational principles. In the 1930s, as the population changed, Washburne met increased opposition, but Winnetkans continued to pride themselves on the school system that had made their village a synonym for innovative education. Community acceptance of Washburne's program was, however, grounded in part on Washburne's ability to demonstrate that the Winnetka program allowed individual children to progress rapidly in their studies and that they were in no way handicapped when they got to high school.

In Lake Forest, the public school system had long been regarded as a service provided by the rich for their servants' children and the children of local tradespeople. By the mid-1930s, community leaders recognized, however, that as new people moved into Lake Forest the schools would have to respond. When superintendent M. G. Davis was brought to Lake Forest to modernize the schools, the way was prepared for innovation. Davis began the process of establishing a new image of the public schools as the schools of the whole community. The schools were now described in progressive terms. When Frederick Quinlan arrived, the community was ready to accept further educational innovation. It should be noted, however, that one of the features on which Lake Forest schools prided themselves was ability grouping—a policy which would assure members of the community's elite that it was alright to send their children to the public schools because these schools would permit the same kind of social sorting process that had been supported by the decision to send children to private schools.

Similarly, as Waukegan began to attract new, more affluent residents after World War II, the schools changed. The major battle over the high school curriculum revealed, however, that here, too, parents were concerned about the ways in which schools tracked children. Those who planned to send their children to college needed to be assured that the high school would provide a differentiated curriculum.

Schools in these places, as in other American communities, reflected community values, and these values were not only different in different communities but they changed as time went on. Because schools are governed by locally elected boards of education and paid for by local taxpayers, it is less likely that schools will be agencies for changing community values than that they will be agencies for reinforcing them.

Moreover, the ways in which education is financed makes it more likely that schools will reproduce social patterns rather than change them. Since schools are so heavily dependent on local property taxes, poorer communities find that they cannot provide the resources needed to support new, experimental programs. Poor children are much more likely to attend schools limited by miserly budgets, with large classes, fewer well-prepared and creative teachers, and limited educational materials. A dramatic illustration of this is the contrast between Waukegan and Lake Forest. In 1961, Waukegan's resources (the assessed valuation per pupil) were less than half those of Lake Forest. Although Waukegan residents paid almost eighteen percent higher taxes than their neighbors, the money devoted to each child's education was thirty-eight percent lower than in Lake Forest. Citizens in the poorer community paid considerably more for the education of their children and received substantially less in return. These inequities make a mockery of Dewey's dream that schools could be agents for creating a more lovely community.[22]

Yet, despite the limits of reform through education, this does not mean that the schools and their administrators are completely powerless. Individuals can (and did) make a difference. The ebullient Carleton Washburne and the energetic Frederick Quinlan did influence the schools of their communities and helped change their communities' views of education. In Waukegan, Wallace Green, president of a reform-minded school board, was able to bring significant change to a traditional school system.

Individual teachers, too, made a real difference in how children were taught and what they learned. A contemporary illustration of the role of individual teachers is provided by Tracy Kidder's *Among School Children,* which tells the story of one year in the life of a fifth-grade teacher in a poor neighborhood of the industrial city of Holyoke, Massachusetts. This account of Chris Zajac and her class of Puerto Rican, black, and white children at Kelly School in a run-down section of this decaying town is not the story of a sorting machine. Chris Zajac, the self-styled "old lady teacher," cares deeply about her children. She lies awake at night worrying about Clarence, a boy with severe psychological problems, and Judith, a bright Puerto Rican girl, struggling not to be defeated by the de-cayed neighborhood where she lives. Zajac is constantly looking for new ways to help the children in her class. Without citing Dewey, she is concerned about the "whole child"—intellectual de-velopment, physical and mental health. She makes a real difference in their lives.[23]

Even within quite conventional school systems there were un-doubtedly individual teachers who, like Chris Zajac, shared the progressives' vision of a school that was based on invoking the natural curiosity of children and that was concerned with the broad needs of individual children. The articles by Waukegan's classroom teachers in the early 1950s revealed a range of educational philoso-phies. Many teachers endorsed progressive ideas; some of them undoubtedly used them in their teaching. In many American class-rooms, behind closed doors, individual teachers, like Chris Zajac, implemented Dewey's ideas. But, as Dewey recognized in 1952, although individual school districts, schools, administrators, and teachers did put Dewey's ideas into practice, schooling in general had changed very little.

The attacks on progressive education after World War II marked the beginning of a new reform movement that rejected Dewey's ideas and argued for a renewed emphasis on teaching fundamentals. In 1957, the Soviet Union's success in launching its space satellite was seen as evidence that we had fallen far behind not only in teaching the basic skills but in science and technology. Accordingly, a new generation of educational reformers launched an extensive pro-gram of curriculum revision—one that emphasized content more than process and the sciences more than the humanities. The "new" math and science programs developed, not by curriculum experts but by academic scientists, were the hallmarks of this reform move-ment.

By the late 1960s, however, public concerns about schooling changed once more. Reflecting a new mood that celebrated freedom more than order, educational reform efforts shifted from promoting new, more rigorous curricula to making schools more attractive to children. The movement for the open classroom apparently replaced the concern for academic rigor. The change can be seen in *Crisis in the Classroom*, a best-selling report on American schools published in 1970. After visiting hundreds of classrooms, journalist Charles Silberman was highly critical of American schools for being joyless, preoccupied with order and control, and obsessed "with routine for the sake of routine." He found a basis for hope, however. Silberman hailed the reforms of the British infant schools and the Americans who followed their examples. These schools' aims, it turns out, were similar to those of the progressives: "The informal English schools demonstrate in practice what Dewey argued in theory."[24] In the late 1960s, Dewey's ideas inspired a new group of educational reformers; a new cycle of reform had begun.

The story of the cycles of educational reform can be discouraging. Efforts to reform schools wax and wane and radically shift their goals. Yet schools remain amazingly resistant to change. In an apt metaphor, historian Larry Cuban compares successive waves of educational reform to storms that create violent waves on the ocean's surface but cause barely a ripple in the depths.[25]

In light of this sobering picture, the crucial question is: can schooling be changed and, if so, how? The history of progressive educational reform in the period from 1930 to 1960 provides some answers.

To begin with, although concern for reforming American education is a recurrent topic for debate, we must recognize defining the problem in these terms is unnecessarily confusing. There *is* no American educational system. Despite the role of the United States Department of Education and a program of school consolidation, education is still overwhelmingly local, not only in its control, but in its operation. The idea of reforming a national educational program is, therefore, a solecism. The phrase "American education" is a convenient term for discussing the operation of over fifteen hundred different school districts. Within most of these, individual teachers have considerable freedom to choose how to approach their task. Although there are nationalizing influences—such as an extensive program of standardized tests and common textbooks—schools are still controlled by local school boards. What goes on in American classrooms depends on the resources and values of the community and the training and personality of individual teachers. Inevitably, the response to demands for change will differ widely even within a single state. Two wealthy suburban Chicago school districts, Winnetka and Lake Forest, responded to the educational thought of the period between the world wars in distinct ways, based in large measure on the different ethos of these communities. Moreover, even within individual schools, teaching methods and approaches will differ, depending on the approach of individual teachers, each of whom works behind a closed door.

The issues of educational reform are not only obscured by the assumption that there is a single system for which we can find a single set of answers but also by a confusion about goals. Often the goals of schools are viewed as having children achieve higher scores on standardized tests. When every school district can claim that their children are "above average," reform will presumably have been successful. Standardized multiple-choice tests have the virtue of allowing us to quantify and to present statistical data on the outcomes of schooling and then to compare the successes or failures of different schools. Test scores have the reassuring aura of representing objective standards that can be applied equally to all schools and providing concrete goals. Testing programs makes clear that the children in some schools consistently achieve higher scores than those in others. But the meaning of these differences is by no means clear. We have not been able to determine the degree to which higher test scores are the product of superior educational approaches as opposed to mere reflections of the social status of residents of the community. Moreover, while these tests measure achievements in certain subjects, there are many valuable aspects of schooling that they do not (and cannot) measure. The real danger, therefore, is that by setting higher test scores as the most important goal, other more important aspects will be slighted. Most likely to be overlooked in any program based on achieving higher test scores are the goals that the progressives emphasized. Under a strict regimen of testing schools might become more uniform and might move closer to developing a single educational system, but in such a system teachers would find few incentives to be spontaneous and creative and the curriculum would be less flexible and less open to innovation.

While focusing on the results of standardized tests establishes narrow goals that slight the aspects of schooling that progressives emphasized, the progressives, in turn, often erred in setting broad, even messianic goals for schools. Dewey's view of the school as a legatee institution led to the view that teachers would become front-line troops in the struggle to overcome broad social problems. When schools are asked not only to provide for the academic and social needs of children but also to overcome the results of centuries of racism, sexism, unequal distribution of wealth, and excessive individualism, they are bound to fail. In order for schools to become more like the democratic communities that Dewey envisioned, American society itself must change in fundamental ways.

Although hopes for a single formula that will transform education and society once and for all are chimerical, significant change within individual schools is not only possible but essential. Schools, like other social institutions, need to rethink and re-evaluate what they do in order to avoid becoming locked into mindless routines. Without continual renewal, even successful schools fail. Winnetka, which had been an exciting place to teach in the Washburne years, had turned earlier reforms into stultified habits by the time Sidney Marland became superintendent. What had been left behind from the Washburne years were the yellowed mimeographed texts; what had been lost was the spirit of Washburne's reforms. Essential for the health of education is the *process* of change. Questioning accepted ways is essential to the health of schools and, therefore, the reiterated demands for change are not signs of failure; they are part of a process that is essential to keeping education vital.

Because it is the process of developing new approaches that is crucial, it must involve principals and teachers directly and intimately. For teachers, like schools, change can be revitalizing. The lesson of the Denver curriculum reforms of the 1920s and 1930s is important. Here teachers were the most important change agents. Similarly, in Winnetka, Washburne (and later Marland) worked closely with teachers in developing new programs. Because the Winnetka curriculum was in large measure the product of the district's teachers, they took great pride in it. Teachers, like those who worked evenings and weekends writing new materials for the Winnetka schools, need to see themselves as important in the educational process. When they are part of the movement for change, they will not only make sure that it works, but they will have undergone the necessary renewal to make it work.

When we recognize that it is the process of change that is valuable, and that this must necessarily involve classroom teachers, it becomes clear why the search for a comprehensive national program for American schools is wrong and ill-fated. Reforms can influence other communities, but they are not replicable from one district to another. While the Washburne's Winnetka program was an attractive model, it would have been a mistake for other districts to copy it. Each community needs to develop its own approach, one that is designed by its own staff and teachers and that is consonant with community values. In order to do this, parents and other interested members of the community must be involved in the process of defining the goals of the schools. The great lesson of the 1950s and the Citizens Committees for the Public Schools, as Sidney Marland demonstrated in Winnetka, was that teachers, administrators, and citizens can cooperate to develop and support new programs.

It is important to recognize that any plan for school reform is necessarily provisional; schools need to emphasize different approaches at different times. As Dewey argued, life itself is a process in which change and development is the only constant. Just as Dewey's goal for the individual is growth, so institutions must grow by responding to changed conditions. Sometimes this means that a school needs to put new emphasis on children's developmental needs. At other times, it will need to re-emphasize academic content. Yesterday's solution will probably become tomorrow's problem.

The theologian Reinhold Niebuhr, whose thought was deeply influenced by John Dewey, noted that there are certain questions "which cannot be solved once for all," questions that must be "continually solved within the framework of the democratic process." For Niebuhr, democracy provides "a method of finding proximate solutions" to such insoluble problems.[26] In the light of this insight, we need to see schooling as a process that is necessarily confronted with continuing demands for reform. Schools have to develop different ways of meeting the changing needs of our society. Schools will always be in need of reform. Within that process, however, it is important to keep in mind John Dewey's hope that schools can become democratic communities that will imbue children with "the spirit of service" and give them "the instruments of effective self-direction."[27]

Tables: School and Community Statistics, 1930-1960

Table 1: School Statistics, 1930–41

	Enrollment	Cost per Pupil	Change in Cost since 1930 in Percent	Teacher/Pupil Ratio
1930–31[1]				
Winnetka	1,929	$191.27	—	20
Lake Forest	649	142.75	—	22
Waukegan	5,003	74.98	—	35
Mundelein	166	63.01	—	33
1935–36[2]				
Winnetka	1,816	$160.55	−16 (2)*	22
Lake Forest	655	148.22	4 (27)	18
Waukegan	4,698	54.97	−27 (−11)	37
Mundelein	170	46.56	−26 (−10)	34
1940–41[3]				
Winnetka	1,422	$226.60	18 (41)	NA[4]
Lake Forest	607	197.54	38 (65)	NA
Waukegan	4,367	67.37	−10 (7)	NA
Mundelein	125	73.74	17 (40)	NA

* Figures in parentheses are calculated for constant dollars.

1. *Thirty-ninth Biennial Report of the Superintendent of Public Instruction of the State of Illinois, July 1, 1930–June 30, 1932,* Appendix A, "School Statistics—1930–1931," pp. 208, 209, 212, 213. Cost per pupil is derived by dividing "Current expenses, 1930–1931" by "Enrollment"; Pupil to teacher ratio is derived by dividing "Enrollment" by the number of teachers.

2. *Forty-first Biennial Report of the Superintendent of Public Instruction of the State of Illinois, July 1, 1934–June 30, 1936,* Appendix B, "School Statistics—1935–1936," pp. 117, 121, 122. The change in cost since 1930 is derived.

3. *Statistical Report of the Superintendent of Public Instruction, State of Illinois for the Year Ended June 30, 1941* (no. 338), pp. 132, 136, 138, 139.

4. The state statistical reports did not include the numbers of teachers in each district for a ten-year period between 1936 and 1946.

Table 2: Teachers' Salaries, 1930–36

	Male Teachers	Female Teachers	Average Salary— Male	Average Salary— Female	Male: Change since 1931 (%)	Female: Change since 1931 (%)
1930–31[1]						
Winnetka	15	80	$3,533	$1,912	—	—
Lake Forest	2	27	2,400	1,854	—	—
Waukegan	6	136	3,270	1,828	—	—
Mundelein	1	4	1,800	1,400	—	—
1935–36[2]						
Winnetka	17	67	$3,223	$2,037	−8.78	−6.52
Lake Forest	5	31	3,251	1,612	35.48	−13.09
Waukegan	5	122	2,448	1,367	−25.14	−25.18
Mundelein	1	4	1,575	1,021	−12.50	−27.05

1. *Thirty-ninth Report of the Superintendent of Public Instruction,* Appendix A, "School Statistics—1930–1931," pp. 208, 209, 212, 213. Figures for average salaries are derived. When these figures are translated into 1991 dollars, Winnetka male teachers earned the equivalent of $28,814 and women earned the equivalent of $15,594.

2. *Forty-first Report of the Superintendent of Public Instruction,* Appendix B, "School Statistics—1935–1936," pp. 117, 121, 122.

Table 3: Percent of Population Under 14 Years of Age in Public School, 1940–41[1]

	Population Under 14 Years of Age	School Enrollment for 1940–41	Percent in Public School
Winnetka	2,149	1,422	66.17
Lake Forest	1,285	607	47.24
Waukegan	7,147	4,367	61.10
Mundelein	*		

* Because Mundelein had more than one school district, there is no meaningful way to present these statistics for the village.

1. These figures are derived from a comparison of data from the 1940 census with enrollment data for the 1940–41 school year. *Sixteenth Census of the United States: 1940 Population,* vol. 2 (Characteristics of the Population), part 2 (Washington, DC: United States Government Printing Office, 1943), pp. 607, 616, 636; and *Statistical Report of the Superintendent of Public Instruction, State of Illinois for the Year Ended June 30, 1941* (no. 338), pp. 136, 138, 139.

Table 4: School Statistics, 1945–61

	Enrollment	Change in Enrollment Since 1946 (%)	Cost per Pupil	Change in Cost since 1946 (%)		Teacher/Pupil Ratio
1945–46[1]						
Winnetka	1,436	—	$254.48	—		20
Lake Forest	616	—	220.31	—		18
Waukegan	3,739	—	115.33	—		27
Mundelein	204	—	81.18	—		29
1950–51[2]						
Winnetka	1,774	24	$370.57	46	(9)*	19
Lake Forest	650	6	378.01	72	(28)	15
Waukegan	3,997	7	213.38	85	(38)	25
Mundelein	355	74	176.21	117	(62)	30
1955–56[3]						
Winnetka	2,089	45	$426.87	68	(13)	21
Lake Forest	987	60	487.50	121	(49)	19
Waukegan	6,566	76	262.40	128	(53)	29
Mundelein	695	241	180.88	123	(50)	33
1960–61[4]						
Winnetka	2,172	51	$559.57	120	(34)	20
Lake Forest	1,346	119	631.20	186	(74)	16
Waukegan	8,891	138	393.63	241	(108)	26
Mundelein	1,549	659	285.38	252	(114)	32

* Figures in parentheses are calculated for constant dollars.

1. *Annual Statistical Report of the Superintendent of Public Instruction, State of Illinois, For the Year Ended June 30, 1946* (Circular Series A, no. 43), pp. 202, 206, 208, 209, 264–65, 278–79.

2. *Annual Statistical Report of the Superintendent of Public Instruction, State of Illinois, For the Year Ended June 30, 1951* (Circular Series A, no. 76), pp. 220–21, 230–31, 258–59, 268–69.

3. *Annual Statistical Report of the Superintendent of Public Instruction, State of Illinois, For the Year Ended June 30, 1956* (Circular Series A, no. 112), pp. 248–49, 258–59.

4. *Annual Statistical Report of the Superintendent of Public Instruction, State of Illinois, For the Year Ended June 30, 1961* (Circular Series A, no. 149), pp. 194–95, 202–3. For this school year, the state's statistics on student-teacher ratio and the per-pupil costs were based on "average daily attendance" instead of "total enrollment," but I've recalculated them so that they are comparable to the figures in previous years.

Table 5: School Tax Statistics, 1960–61[1]

	Assessed Valuation per Pupil (1,000s)	Assessed Value Compared to Lake Forest	Total Tax Rate	Tax Rate Compared to Lake Forest	Per Pupil Expenditure Compared to Lake Forest	Percentage in Private School
Winnetka	$52,683	−18.42(%)	1.480	+3.27(%)	−11.35(%)	28.7(%)
Lake Forest	64,580	—	1.433	—	—	30.0
Waukegan	31,348	−51.46	1.689	+17.86	−37.64	18.7
Mundelein	18,776	−70.93	1.503	+4.88	−54.88	33.8

1. Northeastern Illinois Metropolitan Area Planning Commission, *Suburban Fact Book: Revised with 1960–1961 Data* (n.p.: Northeastern Illinois Metropolitan Area Planning Commission, 1962), table 32 "School District Data"; U. S. Bureau of the Census, *U. S. Population: 1960. General Social and Economic Characteristics, Illinois*. Final Report PC(1)-15C. (Washington, DC: U. S. Government Printing Office, 1962), table 73.

Table 6: Community Characteristics, 1940–60[1]

	1940 Total Population	1950 Total Population	1960 Total Population	Population Change, 1950–60	Population with 1960 Family Income Under $3,000	Population with 1960 Family Income Over $10,000	1960 Black Population	Black Population
Winnetka	12,430	12,105	13,368	10.4(%)	3.3(%)	79.2(%)	252	1.9(%)
Lake Forest	6,885	7,819	10,687	36.7	3.7	53	224	2.1
Waukegan	34,241	38,946	55,719	43.1[2]	8.5	23.5	4,485	8.0
Mundelein	1,328	3,189	10,526	230.1	2.7	23.7	1	0.0

1. Evelyn M. Kitawga and Karl E. Taeuber, *Local Community Fact Book, Chicago Metropolitan Area: 1960* (Chicago: Chicago Community Inventory, University of Chicago, 1963), pp. 4–7; *Suburban Fact Book: Revised with 1960–1961 Data*, tables 4 and 6.

2. A considerable part of this increase was due to annexation; if we allow for this, the growth rate is 26.95 percent: *Local Community Fact Book, Chicago Metropolitan Area. Based on the 1970 and 1980 Censuses.* Chicago Fact Book Consortium, eds. (Chicago: The Chicago Review Press, 1984), p. 294.

Notes

Preface

1. Lawrence Cremin, *The Transformation of the School: Progressivism in American Education, 1876–1957* (New York: Alfred A. Knopf, 1962). See also Lawrence Cremin, *American Education: The Metropolitan Experience* (New York: Harper & Row, 1988).

2. Diane Ravitch, *The Troubled Crusade: American Education, 1945–1980* (New York: Basic Books, Inc., 1983), p. 43.

3. John Dewey and Evelyn Dewey, *Schools of To-Morrow* (New York: E. P. Dutton, 1915).

Chapter One

1. *New York Times*, June 2, 1952. The first sentence of this long obituary calls him "the philosopher from whose teachings has grown the school of progressive education." It goes on to call him "the chief prophet of progressive education" (pp. 1, 21). See also *New York Times*, "Education in Review," June 8, 1952, section 4, p. 11, for an article that discusses Dewey's influence on schools as seen by leading educators.

2. Lawrence Cremin, *The Transformation of the School: Progressivism in American Education, 1876–1957* (New York: Alfred A. Knopf, 1962) was an important work in opening the scholarly examination of progressive education. But, because Cremin's account of the movement is so broad, it fails to describe the movement sufficiently.

For example, Cremin included in the progressive camp those interested in applying scientific testing techniques to education. My reading of the history of progressive education in the post–World War I period does not support this. Carleton Washburne (who served as president of the Progressive Education Association), for example, saw himself as virtually the only educator who belonged both to the Progressive Education Association and the American Educational Research Association (Joseph Baskin's interview with Carleton Washburne at Okemos, Michigan, February 4, 1966—a copy of the tape recording is in my possession). Harold Rugg's autobiographical *That Men May Understand: An American in the Long Armistice* (New York: Doubleday, Doran and Co., Inc., 1941) makes clear that Rugg regarded his interest in progressive education as a shift from his original base in the testing movement (pp. 180–86).

In his latest examination of progressive education, *American Education: The Metropolitan Experience* (New York: Harper & Row, 1988), Cremin again avoided a precise definition. "The movement," he said, "was essentially pluralistic and occasionally even contradictory" (p. 228).

3. Larry Cuban, *How Teachers Taught: Constancy and Change in American Classrooms, 1890–1980* (New York: Longman, 1984), points out that despite a series of issues on which they disagreed, among "pedagogical" progressives there was "a core consensus on what constituted a school focused upon children. For the most part, pedagogical reformers wanted instruction and curriculum tailored to children's interests; they wanted instruction to occur as often as possible individually or in small groups; they wanted programs that permitted children more freedom and creativity . . . ; they wanted school experiences connected to activities outside the classroom; and they wanted children to help shape the direction of their learning" (pp. 43–44).

4. The story of the efforts to apply businesslike standards of efficiency to education is told by Raymond E. Callahan, *Education and the Cult of Efficiency: A Study of the Social Forces That Have Shaped the Administration of the Public Schools* (Chicago: The University of Chicago Press, 1962). David Tyack (who has written several important studies of twentieth-century education) made a useful distinction when he identified these educational reformers as "administrative progressives." See *The One Best System: A History of American Urban Education* (Cambridge, MA: Harvard University Press, 1974), pp. 126–27.

5. Neil Coughlan, *Young John Dewey: An Essay in American Intellectual History* (Chicago: The University of Chicago Press, 1975), p. 75. See also Robert B. Westbrook, *John Dewey and American Democracy* (Ithaca: Cornell University Press, 1991), pp. 34–58.

6. An interview with John Dewey in the *Detroit Tribune*, April 13, 1892, quoted in Richard J. Bernstein, *John Dewey* (Atascadero, CA: Ridgeview Publishing Company, 1966), pp. 31–32.

7. Westbrook, *Dewey and Democracy*, pp. 14, 60–61, notes, however, that "Dewey never completely shook Hegel out of his system" and that he did not completely abandon philosophical idealism until late in the decade of the 1890s."

8. John Dewey, "The Influence of Darwin on Philosophy," reprinted in *American Thought: Civil War to World War I*, Perry Miller, ed., (New York: Holt, Rinehart and Winston, Inc., 1954), p. 214. The essay was originally delivered as a lecture at Columbia University in 1909.

9. Ibid., p. 221.

10. Ibid., p. 223.

11. Jane Addams, "The Subjective Necessity for Social Settlements," [1892] in Christopher Lasch, ed., *The Social Thought of Jane Addams* (Indian-

apolis: The Bobbs-Merrill Company, Inc., 1965), pp. 29–43. The quoted phrase is found on p. 29.

12. Cremin, *Metropolitan Experience*, pp. 176–77.

13. Jane Addams, "A Toast to John Dewey" [1929], in Lasch, *Jane Addams*, p. 177.

14. Christopher Lasch, *Jane Addams*, points out that Addams's and Dewey's ideas were so closely related that it is "difficult to say whether Dewey influenced Addams or Jane Addams influenced Dewey. They influenced each other . . . Hull-House and Dewey's experimental school at the University of Chicago constantly exchanged ideas and personnel" (p. 176).

15. Bernstein, *John Dewey*, pp. 38–39. Alice Chipman Dewey was vitally involved in the school and the school was, in fact, their joint venture.

16. John Dewey, *The School and Society* (1900, rev. ed., 1915; Chicago: The University of Chicago Press, 1956). Cremin, *Metropolitan Experience*, calls this the "greatest of Dewey's educational writings of the Chicago period." Within a year of its publication, "it became Dewey's most widely read book" (p. 169).

17. John Dewey and Evelyn Dewey, *Schools of To-Morrow* (New York: E. P. Dutton, 1915), p. 170.

18. Dewey, *School and Society*, p. 60. Dewey had made a similar point in 1893 while he was still at Michigan: "If I were asked to name the most needed of all reforms in the spirit of education I should say: 'Cease conceiving of education as mere preparation for later life, and make of it the full meaning of the present life.' And to add that only in this case does it become truly a preparation for later life is not the paradox it seems. An activity which does not have worth enough to be carried on for its own sake cannot be very effective as a preparation for something else" (quoted in Dewey's *New York Times* obituary, June 2, 1952, p. 21).

19. Dewey, *School and Society*, pp. 47–48.

20. Ibid., p. 44.

21. Ibid., p. 80.

22. Ibid., p. 36.

23. Ibid., pp. 9, 10, 12.

24. Ibid., p. 29.

25. Ibid., p. 111.

26. Ibid., pp. 106–7, 115.

27. Bernstein, *Dewey*, p. 127. For Dewey's view of science see ibid., pp. 115–29, and Reginald Archambault's "Introduction" in *John Dewey on Education*, Reginald Archambault, ed., (New York: Random House, 1964), pp. xv–xvii.

28. John Dewey, "Progressive Education and the Science of Education," *Progressive Education* 5 (1928): 197–204. This was Dewey's presidential address to the Progressive Education Association in 1928. It is reprinted in *Dewey on Education: Selections*, Martin S. Dworkin, ed., (New York: Teachers College Press, 1959), pp. 113–26. The quoted words are on pp. 117 and 125.

29. John Dewey, *Freedom and Culture* (New York: G. P. Putnam's Sons, 1939), p. 102; quoted in Bernstein, *Dewey*, p. 135.

30. John Dewey, *Democracy and Education: An Introduction to the Philosophy of Education* (1916; New York: The Free Press, 1966), p. 100.

31. Ibid., p. 87.

32. According to a recent study of democratic theory in Dewey's philosophy, "the formation of democratic character . . . [was] at the heart of Dewey's philosophy of education," Westbrook, *Dewey and Democracy*, p. 171.

33. Francis W. Parker, *Talks on Pedagogics* (New York, 1894), p. 450, quoted in Cremin, *Transformation*, p. 132.

34. Cremin, *Transformation*, p. 133; Cuban, *How Teachers Taught*, p. 33.

35. Cremin, *Transformation*, p. 133.

36. Ibid., p. 135.

37. Dorothy Ross, *G. Stanley Hall: The Psychologist as Prophet* (Chicago: The University of Chicago Press, 1972), pp. 358–61.

38. Geraldine Joncich, *The Sane Positivist: A Biography of Edward L. Thorndike* (Middletown, CT: Wesleyan University Press, 1968), pp. 282–96, 308, 359–72, 391–92, 534. Another important figure in the movement to promote efficiency in education was Professor Franklin Bobbitt of the University of Chicago. Bobbitt received his Ph.D. from Clark University where he had worked with G. Stanley Hall. See Callahan, *Cult of Efficiency*, pp. 79–94.

39. Joncich, *Thorndike*, pp. 164, 397–98. In 1929 Thorndike published what Joncich calls "a post-Deweyan" version of an earlier textbook. In *Elementary Principles of Education*, which he wrote in collaboration with his former student, Arthur Gates, he commended Dewey for "brilliantly and steadfastly" upholding the idea that education "is not preparation for life, it is life" (p. 421).

40. Ibid., pp. 268–74.

41. E. L. Thorndike, *Educational Psychology*, vol. 2, p. 16, as quoted in Joncich, *Thorndike*, p. 352.

42. Joncich, *Thorndike*, pp. 312–15, 544.

43. Edward L. Thorndike, "Intelligence and Its Uses," *Harper's Monthly*, May, 1922, quoted in Walter Feinberg, *Reason and Rhetoric: The Intellectual Foundations of 20th Century Liberal Educational Policy* (New York: John Wiley & Sons, Inc., 1975), p. 70.

44. Dewey, *School and Society*, p. 64.

45. Dewey, "Progressive Education and the Science of Education," Dworkin, *Dewey on Education*, p. 119.

46. For a brief account of the impact of the testing movement on American education, see Cremin, *Transformation*, pp. 185–92.

47. John Dewey, "Mediocrity and Individuality," *New Republic* 33 (1922): 35–37, quoted in Cremin, *Transformation*, pp. 190–91. Evelyn Weber, "Conceptions of Child Growth and Learning," in *A New Look at Progressive Education*, James R. Squire, ed. (Washington, DC: Association for Supervision and Curriculum Development, 1972), points out that progressives did not always realize the disparity between their aims and the presuppositions of the "scientific" psychologists of the testing movement (p. 28).

48. Cremin, *Transformation*, pp. 243–45.

49. Ibid., p. 206.

50. Cremin gives a brief account of the impact of Freudianism on progressive education in ibid., pp. 207–15.

51. Addams, "Toast to Dewey," in Lasch, *Jane Addams*, p. 179.

52. A. S. Neill, whose philosophy of education was in the progressive tradition, went so far as to call therapy sessions at Summerhill "private lessons."

53. Biographical information on Kilpatrick is based on Samuel Tenenbaum, *William Heard Kilpatrick: Trail Blazer in Education* (New York: Harper & Brothers Publishers, 1951).

54. Ibid., p. 75.

55. Kilpatrick saw himself as Dewey's interpreter, and until he was fifty years old, he did not regard himself as an innovator. Tenenbaum quotes his diary entry of November 10, 1915: "I shall . . . probably always be little more than the disciple and expounder of Dewey's philosophy. Probably the most I shall do will be . . . to systematize and organize it, coordinate the work of others, and in a few cases carry the whole on further" (p. 208).

56. Ibid., pp. 185–87.

57. Ibid. p. 75. Tenenbaum quotes Dewey telling Kilpatrick: "Since you have asked me specifically . . . about your understanding of my ideas I do say that I would not desire a more sympathetic intelligent interpreter." (The quotation is from a letter from Kilpatrick to his mother, July 16, 1913.) Although Kilpatrick was a disciple of Dewey, Tenenbaum concludes that "In the end, Kilpatrick's educational contributions became really and truly his own, unique and independent" (p. 305).

58. William Heard Kilpatrick, "The Project Method: The Use of the Purposeful Act in the Educative Process," *Teachers College Bulletin*, tenth series, 2 (Oct. 12, 1918): 16.

59. William Heard Kilpatrick, *Remaking the Curriculum* (New York: Newsom & Company, 1936), pp. 31–32. My emphasis.

60. Tenenbaum, *Kilpatrick*, pp. 105, 106. In *Remaking the Curriculum*, Kilpatrick argued that "many pupils, just as many adults, have no need to specialize in the way and along the lines set out by existing school subjects. In fact, it probably hurts most of such pupils to spend time on logically organized subject matter" (p. 105).

61. Kilpatrick, *Remaking the Curriculum*, p. 68.

62. Dewey, *Democracy and Education*, pp. 182–83. Westbrook, *Dewey and Democracy*, p. 104, argues that Dewey "valued mankind's accumulated knowledge as much as the most hidebound traditionalist."

63. Tenenbaum, *Kilpatrick*, p. 177.

64. See John Dewey, *Experience and Education* (New York: The Macmillan Company, 1938): "When education is based in theory and practice upon experience, it goes without saying that the organized subject matter of the adult and specialist cannot provide the starting point. Nevertheless, it represents the goal toward which education should continuously move" (p. 103).

65. Kilpatrick, *Remaking the Curriculum*, pp. 95, 99–107. Kilpatrick does concede that some children will benefit from having subject matter specialists in secondary school.

66. William H. Kilpatrick, "The Essentials of the Activity Movement," *Progressive Education*, Oct., 1924, quoted in Tenenbaum, *Kilpatrick*, p. 163.

67. Tenenbaum, *Kilpatrick*, pp. 287–94. The radicalism of the Social Frontier thinkers should not be exaggerated. David Tyack notes that "left-wing educators were more concerned with the antisocial effects of the profit motive on character—its miseducative quality—than with the dynamics of capital accumulation." Their inspiration was more likely to the *New Republic* than the *New Masses*. See David Tyack, Robert Lowe, and Elisabeth Hansot, *Public Schools in Hard Times: The Great Depression and Recent Years* (Cambridge, MA: Harvard University Press, 1984), pp. 25–26.

68. Ibid., pp. 60–62, 69. For a brief account and analysis of the Frontier group, see Cremin, *Metropolitan Experience*, pp. 187–96.

Chapter Two

1. Anthony Bailey, *America, Lost and Found* (New York: Random House, 1980), pp. 71–74. Some of the material in this chapter was published in my essay, "The Failure of Progressive Education," *Schooling and Society*, Lawrence Stone, ed., (Baltimore: The Johns Hopkins University Press, 1976), pp. 252–63.

2. Lawrence A. Cremin, *The Transformation of the School: Progressivism in American Education 1896–1957* (New York: Alfred A. Knopf, 1962), p. 291. Cremin qualifies this statement by pointing out that reforms proceeded at an uneven pace in different areas.

3. Ibid., pp. 291–308. Cremin does deal with a more or less typical school system, using Robert and Helen Lynds's study of "Middletown." He suggests that the "conservative progressivism" of this city's schools "typifies the influence of progressive education on the pedagogical mainstream during the interbellum era" (p. 305). In his bibliographical essay, Cremin points out that his use of Middletown "is in many respects a literary device at best" (p. 383).

4. Diane Ravitch, *The Troubled Crusade: American Education, 1945–1980* (New York, Basic Books, Inc., 1983), p. 55.

5. U.S. Office of Education, *Biennial Surveys of Education in the United States, 1938–1940 and 1940–1942*, 2 vols. (Washington, DC: United States Government Printing Office, 1947), vol. 2, chapter 1, p. 5; chapter 2, p. 3; chapter 3, p. 24. I have chosen to concentrate on elementary schools because the introduction of progressive ideas into secondary schools was complicated by the problem of meeting college admission standards. There was considerably less pressure on elementary schools to meet a uniform standard of preparation. In many cases, I have used statistics dealing with the late 1930s in order to represent the degree to which the innovations of the progressives of the 1920s and 1930s had actually been adopted.

6. David Tyack, Robert Lowe, and Elisabeth Hansot, *Public Schools in*

Hard Times: The Great Depression and Recent Years (Cambridge, MA: Harvard University Press, 1984), pp. 49, 50–57.

7. U.S. Office of Education, *National Survey of the Education of Teachers,* Bulletin, 1933, no. 10, 6 vols. (Washington, DC: United States Government Printing Office, 1932–35), vol. 2, pp. 42, 36, 162, 174.

8. Ibid., vol. 3, pp. 136–38.

9. Francis E. Peterson, *Philosophies of Education Current in the Preparation of Teachers in the United States,* Teachers College Contributions to Education, no. 528 (New York: Teachers College Bureau of Publications, 1933), pp. 126–27, 131–32.

10. August B. Hollingshead, *Elmtown's Youth: The Impact of Social Classes on Adolescents* (New York: John Wiley & Sons, 1949), pp. 125–26; Robert S. Lynd and Helen Merrell Lynd, *Middletown in Transition: A Study in Cultural Conflicts* (New York: Harcourt, Brace & World, 1937), pp. 236, 411. Hollingshead did his field work in 1940–41 in Morris, Illinois. "Middletown" was based on a study of Muncie, Indiana, in 1936. For a devastating picture of how small towns exploited teachers, see Virgil Scott's autobiographical novel, *The Hickory Stick* (New York: The Swallow Press and William Morrow & Company, 1948).

11. Willard Spalding, "Norwell: A Study of the Environment of School Children" (Ed.D. diss., Harvard University, 1942), pp. 329–30.

12. Herbert B. Bruner et. al., *What Our Schools Are Teaching: An Analysis of the Content of Selected Courses of Study with Special Reference to Science, Social Science, and Industrial Arts* (New York: Teachers College Bureau of Publications, 1941), pp. 205, 208, 209.

13. Ray L. Hamon, "Trends in Types of School Seating," *The Nation's Schools* 16, no. 3 (September 1935): 57–58.

14. See advertisements in the *American School Board Journal* of the period. As late as the 1935–36 academic year, the New York City Board of Education was still specifying that new school buildings should have thirty-five fixed seats in rows in all *new* school buildings. In 1942, the board authorized moveable furniture for new buildings. See Larry Cuban, *How Teachers Taught: Constancy and Change in American Classrooms, 1890–1980* (New York: Longman, 1984), p. 50. On rural black schools, see Tyack, *Public Schools in Hard Times,* p. 32.

15. Another school system that had a well-developed mental hygiene program was Summit, New Jersey. See Charles R. Foster, *Mental Hygiene in New Jersey Schools: An Inquiry into the Influence of Mental Hygiene Concepts on New Jersey School Practice* (New Brunswick, NJ: School of Education, Rutgers University, 1939), pp. 17–26. Summit was well known as a progressive school system.

16. Wilma Walker, "Social and Health Work in the Schools," *Social Work Year Book 1941* (New York: Russell Sage Foundation, 1941), p. 514. The 1935 edition of the *Year Book* reported that there were approximately 175 visiting teachers (an earlier term for school social workers) employed in seventy-one centers but that nowhere did the number of visiting teachers approach the goal set by the White House Conference on Child Health and Protection

of one visiting teacher for every five hundred pupils. See Shirley Leonard, "Visiting Teachers," *Social Work Year Book 1935* (New York: Russell Sage Foundation, 1935), p. 533; Ethel L. Cornell, "The Work of the School Psychologist," University of the State of New York, *Bulletin*, no. 1238 (June 1942): 9. In Ohio, the state made no provisions for school psychologists until 1945, and it was not until 1949 that ten percent of school districts in Ohio had approved units in school psychology. See S. J. Bonham, Jr., and Edward C. Grover, *The History and Development of School Psychology in Ohio* (Columbus, OH: State Department of Education, 1961), pp. 1–3; Lynd and Lynd, *Middletown In Transition*, p. 224.

17. Telephone interview with Luther Gulick, April 1973.

18. Julius B. Maller, *School and Community: A Study of the Demographic and Economic Background of Education in the State of New York*, The Regents' Inquiry into the Character and Cost of Public Education in the State of New York (New York: McGraw-Hill Book Company, Inc., 1938).

19. Leo J. Brueckner et. al., *The Changing Elementary School*, The Regents' Inquiry into the Character and Cost of Public Education in the State of New York (New York: Inor Publishing Co., 1939). Their critique indicates that the members of the inquiry staff generally advocated a moderate version of progressive education: they favored a child-centered curriculum but, like Dewey, they did not believe that teachers should abdicate their own sense of what was important for children to learn.

20. Ibid., pp. 164–65, 171, 47.

21. William S. Gray and Bernice Leary, "Reading Instruction in Elementary Schools," in Brueckner, *Changing Elementary School*, pp. 285–86; William S. Gray and Bernice Leary, *The Teaching of Reading in the Elementary and Secondary Schools in the State of New York*, The Regents' Inquiry into the Character and Cost of Public Education in the State of New York (New York: The Regents' Inquiry, 1938), pp. 24, 44–45.

22. C. L. Thiele and Leo J. Brueckner, "Arithmetic Instruction in Elementary Schools," in Brueckner, *Changing Elementary Schools*, p. 333.

23. Dora V. Smith, *Evaluating Instruction in English in the Elementary Schools of New York: A Report of the Regents' Inquiry into the Character and Cost of Public Education in New York State*, Eighth Research Bulletin of the National Conference on Research in English (Chicago: Scott, Foresman and Company, 1941), p. 64.

24. Ibid., pp. 62, 63.

25. Edgar B. Wesley and Howard E. Wilson, "An Inquiry into Instruction and Achievement in Social Studies," Regents' Inquiry into the Cost and Character of Education in New York State, Elementary Division (typescript, New York State Library, Albany, NY), p. 57.

26. Ibid., p. 39.

27. Paul R. Mort and Francis G. Cornell, *American Schools in Transition: How Our Schools Adapt Their Practices to Changing Needs: A Study of Pennsylvania* (New York: Teachers College Bureau of Publications, 1941), p. 3.

28. Herbert M. Kliebard, *The Struggle for the American Curriculum, 1893–1958* (Boston: Routledge & Kegan Paul, 1986), pp. 223–26.

29. William B. Lauderdale, "A Progressive Era for Education in Alabama, 1935–1951," *Alabama Historical Quarterly* (Spring 1975): 40–61; *Curriculum Bulletin on Orientation* (Alabama State Department of Education, Montgomery, 1927) quoted in ibid., pp. 44–45.

30. Charles A. Harper, *A Century of Public Teacher Education* (Washington, DC: American Association of Teachers Colleges, 1939), pp. 138–42; Earl W. Hayter, *Education in Transition: The History of Northern Illinois University* (DeKalb, IL: Northern Illinois University Press, 1974), pp. 147, 192, 229, 213, 231, 232. Northern Illinois State Teachers College, *Bulletin*, 1926–27, 1940–41. The Northern story was typical. For example, at Eastern Illinois, in 1932–33 fourteen faculty members did not hold a bachelor's degree and twenty-three had only B.A.'s. This "proved to be a source of embarrassment" and, after the North Central Association granted only conditional accreditation in 1933, a large number of faculty members were given leaves of absence to work for higher degrees. See Charles A. Coleman, *Eastern Illinois State College: Fifty Years of Public Service* (Charleston, IL: *Eastern Illinois State College Bulletin*, 189, Jan. 1, 1950), pp. 296–97.

31. Victor Hicken, *The Purple and the Gold: The Story of Western Illinois University* (Macomb, IL: Western Illinois University, 1970), pp. 91–92.

32. Scott, *Hickory Stick*, pp. 206–8, 228–29, 233–35. Scott taught English at a small town high school in Franklin, Ohio, from 1937 to 1941.

33. The impact of the depression on a number of school districts will be discussed in chapters 3 and 4. For an excellent account of the effects of the depression on schools, see Tyack, *Public Schools in Hard Times*, pp. 6–91. Tyack notes that "the first cuts in programs typically struck the subjects last added . . . such as art and music, manual arts and home economics, physical education and health" (p. 161).

34. Donna M. Stephens, *One-Room School: Teaching in 1930s Western Oklahoma* (Norman, OK: University of Oklahoma Press, 1990), pp. 33–157.

35. "The Nation's School Building Needs," *Research Bulletin of the National Education Association* 13, no. 1 (January 1935). The description of the Texas school is quoted in Tyack, *Public Schools in Hard Times*, pp. 181–82.

36. Lynd and Lynd, *Middletown in Transition*, pp. 225–26. What the Lynds reported for Middletown was true elsewhere. As Warren Sussman has pointed out, despite the interest in the Communist Party in the 1930s, the commitment of many of the intellectuals to finding a tradition and their hostility to the anarchic individualism of the 1920s had profoundly conservative implications. See Warren I. Sussman, "The Thirties," in *The Development of an American Culture*, 2d ed., Stanley Coben and Lorman Ratner, eds. (New York: St. Martin's Press, 1983), pp. 215–60.

Chapter Three

1. Dewey held that "the only fundamental agency for good is the *public* school system." Quoted in William W. Brickman's "Introduction" to John Dewey and Evelyn Dewey, *Schools of Tomorrow* (1915; New York: E. P. Dutton, 1962), p. xxv. My emphasis.

2. The politics of Winnetka were controlled by the wealthy residents whose businesses were in Chicago, not Winnetka. See Clarence Elmer Glick, "Winnetka: A Study of a Residential Suburban Community, (M.A. diss., Sociology and Anthropology, University of Chicago, Dec., 1928), pp. 155–57.

3. On the public-spirited ethos of Winnetka, see Michael Ebner, *Creating Chicago's North Shore: A Suburban History* (Chicago: The University of Chicago Press, 1988), pp. 38–40, 83–88, 215–20, and Glick, "Winnetka," pp. 83–85 and passim. Patricia A. Graham, *Progressive Education: From Arcady to Academe. A History of the Progressive Education Association, 1919–1955* (New York: Teachers College Press, 1967), points out that progressive education in the post–World War I period was typically associated with private schools and suburban public school systems that catered to the middle and upper-middle classes (p. 8).

4. Unless otherwise indicated, the summary of educational innovations in Winnetka is based on John L. Tewksbury, "An Historical Study of the Winnetka Public Schools from 1919 to 1946" (Ph.D. diss., Northwestern University, 1962), and Carleton W. Washburne and Sidney P. Marland, Jr., *Winnetka: The History and Significance of an Educational Experiment* (Englewood Cliffs, NJ: Prentice-Hall, Inc., 1963). For a dissenting view, see Corinne Schumacher, "Oversell: Educational Innovation in a Chicago Suburb. An Historical Case Study of the Winnetka Public Schools" (Ph.D. diss., Northwestern University, 1972).

5. Glick, "Winnetka," argues that the wealthiest families in Winnetka did not send their children to the public schools (p. 161). Other sources, however, disagree. Washburne claims that while some parents transferred their children from the public schools to Winnetka Country Day School, others took their children out of the private school and moved them into the public schools.

6. Carleton Washburne, "An Eighty Year Perspective on Education," *Phi Delta Kappan* 45 (Dec. 1963): 146. Washburne told the story of his mother and of his schooling in an interview with Alex Baskin at Okemos, Michigan, Feb. 4, 1966. Professor Baskin provided me with a copy of the tape recording of the interview. According to his daughter, Margaret Plagge, Carleton Washburne's father "wasn't influential on his thinking." (See Grant Pick, "A School Fit For Children," *Reader* 20, no. 21 [March 1, 1991]: 14.)

7. For Burk's criticism of conventional schooling, see Frederic Burk, *A Remedy for Lock-Step Schooling* (San Francisco, 1913). This pamphlet was re-issued by the Winnetka Educational Press in 1935.

8. Washburne tells this story (with obvious relish) in Washburne and Marland, *Winnetka*, p. 17.

9. This early version of programmed instruction is much more congruent with the ideas of G. Stanley Hall and E. L. Thorndike than it is with the ideas of Dewey. Hall's biographer, Dorothy Ross, speculates that Burk may have absorbed Hall's interest in individualized instruction. Hall was a supporter of Preston Search's early efforts in programmed instruction. See *G. Stanley Hall: The Psychologist as Prophet* (Chicago: The University of Chicago

Press, 1972), p. 361. Thorndike called for "a miracle of mechanical ingenuity" that would provide that only someone who had successfully completed a task on page one of a book could see page two. See Geraldine Joncich, *The Sane Positivist: A Biography of Edward L. Thorndike* (Middletown, CT: Wesleyan University Press, 1968), p. 395.

10. Washburne and Marland, *Winnetka*, pp. 78–81.

11. Ross, *Hall*, p. 361. Thorndike's list, published in 1921, was called *The Teacher's Word Book* (see Joncich, *Thorndike*, pp. 392–93).

12. Frances Presler, Frederick Reed, and Florice Tanner, "The Philosophy of the Activity Program," *Group and Creative Activities. Second Grade Units. Southwest Indians* (Winnetka, IL: Winnetka Educational Press, 1932), p. 3; Carleton Washburne, *Adjusting the School to the Child* and an article in *Teacher's World* (1922), quoted in Tewksbury, "Winnetka Schools," pp. 147–48.

13. For Logan's career before he came to Winnetka, see Sheila MacDonald Stearns, "S. R. Logan: Educator for Democracy, 1885–1970," (University of Montana, diss.; Ann Arbor: University Microfilms, International, 1983).

14. Ibid., p. 149.

15. Ibid., pp. 155–82.

16. Carleton Washburne, *What Is Progressive Education: A Book for Parents and Others* (New York: The John Day Co., 1952), pp. 66, 92; Tewksbury, "Winnetka Schools," pp. 331–42.

17. Carleton Washburne, "Girl, J. M.," in J. M. Waddle, "Case Studies of Gifted Children," *The National Society for the Study of Education, Twenty-Third Yearbook*, Guy M. Whipple, ed. (Bloomington, IL, 1924), part 1, pp. 203–7.

18. Washburne and Marland, *Winnetka*, pp. 124–28.

19. Carleton Washburne, "The Philosophy of the Winnetka Curriculum," *The Twenty-Sixth Yearbook of the National Society for the Study of Education*, Guy M. Whipple, ed. (Bloomington, IL, 1926; reprinted, New York, 1969), part 1, p. 219.

20. Harold Rugg praised Washburne's program in Winnetka as being both "society centered and child centered" and notes that Washburne instituted this program and disseminated "his message over America and abroad . . . more successfully than any other superintendent in the history of American education." See *That Men May Understand: An American in the Long Armistice* (New York: Doubleday, Doran and Co., Inc., 1941), p. 304n.

21. Ebner, *Creating Chicago's North Shore*, pp. 38–40, 83–88, 215–20.

22. Lee Benson, *The Concept of Jacksonian Democracy: New York as a Test Case* (1961; New York: Antheneum, 1964), p. 306. Chautauqua, too, had a history of supporting education. Benson quotes a local historian: "In 1824, during the pioneer period . . . while the stumps were still standing on the village green . . . the Old Fredonia Academy was incorporated . . . In the academy, founded by these pioneers, Latin, Greek and the higher branches were thoroughly taught" (Chautauqua History Company, *Centennial History of Chautauqua County* [Jamestown, NY, 1904], vol. 1, pp. 9, 108, quoted in Benson, *Jacksonian Democracy*, p. 306).

23. Ebner, *Creating Chicago's North Shore*, p. 84.

24. Ebner characterizes the community house as the "quintessential expression of Winnetka's public spirited reputation," ibid., p. 217.

25. Helen Hood, *Winnetka: A Suburban Community* (1924), quoted in Glick, "Winnetka," p. 182. Glick (a sociologist) disputes this, arguing that "usually those of different classes do not come at the same time or to the same meetings" (ibid.). But ten years after Glick's study, two Northwestern University graduate students saw in Winnetka "an amazing spirit of social consciousness and a feeling of community unity which embraces all classes." See David G. Monroe and Harry O'Neal Wilson, *City Manager Government in Winnetka (Illinois)* (Chicago: Committee on Public Administration of the Social Science Research Council, 1940), p. 1.

26. Edward C. Banfield and James Q. Wilson, *City Politics* (Cambridge, MA: Harvard University Press and MIT Press, 1963), p. 140, cite Winnetka as an example of a local government that models the "reform ideal." "Winnetkans are in fundamental agreement on the kind of local government they want: it must provide excellent schools, parks, libraries and other community services and it must provide them with businesslike efficiency and perfect honesty. Politics, in the sense of a competitive struggle for office or for private advantage, does not exist."

27. For the views of an opponent of the new junior high school, see Glick, "Winnetka," pp. 159–61.

28. This is the major complaint of Corinne Schumacher's unflattering picture of the Washburne years in Winnetka in her Northwestern University Ph.D. dissertation, "Oversell." She charges that educational reform was imposed on Winnetka by an upper-class elite.

29. According to Monroe and Wilson, *City Manager Government in Winnetka*, Winnetka merchants know their customers are used to service with a capital "S" (p. 2). They also note that Winnetkans "point with pride to the progressive innovations and experiments carried on in their public schools" (p. 1).

30. Carleton Washburne, Mabel Vogel, and William S. Gray, *A Survey of the Winnetka Public Schools* (Bloomington, IL: Public School Publishing Co., 1926). One conclusion of this study was that "A comparative study of the high school freshmen from Winnetka and those of [two similar suburbs] . . . shows that Winnetka freshmen have made a better record in three out of four subjects and in an average of all subjects than have those of the other communities" (p. 83).

31. Tewksbury, "Winnetka Schools," pp. 464–67; Washburne and Marland, *Winnetka*, p. 21.

32. See Seymour B. Sarason, *The Culture of the School and the Problem of Change*, 2d ed. (Boston: Allyn and Bacon, Inc., 1982), esp. pp. 133–34, 194–203. On the failure of the post-Sputnik reforms, see Charles Silberman, *Crisis in the Classroom: The Remaking of American Education* (New York: Random House, 1970), pp. 179–83.

33. Clarence B. Randall, *Over My Shoulder* (Boston: Little, Brown and Company, 1956), pp. 156–57. Randall, who was a vice-president of Inland

Steel, had been president of the board since 1930. He recalls that in his first election he "was swept into office for a three-year term by a total of 19 votes, all of which I am sure were cast by the then members of the school board and the election officials. No one else cared. They fully expected the board to be self-perpetuating." Randall describes himself as "a convert" to progressive education (ibid., p. 156).

34. It is clear that "economy" in government was a major issue. At the same time as the school board was being challenged, the Village Caucus Party was being challenged by an "Economy Party" in the election for town officials and there was a great deal of overlap between that party and the group organized to oppose the school board. See Schumacher, "Oversell," pp. 140–70.

35. Tewksbury concludes that the board's attitude toward innovative education changed in the 1930s, but Washburne's history of the schools disagrees. To my mind, Tewksbury is more convincing. Yet it should be made clear that the change in the tone of the board did not mean a reversal in the sense that the previous program was jeopardized; rather the emphasis shifted to refining previous innovations.

36. Tewksbury, "Winnetka Public Schools," pp. 27–28.

37. Glick, "Winnetka," notes that a large number of people moved to Winnetka at the time their children were ready for school (p. 80).

38. Ibid., pp. 83, 85–86.

39. If the value of the dollar is adjusted for changes in the cost of living, however, the expenditure per pupil was slightly more than in 1930–31. By 1940–41, school spending was up again; Winnetka spent $226.60 per pupil that year. See the Appendix, table 1. It should be noted that the national average per-pupil expenditure in 1930 was $76.70. On average, Illinois schools cut their expenditures by about one-third between 1930 and 1934. See David Tyack, Robert Lowe, and Elisabeth Hansot, *Public Schools in Hard Times: The Great Depression and Recent Years* (Cambridge, MA: Harvard University Press), 1984), pp. 33, 34.

40. Baskin interview with Washburne, 1966.

41. Washburne and Marland, *Winnetka*, p. 41.

42. In the progressive schools of another suburb, Summit, New Jersey, there was a similar concern "not to abandon what the traditionalists like to call 'the fundamentals'" and, when tests revealed weaknesses in reading and arithmetic, the schools took steps to improve instruction in these areas. See Charles R. Foster, *Mental Hygiene in New Jersey Schools: An Inquiry into the Influence of Mental Hygiene Concepts on New Jersey School Practice* (New Brunswick, NJ: School of Education, Rutgers University, 1939), p. 25.

43. "Crow Island Revisited," *Architectural Forum*, Oct. 1955, quoted in Washburne and Marland, *Winnetka*, p. 141. The article goes on: "In 1955 Crow Island appears, if anything, more significant than it did 15 years ago. Time and use—not only here but in many hundred later schools—have proved out the workability of its innovations to a degree that only the wildest optimism in 1940 could have conjectured." In 1990 Crow Island was named as a national landmark: Pick, "School Fit For Children," p. 26.

204 Notes to Pages 56–62

44. Larry Kelly, "No More Grouping By Grades in Winnetka's Novel Laboratory," *Chicago Herald-American*, Feb. 23, 1941.

45. John Dewey and Evelyn Dewey, *Schools of To-Morrow*, (New York: Dutton, 1915), pp. 175–204. John Dewey was responsible for the theoretical parts of the book while his daughter described the school programs.

46. Raymond E. Callahan, *Education and the Cult of Efficiency: A Study of the Social Forces That Have Shaped the Administration of the Public Schools* (Chicago: The University of Chicago Press, 1962), pp. 128–29.

47. Ronald D. Cohen and Raymond A. Mohl, *The Paradox of Progressive Education: The Gary Plan and Urban Schooling* (Port Washington, NY: Kennikat Press, 1979), p. 14.

48. Ibid., p. 13.

49. Dewey and Dewey, *Schools of To-Morrow*, p. 176.

50. Ibid., pp. 128, 136.

51. Callahan, *Cult of Efficiency*, p. 136; Murray Levine and Adeline Levine, *A Social History of Helping Services: Clinic, Court, School and Community* (New York: Appleton-Century-Crofts, 1970), p. 152. See also Lawrence Cremin, *The Transformation of the School: Progressivism in American Education, 1876–1957* (New York: Alfred A. Knopf, 1962), pp. 158–60.

52. "Final Report. Purdue Survey Committee for the Gary Board of Education . . . ," F. B. Knight, Director, (Mimeographed. [n.p., 1941?]), pp. 1–2, 17–18, 49, 41.

53. Larry Cuban, *How Teachers Taught: Constancy and Change in American Classrooms, 1890–1980* (New York: Longman, 1984), pp. 67–75.

54. Ibid., p. 79.

55. Irving Hendrick, "California's Response to the 'New Education' in the 1930s," *California Historical Quarterly* 53:1 (Spring 1974): 26–27.

56. Drummond J. McCunn, "A Study of Pasadena and Its Public Schools: Analysis of the Factors Contributing to Educational Leadership in a Community" (Ed.D. diss., University of California at Los Angeles, Aug. 1950), pp. 10–56, 154.

57. Ibid, pp. 86–95. It is not clear whether the board tried to hire Washburne or whether it tried to hire the superintendent of New Trier High School, also located in Winnetka. See Vincent Booth Claypool, "John Amherst Sexson: Educator" (Ed.D diss., University of California at Los Angeles, June 1948). Supplement: "Additional Interview Notes."

58. California Taxpayers' Association, *Survey of the Pasadena Schools* (Association Report No. 119. Los Angeles, 1931), pp. 104, 141, 118, 123, 34.

59. Ibid., pp. 123, 139–40, 166–67; Charles Wollenberg, *All Deliberate Speed: Segregation and Exclusion in California Schools* (Berkeley: University of California Press, 1976), p. 138.

60. There were, of course, other well-known examples of progressive public school systems in the 1930s, such as Scarsdale and Bronxville, New York, and Summit, New Jersey.

61. A survey of the Gary schools conducted in 1916 by the General Education Board provides evidence that the shop program, especially in the Froeble school, heavily populated by children of immigrants, was much

more narrowly vocational than the Deweys' report suggests. See Cohen and Mohl, *The Paradox of Progressive Education*, pp. 90–91.

62. Ibid., p. 29. Although they had worked together harmoniously for many years, during the New Deal era, Wirt's increasing political conservatism and Barrows' increasing radicalism led to a split. See ibid., pp. 10–34.

63. Jesse Newlon's 1923 report to the Denver Board of Education, quoted in Cremin, *Transformation*, p. 299.

64. Cuban, *How Teachers Taught*, p. 74. On teachers' sense of isolation, see Sarason, *The Culture of the School*, pp. 133–34.

65. Levine and Levine, *History of Helping Services*, pp. 151–52. Seymour Sarason, who has studied the process of change in schools, concludes that for reforms to have any chance of success, they must involve teachers. See *The Culture of the School*, p. 194.

Chapter Four

1. Michael Ebner, *Creating Chicago's North Shore: A Suburban History* (Chicago: The University of Chicago Press, 1988,) notes that "People whose social reputations were associated with Lake Forest lived their lives as if they held membership in an American royalty" (p. 201).

2. Frederick Mercer Van Sickle, "A Special Place: Lake Forest and the Great Depression, 1929–1940" (senior thesis, Lake Forest College, 1983).

3. Clarence Elmer Glick, "Winnetka: A Study of A Residential Suburban Community" (M.A. diss., Sociology and Anthropology, University of Chicago, Dec. 1928), pp. 75, 124, 127. In 1926, Winnetka was the home of 203 families listed in the Chicago Social Register; Lake Forest, 200 (p. 190). But, Glick notes, Lake Forest families were more involved in Chicago society events than Winnetka's residents (p. 191). Ebner, *Creating Chicago's North Shore*, speaks of Lake Forest's reputation as "the haven of Chicago's society set" (p. xviii) and points out that Lake Forest's reputation as a "fashionable suburb" was "well established by the 1870s" (p. 77).

4. See Lee Benson, *The Concept of Jacksonian Democracy: New York as a Test Case* (1961; New York: Atheneum, 1964), p. 313 and passim. Benson's distinction between "Yankees" and "Yorkers" was developed from a point made by the historian of New York, Dixon Ryan Fox.

5. The "blue-stocking" comment comes from a conversation with a woman who grew up in Lake Forest in the 1930s as a member of one of the leading families. Edward Arpee, *Lake Forest, Illinois: History and Reminiscences* (Lake Forest, IL, 1963), pp. 244–47, tells the story of the failure of Lake Forest to support a community center in 1948. See also *Lake Forester*, Feb. 20, 1948, p. 4.

6. Significantly, as Ebner notes, while Lake Forest was from its beginnings "officially dry, this virtue was rarely treated with the passion accorded temperance elsewhere" (*Creating Chicago's North Shore*, p. 28).

7. My research on the schools of Lake Forest and Waukegan was assisted by Christine McLennan and Samara Way.

8. Lucia Boyden Prochnow, *Lake Forest Country Day School: The First Cen-*

tury (Lake Forest, IL: Lake Forest Country Day School, 1988), pp. 8–20. Carleton Washburne visited in 1932 and "evaluated the Lake Forest Country Day School very favorably, suggesting only that there be better coordination between strictly academic work and group activities" (p. 13). By 1936, however, the school had become much more conservative (p. 15).

9. *Waukegan News-Sun*, Sept. 25, 1939, pp. 1, 8.

10. Ebner, *Creating Chicago's North Shore*, pp. 27–30, 68.

11. Ibid., pp. 203–9; "Local Public Schools Undergo Many Changes in Eighty-Three Years," *Lake Forester*, July 27, 1945, pp. 24, 76.

12. Marc A. Rose, "The Most Unforgettable Character I've Met," *The 30th Anniversary Reader's Digest Reader* (Pleasantville, NY: The Reader's Digest Association, Inc., 1951), p. 378 (reprinted from *Reader's Digest*, Feb. 1943).

13. "Local Public Schools Undergo Changes," *Lake Forester*, July 27, 1945, pp. 24, 76.

14. "Grade Four. Tentative Course of Study for 1928–1929" (typewritten ms., Lake Forest Board of Education).

15. Ibid.; the *Lake Forester* reported to the community on Sept. 22, 1932, that newly instituted educational guidance courses at the upper school included instruction in good manners (p. 6).

16. Lake Forest Board of Education, "Minutes," ms., Lake Forest Board of Education Offices, Dec. 7, 1933. In 1938, the new superintendent, M. G. Davis, recommended dropping the policy of giving each child a Christmas stocking. The board voted to continue it. Board "Minutes," Dec. 6, 1938.

17. Board "Minutes," June 2, 1936, pp. 144–45.

18. *Lake Forester*, May 8, 1931, pp. 1, 30. Significantly, the name chosen— "upper school"—was often used for the upper grades in private schools.

19. "Local Schools Undergo Changes," *Lake Forester*, July 27, 1945, pp. 24, 76; *Lake Forester*, May 8, 1931; Board "Minutes," April 6, 1931; Robert Vandervoort, interview, July 23, 1974. Vandervoort had taught science in the school of which Loos had been principal. He was brought to Lake Forest to begin the science program in the upper school. Vandervoort says that although Baggett was still superintendent, by then "Loos was running things."

20. Board "Minutes" of April 11, 1930; July 18, 1930; Feb. 5, 1935; May 7, 1935; April 7, 1936; John E. Baggett, "Candidates for the 'Special Help' room, Halsey School 1930–1931" (undated typewritten ms., Lake Forest Board of Education); Board "Minutes," May 8, 1928.

21. *Lake Forester:* June 13, 1935, p. 1, and Feb. 13, 1936, p. 3; Board "Minutes," July 7, 1931.

22. Lake Forest also increased the average salary paid to male teachers by nearly two-thirds (measured in constant dollars). See Appendix, table 2.

23. See Appendix, table 1. For the lack of impact of the depression, see Van Sickle, "Lake Forest and the Great Depression."

24. *Lake Forester*, Sept. 25, 1931, pp. 1, 19; Board "Minutes," Nov. 1, 1932.

25. Board "Minutes," Feb. 25, 1930; April 5, 1933; June 5, 1934.

26. See Appendix, table 3. While the Census provides the number of children in different age groups actually attending school for larger towns

such as Winnetka, it does not give these figures for smaller communities such as Lake Forest. *Sixteenth Census of the United States: 1940 Population,* vol. 2 (Characteristics of the Population), part 2 (Washington, DC: United States Government Printing Office, 1943), pp. 607, 616. In order to make a meaningful comparison, therefore, I am comparing the percentages of the under-fourteen-years-old population enrolled in public school (although some of those children were too young to be in school). It is possible to make another comparison, although the figures are based on different criteria for the two communities: in Winnetka about 95 percent of the 5–13-year-olds reported as actually going to school were enrolled in the public schools while in Lake Forest about 66 percent of the total number of 5–14-year-olds were enrolled in the public schools. (These figures were derived by comparing the census figures to the 1940–41 enrollments reported in the *Statistical Report of the Superintendent of Public Instruction, State of Illinois, for the Year Ended June 30, 1941* [no. 338], pp. 136, 138.)

27. Frank S. Read, interview, Feb. 24, 1983, quoted in Van Sickle, "A Special Place," p. 57.

28. In 1932, the superintendent predicted that the children of wealthy families were now expected to attend the public schools in greater number (*Waukegan News-Sun,* Aug. 31, 1932, p. 5). There is no evidence that this shift occurred during the 1930s.

29. To ease these obviously painful decisions, Baggett was given the title of "Superintendent emeritus" and Loos was given a leave of absence to "continue his university studies." See: F. J. Held to the Mayor and City Council, April 7, 1936, Board "Minutes," April 7, 1936. The decision had been made in February (Board "Minutes," Feb. 4, 1936), but Baggett's retirement was not announced until April (*Lake Forester,* April 2, 1936, p. 1). Apparently, the board's action was sufficiently controversial that it had to defend itself by writing the letter to the mayor and council.

30. *Lake Forester,* July 9, 1936, p. 1.

31. Board "Minutes," Oct. 6, 1936; Nov. 5, 1936; Jan. 5, 1937.

32. Board "Minutes," Feb. 2, 1937; June 8, 1937.

33. Davis suggested that the failure to appreciate public education in Lake Forest might be because the local private schools "for selfish reasons" had "misinformed many people" by exaggerating "the importance of attending private elementary schools" (Board "Minutes," Nov. 9, 1936). *Lake Forester,* Nov. 10, 1938, p. 4. Offering Latin had first been discussed in August (Board "Minutes," Aug. 2, 1938). On Lake Forest's "private school tradition," see Ebner, *Creating Chicago's North Shore,* p. 172.

34. *Lake Forester,* Jan. 19, 1939, p. 6 (see also the issue of Sept. 7, 1939, p. 1); Oct. 15, 1936, p. 1; Oct. 22, 1936, p. 1; March 25, 1937, p. 4.

35. Lake Forest Public Elementary Schools, *Your Schools at Work* (Lake Forest, IL: Lake Forest Public Schools, 1940), pp. 8–9.

36. Ibid., p. 9; Vandervoort interview.

37. *Your Schools at Work,* p. 37. Val Hayward (who had been the faculty advisor to the student council) told me of the role of the superintendent in the council elections. Interview with Val Hayward, Aug. 1974.

38. *Your Schools at Work,* p. 32.

39. "Lake Forest Public Schools on Parade," photography by Ward McMasters. The film is in the Lake Forest Board of Education Office. I have a video copy in my possession. I showed the film to Julie Massey, who has been a supervisor of student teachers at Lake Forest College. She saw "more similarities than differences" between the practices shown in the film and what might be found today in a similarly affluent school district.

40. Christine McLennan, unpublished paper, "Progressivism in Education: Waukegan"; Waukegan Board of Education, "Minutes," ms., Waukegan Board of Education Offices, June 16, 1927.

41. *News-Sun,* Aug. 19, 1930, pp. 1–2; Oct. 15, 1930, p. 4; Oct. 7, 1930, p. 4; Dec. 10, 1931, p. 1; Dec. 14, 1931, p. 12; *Chicago Tribune,* Dec. 13, 1931, p. 9.

42. *News-Sun,* Feb. 26, 1932, p. 4; Feb. 26, 1932, p. 1; Feb. 29, 1932, p. 1; March 15, 1932, p. 1. *Chicago Tribune,* March 16, 1932.

43. *News-Sun,* Sept. 1, 1932, p. 1; Sept. 3, 1932, p. 1; Oct. 12, 1932, p. 1; Oct. 14, 1932, p. 1; Oct. 25, 1932, p. 1; Nov. 16, 1932, p. 1. The newspaper urged readers to "oppose the attempt to reduce the quality of teaching or to eliminate other life-enriching elements in our schools" (Nov. 16, 1932, p. 4).

44. *News-Sun,* Jan. 4, 1933, p. 1; March 15, 1933, p. 6; May 12, 1933, p. 1; May 18, 1933, p. 4.

45. David Tyack, Robert Lowe, and Elisabeth Hansot, *Public Schools in Hard Times: The Great Depression and Recent Years* (Cambridge, MA: Harvard University Press, 1984), p. 43.

46. *News-Sun,* March 15, 1932, p. 1; Board "Minutes," April 4, 1932; *News-Sun,* March 15, 1933, p. 6; Jan. 2, 1934, p. 1; May 12, 1933, p. 1.

47. If the value of the dollar is adjusted for changes in the cost of living, the decline was nine percent; see Appendix, tables 1 and 2.

48. Board "Minutes," Nov. 8, 1935; April 4, 1932; Nov. 5, 1932.

49. *News-Sun,* Dec. 31, 1935, p. 7; Waukegan "Curriculum Plans, 1933," ms.; "Course of Study in Civics," 1934, typewritten ms. These records were in the board's files in 1975, stored in one of the schools, but they can no longer be located and have probably been discarded. I have a copy of the civics course of study in my possession.

50. *News-Sun,* Sept. 15, 1939, p. 12; Sept. 12, 1939, p. 6; Sept. 14, 1939, p. 4. See Appendix, table 1.

51. Waukegan "Curriculum Plans, 1937," ms.; *News-Sun,* Sept. 30, 1939, p. 1.

52. Interview with H. R. McCall, July 22, 1986.

53. Connie Purcell and Ricki Mandell, *Memories of Mundelein* (Fox Lake, IL: Mandell and Associates, n.d.), pp. 7–14.; Mundelein Chamber of Commerce, "Welcome to Mundelein," [1962], p. 1. Mark Maley, "Mundelein: remember its early days," *Libertyville Independent Register,* Feb. 2, 1984. The town had been called Mechanics Grove, Holcomb, Rockefeller, and Area before it found its new identity. In order to have sufficient population to

incorporate as a village, it briefly joined with the neighboring community of Diamond Lake to form the village of Rockefeller.

54. Maley, "Mundelein: remember its early days"; Class Records, 1924–1925," ms. book, Mundelein Board of Education. My research on Mundelein was assisted by Katherine Amato-Von Hemert.

55. Mundelein Board of Directors, Records, ms. books, July 10, 1930; *News-Sun,* Aug. 23, 1930; Board Records, March 19, 1932; Feb. 1, 1933; *News-Sun,* April 29, 1933, p. 2. At their March 19, 1932, meeting the directors had called for the 1932–33 school year to be nine months and twenty days long.

56. Board Records, Sept. 5, 1933; Oct. 2, 1933; Oct. 27, 1933; Dec. 21, 1933. In 1920–21 there had been forty children in the combined first and second grade class (Classroom Records, ms. books, 1920–21 and 1930–35); Linda Alfredson, "A Little red-brick school lives on," *Independent Register,* May 27, 1976, p. 1b.

57. See Appendix, table 4. In 1944, the district spent only $52.40 per pupil. In 1943, on the other hand, it had spent $75.22 (Superintendent of Public Instruction, State of Illinois, *Annual Statistical Report,* 1943, p. 142; 1944, pp. 248–49).

58. Katherine Amato-Von Hemert's interviews with former teachers: Abbie Dolton, Ruth Rouse, and Genevieve LaMagdeleine, July 1975.

59. Tyack, *Public Schools in Hard Times,* pp. 1–2.

60. Larry Cuban, *How Teachers Taught: Constancy and Change in American Classrooms, 1890–1980* (New York: Longman, 1984), pp. 7–8.

61. Ibid., p. 55. See Also Diane Ravitch, *The Great School Wars: New York City, 1805–1973* (New York: Basic Books, 1974). Ravitch points out that, surprisingly, progressives found their great advocate in superintendent Harold Campbell, a conservative. They did not realize, however, "that the slogans of progressivism changed their meaning in the context of a massive school system" (pp. 236–37).

62. Cuban, *How Teachers Taught,* pp. 61–63.

63. The report card from P.S. 6 was for the second semester of eighth grade, June 1946. By contrast, my report card from a suburban school in California, San Mateo Park School, integrated grades for subjects with grades for character traits and did not use numbers, using only grades of "S," "I," and "U." Even in subject matter, the grades reflected behavior more than learning. For example, there was a grade for "Is interested in Nature and Science" rather than a grade for achievement in that subject. The card devoted a great deal of space to "Teacher's Comments." In an explanatory note, the San Mateo card noted: We consider the regular school subjects to be very important; however, we believe that proper habits of conduct making for better character are more important." The San Mateo report card was for the fourth grade for 1941–42. The upper grades used the same format. For a description of progressive report cards in Summit, New Jersey, see Charles R. Foster, *Mental Hygiene in New Jersey Schools: An Inquiry into the Influence of Mental Hygiene Concepts on New Jersey School Practice* (New Brunswick, NJ: School of Education, Rutgers University,

1939), pp. 21–22. In Summit, the report card noted that "Personality and social traits should receive more emphasis than school achievement."

64. Samuel Tenenbaum, *William Heard Kilpatrick: Trail Blazer in Education* (New York: Harper & Brothers Publishers, 1951), p. 249. Tenenbaum wrote an article about his disappointment: "The Project Method: A Criticism of its Operation in the School System," *Science and Society* 49 (June 17, 1939): 770–72.

65. Joseph Calguire, "Union Township Schools and the Depression, 1929–1938," *New Jersey History* 93 (Autumn–Winter 1975): 115, 120. It should be noted that unlike the schools of Winnetka, Waukegan, Lake Forest, and Mundelein, which were elementary school districts, the Union Township schools included the high school grades.

66. *Union Register,* March 3, 1934, quoted in Calguire, "Union Township and the Depression," p. 121.

67. Calguire, "Union Township and the Depression," pp. 122–25.

68. Robert L. Greet, "The Plainfield School System in the Depression: 1930–1937," *New Jersey History* 110 (Summer 1972): 69–82.

69. According to one newspaper's historical account, "Teachers were forced to accept and teach the new 'progressivism.' Many (who) . . . 'bootlegged' the three R's in defiance of official pronouncements . . . (and) any who voiced opposition were called 'unprofessional,' 'uncooperative,' or 'old-fashioned.' They were passed over when it came to promotions." "A History of the San Francisco Schools," *San Francisco Progress,* April 29, 1959, p. 1, quoted in Lee Stephen Dolson, Jr., "The Administration of the San Francisco Public Schools, 1847 to 1947" (Ph.D. diss., University of California, Berkeley, 1964), p. 453.

70. Dolson, "The Administration of the San Francisco Public Schools," pp. 317, 628, 584 and passim; Ruth H. Grossman, "Development of Social Studies Curricula in the Public Schools of New York City and San Francisco, 1850–1952," (Ph.D diss., University of California, Berkeley, 1964), pp. 183, 267.

71. For an example, see the *San Francisco Examiner,* Sept. 25, 1945. The attack on progressive education began at the top of the first page and continued on page 12. In addition, the newspaper ran two columns of letters from parents supporting the newspaper's views on progressivism. Irving Hendrick, "California's Response to the 'New Education' in the 1930s," *California Historical Quarterly* 53:1 (Spring 1974), points out that Los Angeles schools were more firmly in the progressive camp than those of San Francisco, where there was "no clearly defined position toward progressivism." Yet, even in San Francisco, "Apparently the progressive tide had been too strong for alert teachers and administrators to resist, with or without official policy" (p. 32).

72. Dolson, "San Francisco Schools," pp. 659–61; *San Francisco Chronicle,* Feb. 25, 1942, part 2, p. 1; *San Francisco News,* June 17, 1942, p. 2; *San Francisco Examiner,* April 7, 1943, p. 12. Rugg has given his own account of the battle over his books. See Harold Rugg, *That Men May Understand: An American in the Long Armistice* (New York: Doubleday, Doran and Co., Inc.,

1941), pp. 3–95. Opponents of progressive education continued to criticize the San Francisco schools throughout the war years. In 1945, they finally captured a majority on the board, setting the scene for a major confrontation with Nourse's successor, Curtis Warren. Unlike Nourse, Warren was willing to take strong positions on educational issues. In addition, he angered his opponents by supporting Henry Wallace's Progressive Party campaign for the presidency in 1948. See: *Examiner*, Dec. 20, 1944, pp. 1, 3; Dolson, "San Francisco Public Schools," pp. 621–23, 646, 650, 643.

73. *Examiner*, Sept. 25, 1942, p. 12; Sept. 19, 1942, p. 6. Enrollment figures indicate the basis for Nourse's argument: in 1920, only 7 percent of San Francisco public school pupils completed high school; by 1930, the number completing high school was up to 29 percent. By 1939, 86 percent of all pupils who began first grade finished high school (Dolson, "San Francisco Public Schools," p. 575).

74. This is ironic in view of Dewey's idea that progressive education would be the way to promote harmony between social classes. See David John Hogan, *Class and Reform: School and Society in Chicago, 1880–1930* (Philadelphia: University of Pennsylvania Press, 1985) p. 88.

Chapter Five

1. N[orman] C[ousins], "Modern Man is Obsolete," *Saturday Review* 28, no. 33 (August 18, 1945), p. 5.

2. United States Bureau of the Census, "Forecasts of Population and School Enrollment in the United States," *Current Population Reports, Population Estimates*, Series P-25, no. 18, (Washington, DC: United States Government Printing Office, February 1949), p. 4. The Census Bureau estimated that the increase would be forty-six percent between 1947 and 1957; thereafter it predicted a gradual decline. The actual increase in elementary enrollment from 1949 to 1959 was about forty-two percent. See United States Bureau of the Census, *Education in the United States: 1940–1983* (Special Demographic Analysis, CDS-85-1, Washington, DC: United States Government Printing Office, 1985), p. 24.

3. Citizens Federal Committee on Education, *Citizens Look at Our School-houses. A Progress Report . . .* (Washington, DC: Federal Security Agency, Office of Education, November 1950), pp. 6–7; Ray L. Hamon, "The Race Between School Children and Schoolhouses," *School Life* 32, no. 1 (October 1949): 8–9; Census Bureau, "Forecasts of Population" (1949), p. 5; United States Bureau of the Census, *Education of the American Population*, by John K. Folger and Charles B. Nam (*A 1960 Census Monograph*) (Washington, DC: United States Government Printing Office, 1967), p. 8. According to the *New York Times*, enrollment *increases* in the 1950s were over sixteen million (including students enrolled in private schools and in colleges) and approximated the total population of New York State (September 3, 1961, sect. 4, p. 7).

4. I. L. Kandel, *The Impact of the War Upon American Education* (Chapel Hill, NC: University of North Carolina Press, 1948), pp. 19, 61, 65. Kandel

reports that according to a National Education Association estimate, one-third of the competent teachers employed in the 1940–41 school year left the profession during the war (p. 65).

5. Ibid., pp. 17, 43–45, 46–52, 275. For an example of the demand that schools respond to the wartime disruption of the family and combat delinquency, see *Youth in Crisis*, The March of Time, Time/Life Films, vol 10, no. 3 (1943). On the fear of delinquency, see James Gilbert, *A Cycle of Outrage: America's Reaction to the Juvenile Delinquent in the 1950's* (New York: Oxford University Press, 1986), pp. 24–41.

6. *New York Times*, Feb. 10, 1947, pp. 1, 20; Feb. 18, 1947, pp. 27, 30; Feb. 21, 1947, pp. 1, 10.

7. *New York Times*, Feb. 18, 1947, pp. 27, 30; Feb. 19, 1947, pp. 27, 28.

8. United States Office of Education, *Report of the Status Phase of the School Facilities Survey* (Washington, DC: United States Government Printing Office, 1953), pp. 59, 109, 123. The survey, which was conducted in March 1951, included thirty-nine states plus Alaska, Hawaii, Puerto Rico, and the Virgin Islands (pp. 29, 37); Anne Moody, *Coming of Age in Mississippi* (1968; New York: Dell Publishing Co., Inc., 1970), p. 21. The figures on the black schools of Alabama are from a Columbia University report on illiteracy as reported in the *New York Times*, March 21, 1953, p. 14.

9. *New York Times*, Feb. 10, 1947, pp. 1, 20; Feb. 15, 1947, pp. 17, 30; Feb. 19, 1947, pp. 27, 28.

10. *New York Times*, Feb. 10, 1947, pp. 1, 20; Feb. 13, 1947, pp. 25, 27; Feb. 15, 1947, pp. 17, 30.

11. Marshall O. Donley, *Power to the Teacher: How America's Educators Became Militant* (Bloomington, IN: Indiana University Press, 1976), pp. 36–38.

12. Edwin H. Miner, "Help Wanted—Teachers," *School Life* 21, no. 1 (Oct. 1949): 4–7, 13; Emery M. Foster, "Magnitude of the Nation's Educational Task Today and in the Years Ahead," *School Life* 22, no. 6 (March 1950): 88–89.

13. In September 1950 Benjamin Fine reported that the situation of the schools was "growing steadily worse because of rapid enrollment increases and a developing shortage of necessary materials and labor." Educational leaders, he reported, were urging that "if priorities must be set up for the allotment of building materials and supplies, schools should be ranked with hospitals and second only to military requirements. Otherwise the nation's free public school system will deteriorate as dangerously as it did during World War II" (*New York Times*, "Education in Review," Sept. 24, 1950, section 4, p. 11; Sept. 10, 1950, section 4, p. 11).

14. The word ideology requires clarification because it has been sometimes been used as a pejorative term to describe a system of ideas that justifies special class interests. This is not what I mean when I use the term. The definition I use is close to that of Talcott Parsons, *The Social System* (Glencoe, IL: The Free Press, 1951). Parsons defines an ideology as "an empirical belief system held in common by the members of *any* collectivity" (p. 354). It is "a system of ideas which is oriented to the evaluative

integration of the collectivity, by interpretation of . . . the situation in which it is placed, the processes by which it has developed to its given state, the goals to which its members are collectively oriented and their relation to the future course of events" (p. 349). See also Mostafa Rejai, "Ideology," in *Dictionary of the History of Ideas: Studies of Selected Pivotal Ideas*, Philip P. Wiener, ed., (New York: Charles Scribner's Sons, 1973), vol. 2, pp. 552–59, and Edward Shils, "Ideology: The Concept and Function of Ideology," in *International Encyclopedia of the Social Sciences*, David L. Sills, ed. (New York: The Macmillan Co. & The Free Press, 1968), vol. 7, pp. 66–75. According to Shils, what I am calling ideologies should be called "outlooks" or "creeds"—that is a "patterns of cognitive and moral beliefs" that tends to "lack one authoritative and explicit promulgation." Outlooks are differentiated from ideologies in being "pluralistic in their internal structure" and in not being "systematically integrated" (p. 66). "Creeds" are like ideologies, but "have much less orthodoxy." Its followers "will take from this creed what he wants" (pp. 66–67). On the other hand, Francis X. Sutton et al., *The American Business Creed* (Cambridge, MA: Harvard University Press, 1956), use "creed" and "ideology" as synonyms. They define ideology as a description of "any system of beliefs publicly expressed with the manifest purpose of influencing the sentiments and actions of others." They see ideologies as "selective in subject matter and in use of empirical evidence and logical argument. They are simple and clear-cut even when their subject matter is complicated. They are expressed in language that engages the emotions, as well as the understanding, of their readers and listeners" (pp. 2–3).

15. Lawrence A. Cremin, *The Transformation of the School: Progressivism in American Education, 1876–1957* (New York: Alfred A. Knopf, 1962), p. 328.

16. David Tyack has called the proponents of administrative efficiency "administrative progressives"—see David Tyack, *The One Best System: A History of American Urban Education*, (Cambridge, MA: Harvard University Press, 1974), pp. 182–98. Tyack notes that the administrative progressives "had little in common in aim either with the small libertarian wing of educational progressivism or with the small group of social reconstructionists" (p. 196). Dewey frequently warned that the reliance on scientific testing could undermine the egalitarian goals of a liberal philosophy of education.

17. Diane Ravitch, *The Troubled Crusade: American Education, 1945–1980* (New York: Basic Books, Inc., 1983), p. 47, has characterized post–World War II progressivism as "a bastard version, and in important ways, a betrayal of the new education" Dewey called for.

18. Before World War II, progressivism had had only a very limited impact on high schools even in California, which apparently led the nation in implementing progressive reforms at the elementary level. See Irving Hendrick, "California's Response to the 'New Education' in the 1930s," *California Historical Quarterly* 53, no. 1 (Spring 1974): 35.

19. The roots of life adjustment can be seen in the 1930s. For example, the 1934 *Report of the Superintendent* of the San Francisco Public Schools

argued that although "the college preparation idea has always dominated our high schools," only thirty percent of San Francisco high school graduates undertook any postsecondary education. The report pointedly asked: "Should preparation for 30 determine preparation for 100?" Under new conditions, the high school should deal with such subjects as "making a home, getting a living, keeping healthy, using leisure" [pages are not numbered]. The movement for a new high school curriculum was rooted in the most ambitious project of the Progressive Education Association—the famed Eight-Year Study which fostered experiments in the secondary school curriculum: Cremin, *Transformation*, p. 333.

20. Educational Policies Commission, *Education for All American Youth* (Washington, DC: National Education Association, 1944), p. 3; Federal Security Agency, *Life Adjustment Education for Every American Youth* (Washington, DC: United States Office of Education, [1948]), pp. iii, 4–5. The basis for Life Adjustment was the famous Prosser resolution of 1945. Prosser asserted that precollege education was suitable for twenty percent of American youth while vocational education was suitable for another twenty percent. Prosser then went on to say: "We do not believe that the remaining 60 percent of our youth of secondary age will receive the life adjustment training they need" (ibid., p. 15, n. 2). The resolution was later revised, dropping the percentage figures (pp. 18–19, n. 5). For a short history of the movement, see ibid., pp. 15–22, and Ravitch, *Troubled Crusade*, pp. 60–69.

21. Barry M. Franklin, *Building the American Community: The School Curriculum and the Search for Social Control* (Philadelphia: The Falmer Press, 1986), pp. 147–51. The date of the Tulsa program was 1940.

22. Minneapolis Public Schools, *A Primer for Common Learnings*, (Minneapolis, MN: Board of Education, 1948), pp. 7–8, quoted in Franklin, *Building the American Community*, p. 153.

23. S. J. Bonham, Jr., and Edward C. Grover, *The History and Development of School Psychology in Ohio* (Columbus, OH: State Department of Education, 1961), p. 3, table 1 and table 2.

24. The University of the State of New York. The State Education Department, *Fifty-Second Annual Report of the Educational Department* (Albany: The State University of the State of New York, 1958), vol. 2, p. 83.

25. David G. Salten, Victor B. Elkin, and Gilbert M. Trachtman, "Public School Psychological Services: Recent Growth and Further Potential," part I, *Educational Administration and Supervision* 42 (1956): 101, 105.

26. Warren G. Findley, "Student Personnel Work—Elementary and Secondary," *Encyclopedia of Educational Research*, 3d ed., Chester W. Harris, ed. (New York: The Macmillan Co., 1960), p. 1430; Salten, Victor, and Trachtman, "Public School Psychological Services," p. 100.

27. Ronald K. Goodenow, "The Progressive Educator, Race and Ethnicity in the Depression Years: An Overview," *History of Education Quarterly* 15, no. 4 (Winter 1975): 374. Goodenow points out, however, that the progressives' commitment to racial and ethnic diversity was limited by their fail-

ure to recognize the class issues involved in discrimination against blacks and immigrants (pp. 365–94).

28. For a searching critique of the liberal ideology of the era, see Reinhold Niebuhr, *The Children of Light and the Children of Darkness* (1944; New York: Charles Scribner's Sons, 1953).

29. Lucille H. Hildreth, *Child Growth Through Education: Effective Teaching in the Modern School* (New York: The Ronald Press Company, 1948), p. 208.

30. National Education Association, Committee on International Relations, *Education for International Understanding in American Schools* (Washington, DC: National Education Association, 1948); Association for Supervision and Curriculum Development, *Organizing the Elementary School for Living and Learning* (Washington, DC: National Education Association, 1947), pp. 166–68.

31. Carleton Washburne, *The World's Good: Education for World-Mindedness* (New York: John Day, 1954), pp. 3, xi, and passim.

32. Richard W. Streb, "A History of the Citizenship Education Project: A Model Curricular Study" (Ed.D. diss., Teachers College, 1979 [Ann Arbor: University Microfilms, International, 1982]), pp. 1, 93–94, 98–99. By January 1951 the Carnegie Corporation had granted over a million dollars to the CEP—"the largest amount ever given" for an educational project. In 1953 the Corporation notified the project that it would fund it for three more years with a grant of an additional $700,000 (ibid., pp. 219–20). For a brief survey of other citizenship education activities in this period, see Erling M. Hunt, "Recent Programs for Improving Citizenship Education," National Council for the Social Studies, *Education for Democratic Citizenship. Twenty Second Yearbook. 1951*, Ryland W. Crary, ed. (Washington, DC: National Council for the Social Studies, 1952), pp. 110–23.

33. Carnegie Corporation of New York, *Annual Report, 1948* (New York: Carnegie Corporation of New York, 1948) quoted in Streb, "Citizenship Education Project," p. 102.

34. Streb, "Citizenship Education Project," pp. 34, 261. The link between citizenship education and Cold War issues can also be seen in Ryland Crary's "Preface," *Education for Democratic Citizenship*. He argues for the teaching for "civic competence" by asserting that "the tawdry dogmas of communism itself are the very demonstration of a lack of civic competence" (p. vii).

35. According to Alan Felix, who was in charge of the committee that drew up the laboratory procedures, "CEP was really an attempt to implement Dewey's ideas—to learn by doing," Streb, "Citizenship Education Project," pp. 2, 12, 14, 26, 36, 149, 152.

36. Charles W. Sandford, Harold C. Hand, and Willard B. Spaulding, eds., *The Schools and National Security: Recommendations for Elementary and Secondary Schools* (New York: McGraw-Hill, 1951), pp. vii, 1–2, 103.

37. Despite its enrollment in the Cold War, the Citizen Education project found it was not immune from the anticommunist hysteria of the early 1950s. In 1951, *Chicago Tribune* reporter and editorial writer Frank Hughes attacked it for promoting leftist, pro-New Deal, and "One World" ideas.

These charges received widespread publicity and were republished as a pamphlet: "Leftists Views Rule Columbia Citizen Course." Russell protested that he had "no truck with socialism" and had carefully chosen his associates from the "[m]iddle-of-the-road—neither left nor right." Moreover, a study of project materials by a committee of the National Association of Manufacturers found that many more were oriented toward the Right rather than the Left of the political spectrum. Streb, "Citizen Education Project," pp. 286–95.

38. Arthur Bestor, *Educational Wastelands: The Retreat from Learning in Our Public Schools* (Urbana, IL: The University of Illinois Press, 1953), p. 99.

Chapter Six

1. A great deal was written about the Pasadena school crisis. David Hulburd, *This Happened in Pasadena* (New York: The Macmillan Company, 1951) is a good journalistic account. The National Education Association's Commission for the Defense of Democracy Through Education investigated the Pasadena situation and produced a report, *The Pasadena Story: An Analysis of Some Forces and Factors That Injured a Superior School System* (Washington, DC: National Education Association, 1951). For a defense of Goslin's opponents, see Mary L. Allen, *Education or Indoctrination* (Caldwell, ID: The Caxton Printers, Ltd., 1955).

2. The community was clearly changing. Between 1939 and 1951 the number of employees in manufacturing in Pasadena rose from 1,000 to 12,000. Between 1930 and 1950 the school district's population increased sixty percent. While the district's "non-white" population had been four percent in 1940, ten years later "non-whites" represented over nine percent of the school district's population. See Clyde M. Hill and Lloyd N. Morrisett, *Report of the Survey of the Pasadena City Schools: A Cooperative Study, 1951–1952* (Pasadena: City Board of Education, 1952), pp. 18, 56, 52–53.

3. Charles Wollenberg, *All Deliberate Speed: Segregation and Exclusion in California Schools* (Berkeley: University of California Press, 1976), pp. 138–40.

4. On Sexson, see Vincent Booth Claypool, "John Amherst Sexson: Educator" (Ed.D diss., University of California at Los Angeles, June 1948).

5. NEA, *Pasadena Story*, pp. 33–34.

6. As the *New York Times* (Aug. 18, 1952) pointed out, Goslin's "dismissal became a cause célèbre because Dr. Goslin, while denounced in some local quarters as a radical, was widely regarded as typifying the moderately progressive school of educational thought" which "has been under attack in a number of communities" (p. 1).

7. After Goslin's departure, the Pasadena schools were the subject of an extensive school survey. A special condensed version was published to allow the people of Pasadena to sort out the issues for themselves: Clyde M. Hill and Lloyd N. Morrisett, *Pasadena Faces the Future: Abridged Report of the Cooperative Study of the Pasadena City Schools* (Pasadena, CA: Pasadena City Schools, 1952). The survey committee concluded that there was no

evidence that the school program had changed significantly since the 1931 school survey. The Pasadena schools offered "a balanced combination of drill periods and related activities which made applications of the skills learned" but they did not have "a typical activities curriculum." Furthermore, the survey team (which included laypeople from the community) found no evidence of indoctrination in socialism and communism and no evidence that the education of "the whole child" meant, as the critics had charged, that the schools were taking over the functions of the home, church, and community to prepare children for collectivism (pp. 50–51, 62, 21, 43–44). Allen, *Education or Indoctrination*, argues that Goslin did change the curriculum, but covered his tracks (p. 72).

8. Allen Zoll is a shadowy figure. A supporter of Father Coughlin and other anti-Semites in the 1930s, in 1948 he founded the National Council for American Education, dedicated to eradicating "Socialism, Communism and all forms of Marxism from the schools and colleges of America, and to stimulate sound American education." One of his many pamphlets was entitled "Progressive Education *Increases* Delinquency." Hulburd, *Pasadena*, pp. 87–89.

9. NEA, *Pasadena Story*, p. 7. The *New York Times*, for example, observed that the Goslin case "epitomizes on a nation-wide scale the continuing attack on progressive education," "Education in Review," Dec. 10, 1950, section 4, p. 11. For a report on contemporary attacks on progressive education in other communities, see Morris Mitchell, "The Battle for Free Schools: Fever Spots in American Education," *Nation* 173, no. 17 (Oct. 27, 1951), pp. 344–47.

10. Elaine Tyler May, *Homeward Bound: American Families in the Cold War Era* (New York: Basic Books, Inc., 1988), pp. 10–15.

11. The survey of 168 newspapers published during a twelve-week period in 1951 was conducted by the NEA. The results are summarized in American Association of School Administrators, *American School Curriculum. Thirty-First Yearbook* (Washington, DC: American Association of School Administrators, 1953), pp. 285–86.

12. *New York Times*, May 25, 1952, pp. 1, 58. A few weeks later, Fine reported that the Department of Classroom Teachers of the NEA "'viewed with alarm' the growth of censorship in the nation's schools" (*New York Times*, July 1, 1952, p. 21). For brief descriptions of some of these censorship groups, see Mitchell, "Fever Spots," pp. 344–47.

13. *New York Times*, "Education in Review," July 9, 1950, section 4, p. 9; Feb. 25, 1951, section 4, p. 9; July 6, 1952, section 4, p. 9.

14. *New York Times*, "Education in Review," July 6, 1952, section 4, p. 9; *Chicago Tribune*, March 9, 1952, p. 11. The *Tribune* article that hailed the elimination of references to the UN from the new civics course also attacked the course it had replaced as an example of progressive education. The aim of that course had been stated in progressive terms: to "create an awareness of the certainty of change" and to develop the ability to recognize and to analyze these changes. But, the *Tribune* ominously warned, "the first aim of all Communists and socialists is to 'change' American govern-

ment into their pattern." Moreover, the old course had equated the government of the United States with "Great Britain, under socialism" and used a textbook (Frank A. Magruder, *American Government*) whose "socialist and communist bias" had been previously "exposed" by the *Tribune*.

15. *New York Times*, "Education in Review," July 6, 1952, section 4, p. 9. In 1953 an NEA survey reported that "criticism of teachers and of schools has become more common" and "[s]ubjects that in former days were accepted as commonplace are now suspect." These subjects included communism, socialism, UNESCO, and the UN. Two-thirds of the superintendents who participated in the survey acknowledged that there was now less academic freedom than there had been in 1940 (*New York Times*, "Education in Review," July 5, 1953, section 4, p. 7).

16. *New York Times*, "Education in Review," July 6, 1952, section 4, p. 9. The breach with the Legion was healed; in November 1953 the Legion joined the NEA in sponsoring American Education Week (*New York Times*, "Education in Review," Nov. 8, 1953, section 4, p. 9).

17. *New York Times*, "Education in Review," Sept. 14, 1952, section 4, p. 9; "School Board vs. Communism in Schools," *American School Board Journal* 126 (June 1953): 54; *New York Times*, "Education in Review," Feb. 22, 1953, section 4, p. 9.

18. *New York Times*, "Education in Review," July 4, 1954, section 4, p. 7.

19. "This We Do Believe," *School Review* 60 (May 1952): 256–57.

20. Raymond F. Howes, ed., *Causes of Public Unrest Pertaining to Education. Selected Addresses and Statements Presented at the Harvard Summer School Conference on Educational Administration* (American Council on Education Studies, Series I, Reports of Committees and Conferences, 17, no. 56, [Oct. 1953]), pp. 8, 32.

21. Mortimer Smith, *And Madly Teach: A Layman Looks at Public School Education* (Chicago: Henry Regnery Company, 1949), pp. 4, 7. Norman Cousins, in a discussion of "The Great Debate in American Education," listed four "misconceptions" about educators. The first of these was that educators were a closed group that communicate in a specialized jargon to exclude the public (*Saturday Review* 37 [Sept. 11, 1954], p. 12).

22. Albert Lynd, *Quackery in the Public Schools* (Boston: Little, Brown and Company, 1953), pp. 205–6, 52, 216, 211.

23. Arthur Bestor, *Educational Wastelands: The Retreat from Learning in Our Public Schools* (Urbana, IL: The University of Illinois Press, 1953), pp. 51–52, 45–46, 47–48, 50.

24. The word "progressive" bore an additional burden for public school people after it was used as the name of Henry Wallace's third party in 1948.

25. For example, at its annual convention in 1951, the NEA "presented evidence that the public schools are teaching the 3R's more efficiently and more effectively than they were thirty years ago" (*New York Times*, "Education in Review," July 8, 1951, section 4, p. 9). A year later, the Association for Supervisors and Curriculum Development of the NEA argued that "the basic skills of reading, writing and arithmetic" are "best developed in a total, meaningful setting, not in isolated periods of the school day" and

that "children who are taught by the modern methods outstrip their parents and grandparents in the Three R's" (quoted, *New York Times*, Oct. 29, 1952, p. 34). See also William S. Gray and William J. Iverson, "What Should Be the Profession's Attitude Toward Lay Criticism of the Schools?" *Elementary School Journal* 53, no. 1 (Sept. 1952): 3; Carleton Washburne, *What Is Progressive Education? A Book for Parents and Others* (New York: John Day Company, 1952), pp. 40–49, 93–104, 111–17.

26. When the Progressive Education Association disbanded, its officers tried to make it sound like a victory instead of a defeat. They announced that "the organization's work had been accomplished, [and] that there was no longer any need for the group's efforts." Quoted by Fred M. Hechinger, "Education in the News," *Saturday Review* 38 (Sept. 10, 1955), p. 29.

27. Albert Lynd, for example, began his book with a comprehensive account of this support for public education. He explained that he had served on his local school board after being elected on a platform that called for a new building program. He not only supported federal aid to public schools, but he opposed any use of public funds to support private education. Moreover, he did "not agree with those who denounce the public schools as 'godless,' merely because they are nonreligious." Nonetheless, Lynd pointed out, "many public school Educationists cannot bring themselves to believe that any criticism of their enterprise can be honestly motivated. . . . By the canons of Educationism, all critics must be tax misers, clerical conspirators, ultrareactionaries, [or] paid hirelings of crypto-Fascist organizations" (*Quackery in the Public Schools*, pp. 4–9).

28. According to the *New York Times*, delegates to the 1953 NEA Convention listed "Good public relations . . . as the most important need" in the campaign to fight attacks on the schools ("Education in Review," July 5, 1953, section 4, p. 7).

29. David B. Dreiman, *How to Get Better Schools: A Tested Program* (New York: Harper & Brothers, 1956), p. 65. Roy E. Larsen, "A Citizen Looks at His Schools," *Critical Issues and Trends in American Education, The Annals of the American Academy of Political and Social Science*, 256 (Sept. 1949): 160–66; "By & For the Public," *Time*, vol. 44 (May 23, 1949), pp. 79–80; *Do Citizens and Education Mix? A Community Guide to School Study* (Hartford: Governor's Fact Finding Commission on Education, 1950), p. 5. Norman Cousins, editor of the *Saturday Review*, served as chairman of the Connecticut commission.

30. Fred M. Hechinger, *An Adventure in Education: Connecticut Points the Way* (New York: Macmillan, 1956), pp. 38–40, 43–45.

31. *How Do We Pay for Our Schools?: A Guide to Understanding Public School Finance* (New York: National Citizens Commission for the Public Schools, 1954), pp. 76, 17, 26, 5; "*How Can We Help Get Better Schools?*" (New York: National Citizens Commission for the Public Schools, [1951]), pp. 15, 21, 22. The 1954 publication lists an "Advisory Panel of Educational Consultants"; one of the six was Dr. Willard Goslin, Professor of Education at George Peabody College for Teachers. Another was Dr. Benjamin Spock (p. 76).

32. Dreiman, *Better Schools*, p. 75. Between 1949 and 1955 newspapers

ordered 53 thousand mats for better schools advertisements from the Advertising Council; radio and television stations broadcast $8 million worth of announcements supporting the campaign: Fred M. Hechinger, "The NCCPS Bows Out," *Saturday Review* 38 (Feb. 19, 1955): 35–36.

33. "The Fight for Better Schools," and "Schools March On!" The March of Time, Time/Life Films, vol. 15, no. 10 (1949) and vol. 16, no. 7 (1950).

34. *New York Times*, "Education in Review," July 12, 1953, section 4, p. 9; Albany Know Your Schools Committee, "Report," (Mimeographed, Albany, New York, 1949), pp. 5, 7, 8, 9.

35. Robert K. Blair, "Albany Makes A Start," *Saturday Review* 36 (Sept. 12, 1953), pp. 22, 66–67.

36. *New York Times*, "Education in Review," Aug. 24, 1952, section 4, p. 9; P. Bernard Young, Jr., "Norfolk Keeps Its Head Above Water," *Saturday Review* 36 (Sept. 12, 1953): 21–22, 62. Young was the editor of the Norfolk, Virginia, *Journal and Guide* and a member of Norfolk's Citizens Advisory Committee on Schools.

37. The Commission member was Mrs. Eugene Meyer (of the *Washington Post*), who spoke at a meeting of the American Association of School Administrators: *New York Times*, "Education in Review," Feb. 22, 1953, section 4, p. 9.

38. *Do Citizens and Education Mix?*, pp. 5, 62, 146, 150–51.

39. Association of School Administrators, *American School Curriculum*, p. 281.

40. "What U.S. Thinks About its Schools—Roper Survey Finds Both Complacency and Dissatisfaction," *Life*, vol. 29, part II, (Oct. 16, 1950), pp. 11–18. *Life's* interpretation of the survey differs from mine; *Life* held that "only" 33.4 percent of the respondents said they were satisfied with the schools and that 38.2 percent were "only fairly satisfied" (p. 11). I believe that the fact that less than twenty percent of the people were dissatisfied is more significant.

41. Kenneth B. Henderson and Harold C. Hand, "To What Extent is the General Public in Sympathy with the Current Attacks on the Schools?" *Progressive Education* 29 (Jan. 1952): 110–13.

42. *Chicago Daily News*, Oct. 3, 1955; "Report Covering the Florida Conference on Education, Tallahassee, Sept. 28–29, 1955" (mimeographed, National Institute for Education Library, Washington, DC), pp. 1–3.

43. Committee for the White House Conference on Education, *Table Reports. Topic I "What Should Our Schools Accomplish?"* (mimeographed, National Institute for Education Library, Washington, DC), passim; The Committee for the White House Conference on Education, *A Report to the President* (Washington, DC: United States Government Printing Office, 1956), pp. 8–13. Agreement was not, of course, unanimous. In an article entitled "Dissent at Table 40," *Time* cited Joel H. Hildebrand, emeritus professor of chemistry from the University of California, who charged that the conference report "did nothing more than echo an educationist party line" and that in an effort to create harmony, dissident views were not expressed in the reports (Dec. 19, 1955, p. 57).

44. Eisenhower's impromptu remarks at the Dartmouth Commence-
ment exercises received a three-column headline on page 1 of the *New York
Times* (June 15, 1953, pp. 1, 10). At the 1954 meeting of the NEA, its National
Commission for the Defense of Democracy Through Education reported
that critics of the school had been less effective than in earlier years (*New
York Times*, "Education in Review," July 4, 1954, section 4, p. 7). In 1956
Benjamin Fine reported on the continuing enrollment crunch and the shortage of classrooms and teachers. He acknowledged, however, that "For so
long the cry of 'crisis' has been heard that it has lost its sharpness." He
pointed to "a bright spot on the educational scene," the rise in public interest in education exemplified by the citizens' committees (*New York Times*,
"Education in Review," Sept. 9, 1956, section 4, p. 11).

45. Fred M. Hechinger, "Education in the News," *Saturday Review* 38
(Sept. 10, 1955), pp. 57, 29.

46. Ronald Lora, "Education: Schools as Crucible in Cold War America,"
Reshaping America: Society and Institutions, 1945–1960, Robert H. Bremner
and Gary W. Reichard, eds. (Columbus, OH: Ohio State University Press,
1982) pp. 242–43.

47. Fred M. Hechinger, "Education in the News," *Saturday Review* 38
(Sept. 10, 1955): 29; National Center for Education Statistics, *The Condition
of Education. 1976 Edition.* (Washington, DC: United States Government
Printing Office, 1976), p. 180. By 1974, the share of the GNP devoted to
education had risen to 7.8 percent.

48. United States Office of Education, *Biennial Survey of Education in the
United States—1954–1956* (Washington, DC: United States Government
Printing Office, 1959), chapter 2, (Statistics of State and Local School Sys-
tems), table 41, p. 110.

49. White House Conference on Education, *A Statistical Survey of School
District Organization in the United States, 1954–1955* (Washington, DC, 1955),
p. 3. In 1947–48, there were 83,815 operating school districts in the United
States; in 1954–55, this figure had been reduced to 51,596. In 1947–48, there
were 77,832 one-teacher schools. By 1954–55, this had been reduced by
almost 50 percent to 39,061. For a spirited defense of one-room schools and
a rebuttal to the view that consolidation represented "progress," see Wayne
E. Fuller, *The Old Country School: The Story of Rural Education in the Middle
West* (Chicago: The University of Chicago Press, 1982).

50. In 1946–47 only about 26 percent of the pupils enrolled in the first
grade had attended public kindergartens the year before. By 1954–55, this
had increased to approximately 40 percent. These figures are derived from
United States Office of Education, *Biennial Survey—1954–1956*, chapter 2
("Statistics of State School Systems: 1955–1956"), p. 58. The percentages are
based on a comparison between the enrollments in the first grade and the
enrollments in public kindergartens the year before. This does not, of
course, take into account the children who did not attend public kindergartens because their parents kept them at home or put them into a private
program. Nonetheless, the *change* from 26 to 40 percent does reflect the
greater availability of kindergartens. In 1944–45, 3.2 percent of all public

elementary pupils were enrolled in kindergarten; in 1955–56, the comparable figure was 5 percent. United States Office of Education, *Biennial Survey—1954–1956*, chapter 2 ("Statistics of State School Systems: 1955–1956"), p. 58. As late as 1955 the white delegates to the Georgia preliminary White House Conference recommended "serious study" of whether kindergartens should be part of the public school system: *The Georgia Conferences Preceding the White House Conference on Education* (Athens, GA, 1955) p. 9.

51. The growth of elementary school guidance and counseling after 1955 was "phenomenal" according to Harold F. Cottingham, "Counselling—Elementary Schools," *Encyclopedia of Educational Research*, Robert L. Ebel, ed. (London: The Macmillan Co., 1969), p. 229. Yet, a 1975 dissertation notes that in the early 1960s "the profession of school psychology was relatively new" and that school social workers were "still relatively rare except in large metropolitan areas" (James Ray Kennedy, "The Mental Hygiene Movement in American Education" [diss., University of Pittsburgh, 1975], pp. 110, 118).

52. *New York Times*, "Education in Review," Nov. 6, 1955, section 4, p. 9.

53. Figures derived from *Annual Statistical Report of the Superintendent of Public Instruction, State of Illinois, for the Year Ended June 30, 1945* (Circular Series A, no. 33), pp. 426–27 and *Annual Statistical Report . . . for the Year Ended June 30, 1955* (Circular Series A, no. 106), pp. 337–38. In both cases, the figures excluded Chicago schools and rural schools. In the case of rural schools five percent of the teachers had degrees in 1944–1945 while thirteen percent had degrees in 1954–55.

54. "The Status of the American Public-School Teacher," *National Education Association Research Bulletin* 25, no. 1 (Feb. 1957): 30, 57, 33, 59, 62. The study reported that over 86 percent of elementary teachers were women. The typical woman teacher was 45.5 years old, married with one child, and was an active church member. She held a bachelor's degree and had taught for 15.4 years. There were 30.8 pupils in her class (p. 41).

Chapter Seven

1. "The New Mood," *Time* 71, (March 3, 1958), pp. 39–40.

2. Albert Lynd, *Quackery in the Public Schools* (Boston: Little, Brown and Company, 1953), p. 33; Gordon K. Chalmers and Maurice R. Ahrens, "Is There Quackery in Our Schools?" *Saturday Review* 36 (Sept. 12, 1953), pp. 26–27. Ahrens, who is identified as director of curriculum, Corpus Christi Public Schools, conceded "There have been improvements . . . particularly in methods of teaching, but essentially the same subjects are being taught that were taught fifty years ago." Moreover, "instruction is still largely dependent upon textbooks which, although somewhat improved, are similar in organization and content to the textbooks of a half century ago."

3. Allison Davis, "Developing an Improved Primary Curriculum," *Educational Leadership* 7 (Dec. 1949): 175–78.

4. Ralph W. Tyler, "Educability and the Schools," in American Association for the Advancement of Science, *Centennial: Collected Papers Presented at*

the Centennial Celebration . . . (Washington, DC: American Association for the Advancement of Science, 1950), p. 46. See also: W. A. Saucier, *Theory and Practice in the Elementary School* (1941; New York: The Macmillan Co., 1951). In the 1951 edition, the author concludes that in the "typical" elementary school classroom, the "primary concern" is "the teaching of facts." He conceded that "some teachers claim that they advocate higher objectives for the pupil than the memorization of facts, but they do not reveal this in practice" (p. 101).

5. Earl Conrad, *The Public School Scandal* (New York: The John Day Co., 1951).

6. Association of School Administrators, *American School Curriculum. Thirty-First Year Book* (Washington, DC: American Association of School Administrators, 1953), pp. 57–70. Written with the knowledge that it might well add fuel to the fire, the report was careful to put its references to progressive education in quotation marks and to avoid taking a stand on such controversial issues as the core or the experience curriculum. The book identified the four curriculum patterns as: Subject, Broad-Fields, Core, and Experience. The Broad-Fields Curriculum is defined as one in which there is some integration or correlation across disciplinary lines, such as substituting social studies for separate courses in history and geography. The Core Curriculum is defined as one in which an integrated curriculum is "centered upon life today."

7. Leroy K. Pinnell, *Functionality of Elementary School Desks* (University of Texas, Bureau of Laboratory Schools, Publication no. 5, Austin: The University of Texas, 1954), pp. 63–64, 146.

8. Barry M. Franklin, *Building the American Community: The School Curriculum and the Search for Social Control* (Philadelphia: The Falmer Press, 1986), pp. 147–51; 153–55.

9. In 1954, the *Saturday Review* devoted an entire issue to the strident debate about education. It identified several important issues that were at the heart of the debate: criticism of teaching methods, the need for new classrooms, desegregation, juvenile delinquency, and threats to academic freedom: Norman Cousins, "The Great Debate in American Education," *Saturday Review* 37 (Sept. 11, 1954), pp. 11–13, 47; Benjamin Fine, "Mrs. Grundy vs. Teacher," *Saturday Review* 37 (Sept. 11, 1954), p. 29.

10. Washburne had served as the Director of Education for the Allied Military Government in Italy and then became a member of the faculty at Brooklyn College in New York. He was succeeded by Assistant Superintendent Rae Logan, who served from 1943 until 1946. Logan was followed by Harold Shane (1949–50) and Gilbert Wiley (1950–56). Wiley resigned because of ill-health. See *Winnetka Talk*, Feb. 9, 1956, p. 24, and March 15, 1956, p. 3.

11. The Winnetka Board of Education, "Report for 1952–1953," printed in *Winnetka Talk*, Sept. 17, 1953.

12. Carleton W. Washburne and Sidney P. Marland, Jr., *Winnetka: The History and Significance of an Educational Experiment* (Englewood Cliffs, NJ: Prentice-Hall, Inc., 1963), pp. 128, 159, 165, 171.

13. Washburne's power was in large part based on his ability to persuade and it was exercised within a democratic framework. See Carleton Washburne, "What is Progressive School Administration?" *Progressive Education* 12 (1935): 219–23.

14. Washburne and Marland, *Winnetka*, pp. 165–66. The description of the superintendents' new view of their role is quoted by Marland from the 1950 edition of the *Encyclopedia of Educational Research*.

15. Wheeling, a suburb west of Winnetka, reported a 683 percent increase in population (Northeastern Illinois Metropolitan Area Planning Commission, *Suburban Fact Book. Revised With New Tables and 1960–1961 Data* [Chicago: Northeastern Illinois Metropolitan Area Planning Commission, 1962], table 4). The median age of Winnetka residents in 1960 was thirty-eight; only adjacent Kenilworth, also a mature suburb, had a slightly older population with a median age of thirty-nine. In sharp contrast, Rolling Meadows (a western suburb) had a median age of only eighteen (ibid., table 6). Sidney P. Marland, Jr., Winnetka's superintendent in the mid-1950s noted that "we are not preoccupied with the hysterical demands of building more and more schools as so many suburban communities are; we are not faced with a critical teacher shortage" (Marland, "One Hundred Years of Education" [An Address Before the Winnetka Women's Club, January 20, 1959], reprinted in Winnetka Board of Education, *Report*, 1959). See Appendix, tables 4 and 6.

16. "Marland, Sidney P(ercy), Jr.," *Current Biography Yearbook, 1972*, Charles Moritz, ed. (New York: H. W. Wilson Company, 1973), pp. 311–13; Washburne and Marland, *Winnetka*, p. 165.

17. Mary Ellen Singsen, "We Work Together in School Planning," *Childhood Education* 27 (May 1951): 424.

18. Washburne and Marland, *Winnetka*, pp. 176, 181, 182. Many of Marland's ideas about education were announced in a speech he gave to the faculty in 1957, which is reprinted (with comments) in ibid., pp. 178–86.

19. Of the 106 teachers in the Winnetka schools in the 1956–57 school year, only 38 had worked with Washburne for even a brief period (ibid., pp. 196–97).

20. Ibid., pp. 181, 182, 183.

21. Ibid., pp. 194, 172, 183. Significantly, in 1968 after Marland had moved on to the superintendency of Pittsburgh schools, he lost a pitched battle with the teachers over their right to be represented by the American Federation of Teachers and to bargain collectively. Subsequently, organized labor opposed his nomination as U. S. Commissioner of Education, citing his "anti-unionism." See "Marland," *Current Biography*, pp. 311–12.

22. Washburne and Marland, *Winnetka*, pp. 186–92. The quotation is on p. 192.

23. Ibid., pp. 209–26; the quotations are from pp. 212, and 214. See also Mildred Whitcomb, "How to Make 'Progressive' Education Work," *Nation's Schools* 70, no. 4 (Oct. 1962): 58–60, 106, 108, 110.

24. Washburne and Marland, *Winnetka*, p. 275.

25. Ibid., p. 184.

26. Ibid., pp. 324–37.

27. Ibid., p. 310.

28. Carleton Washburne, "Ripeness," *Progressive Education* 13 (February 1936): 126–30.

29. In 1961, Winnetka was still committed to Washburne's idea that educational practices should be based on research. In its annual report, the board of education took pride in the fact that the "schools have served and should continue to serve as an educational laboratory for the pursuit and discovery of ever better ways to teach and to learn" ("Beliefs and Objectives of the Winnetka Schools," Winnetka Board of Education, *Annual Report*, 1961; reprinted in Washburne and Marland, *Winnetka*, p. 232).

30. The population in 1940 had been 6,885. Although the population density per square mile increased from 523 to 703, Lake Forest was still, by far, the least densely populated of all north shore communities (Winnetka, by contrast, had a population density of 3,518 per square mile). Between 1950 and 1960, there was a 47 percent increase in the number of housing units in Lake Forest and 48 percent of the houses in town had been built since 1950 (the corresponding figure for Winnetka was only 16 percent). See *Suburban Fact Book* (revised with 1960–61 data), table 4, table 5; table 12, table 13; *Suburban Fact Book, 1950–1960*, table 15A. See Appendix, table 6.

31. Figures from the Annual *Statistical Report of the Superintendent of Public Instruction, State of Illinois* show that the Lake Forest public elementary schools enrolled 618 pupils in the 1945–46 school year. Enrollments began to climb rapidly in the 1950–51 school year and by 1955–56 totaled 987. The next year, enrollment jumped to 1,145 and in 1960–61 the schools enrolled 1,346. In 1945–46, Lake Forest had thirty-five teachers; in 1960–61, it had eighty-two. In this period, per capita costs had risen from $220.31 per pupil to $631.20 per pupil. See Appendix, table 4.

32. For the story of the Lake Forest Schools under Baggett and Davis, see chapter 4. Quinlan, who came from New York State, had been a principal in Katonah and then Pleasantville; he had attended Union College and Columbia University Teachers College (*Lake Forester*, August 11, 1944, p. 3).

33. *Lake Forester*, Dec. 16, 1943, pp. 3, 22; Aug. 11, 1944, p. 3.

34. Lake Forest Board of Education, "Minutes," ms., Board of Education Office, Feb. 6, 1945.

35. Board of Education, "Minutes," June 5, 1945 (my italics).

36. Frederick Quinlan, "The Schools Are Yours," *Lake Forester*, Nov. 7, 1947, p. 3.

37. Board of Education Scrapbook, Board of Education Office, Jan. 1948.

38. *A Statement of the Curriculum. Lake Forest Public Schools. Grades 1–8.* (Lake Forest, IL: Lake Forest Public Schools, 1949). A revised version, published in 1953, did not reflect any major changes. For PTA discussions of the curriculum, see: *Lake Forester*, Oct. 28, 1949, p. 5; Nov. 11, 1949, p. 3; Aug. 2, 1951, p. 22; Nov. 3, 1956, p. 4; Nov. 22, 1956, p. 3; March 7, 1957, p. 19; Board of Education, "Minutes," Feb. 4, 1958.

39. *Lake Forester*, April 20, 1945, p. 3; May 4, 1945, p. 3. Before 1946, children in grades K–4 from the eastern parts of town had been taught in

the upper school building; now they would attend Halsey, a few blocks away.

40. On the Home School Relationship Committee, see Board of Education, "Minutes," Oct. 6, 1953, and Oct. 2, 1956.

41. *Lake Forester,* Feb. 11, 1954, p. 4.

42. Much of the information on Quinlan is based on interviews: with Professor Ned Reichert (former chair of the Lake Forest College Education Department), June 10, 1986; Professor Rosemary Hale, June 4, 1986; Philip Speidel (former School Board member), July 1, 1986. The direct quotations are all from the recollections of Professor Reichert.

43. Interview with Professor Hale, June 4, 1986.

44. Interview with Val Hayward, July 11, 1974.

45. Frederick F. Quinlan, "Faculty Meetings During School Hours," *American School Board Journal* 113 (July 1946): 46.

46. Board of Education, "Minutes," Jan. 8 and Oct. 8, 1946.

47. Board of Education, "Minutes," Sept. 16, 1947, and Sept. 13, 1949; *Lake Forester,* Sept. 3, 1948, p. 7; July 27, 1950, p. 39; Aug. 31, 1950, pp. 3, 7.

48. *Lake Forester,* March 28, 1957, p. 9.

49. "The Story of APSS," *Associated Public School Systems, 13th Annual Conference,* Oct. 1961, pp. vii–ix.

50. Board of Education, "Minutes," June 6 and Sept. 12, 1950, Feb. 6, 1951; *Lake Forester,* Oct. 19, 1950, p. 5.

51. *Lake Forester,* Nov. 30, 1950, p. 5; Board of Education, "Minutes," Feb. 6, 1951.

52. *Lake Forester,* Oct. 19, 1950, p. 5.

53. Board of Education, "Minutes," Feb. 6, 1945; *Lake Forester,* April 20, 1945, p. 1, and May 4, 1945, p. 1.

54. *Lake Forester,* July 30, 1948, pp. 37, 40.

55. *Lake Forester,* Oct. 4, 1946, p. 17.

56. *Lake Forester,* May 16, 1947, p. 6.

57. Board of Education, "Minutes," April 5, 1949. The *Lake Forester,* March 25, 1949, p. 10, described the new procedures but noted that they had begun two years earlier.

58. Orville. B. Peterson, "Remedial Reading," *Illinois Education* 37 (Feb. 1949): 205, 227; *Lake Forester,* March 4, 1949, pp. 3, 26; Frank Bright, "Base Primary, Intermediate Curriculum on Sound, Firm Instructional Program," *Lake Forester,* Jan. 13, 1955, p. 13. The latter article provides, incidentally, a wonderful example of high level educational gobbledygook: "A sound instructional program initially is determined by the place a given school is to have within the interdependent system of which it is a functional part."

59. The only attack on "fads and frills" in the curriculum that I found in the *Lake Forester,* a letter from a "Worried Parent," was directed mostly at the high school: May 22, 1958, p. 24. The letter tied concern for American education directly to the launching of Sputnik, the Soviet space vehicle.

60. Quinlan reported to the board on how the schools dealt with gifted children: Board of Education, "Minutes," Jan. 3, 1956; *Lake Forester,* July 29,

1956, p. 28; John C. Pearson, "Certainly, We Group Our Students," *Phi Delta Kappan* 39 (May 1958): 358.

61. Interview with Professor Reichert, June 10, 1986.

62. Board of Education, "Minutes," Feb. 10, 1947.

63. Board of Education, "Minutes," Nov. 2, 1954, and May 3, 1955. At various times in the period from 1944 to 1959 the schools employed physicians, dentists, and nurses but no psychologists or school social workers. See "Teachers Annual Report File," ms., Lake Forest Board of Education Office.

64. Quinlan submitted a letter of resignation to the board on September 10, 1957; it was accepted at the next meeting and announced publicly on October 17. Before leaving Lake Forest, Quinlan thanked the board for its "consistent and generous support through the years" and there is no indication that Quinlan was encouraged to resign (Board of Education, "Minutes," Sept. 10 and Oct. 8, 1957). Quinlan's successor, Albert Poole, was a principal in Lake Forest. At least two candidates from other communities had been invited to Lake Forest for interviews (*Lake Forester*, March 27, 1958, p. 3.; Board of Education, "Minutes," Feb. 4, 1958).

Chapter Eight

1. *Waukegan News-Sun,* May 20, 1941, p. 1; May 16, 1942, p. 1. Green was the manager of the Waukegan branch of a family-owned marine construction company, *News-Sun,* Jan. 12, 1961, pp. 1, 10.

2. *News-Sun,* Jan. 31, 1942, p. 1; Feb. 14, 1942, p. 1; Feb. 18, 1942, pp. 1, 2; Feb. 21, 1942, p. 1; Feb. 26, 1942, p. 1; March 7, 1942, p. 6; March 9, 1942, p. 1; *Chicago Tribune,* March 7, 1942, p. 14.

3. Interview with H. R. McCall, Waukegan, IL, July 22, 1986; *News-Sun,* May 16, 1942, p. 1; May 19, 1942, p. 1; July 10, 1943, p. 1. After the third resignation, the newspaper noted (with evident disgust) that "Waukegan's New Deal administrators last night took a firmer hold on the Waukegan Grade school system" (July 20, 1943, p. 1).

4. Waukegan Board of Education, "Minutes," ms., Waukegan Public Schools Central Office, Nov. 13, 1944; *Chicago Tribune,* Nov. 15, 1944, p. 5; *News-Sun,* Nov. 14, 1944, pp. 1, 8; Dec. 4, 1944, p. 2; Dec. 12, 1944, p. 1; Jan. 9, 1945, p. 1; Nov. 13, 1946, p. 14. Many teachers, loyal to Clark, resented the way in which the board forced his retirement and retaliated by opposing the in-service program: *News-Sun,* Feb. 13, 1945, pp. 1, 8. By this time, however, the board was paying little attention to Clark. It did not make him a member of a special faculty-administration council appointed to determine needed changes in the curriculum (Board of Education, "Minutes," Feb. 12, 1945).

5. *News-Sun,* April 6, 1945, p. 1; Oct. 12, 1964, p. 12; McCall interview.

6. Out of the ten schools, one had been built in 1860 and two others in 1889 and 1890. See "Waukegan, Illinois Comprehensive City Plan, 1959," A. Gardner and Associates, Inc., Chicago (typescript, Waukegan Public Library), p. 59.

7. McCall interview; Committee on Field Services, Department of Education, University of Chicago, "Survey Report, School Buildings and Equipment, Board of Education, Waukegan City School District 61, Waukegan, Illinois" (Dittoed, 1948; copy in Regenstein Library, University of Chicago), pp. 1–2, 21.

8. McCall interview; Board of Education, "Minutes," April 10, 1947, indicate that the schools employed 35 non-B.A. teachers. Teachers without bachelor's degrees were no longer being hired.

9. The earlier manual is found in the Board of Education, "Minutes," Sept. 10, 1945, while the 1948–49 Superintendent's Manual was found in the Board of Education files.

10. Board of Education, "Minutes," Nov. 11, 1946; *News-Sun*, Dec. 16, 1946, p. 2. Copies of the report cards, with a printed letter of explanation, were found in the files of the Board of Education and I made copies of them. The original files have been destroyed since I originally looked at them. One of McCall's letters of explanation is dated January 1947.

11. *News-Sun*, April 9, 1946, pp. 1, 4; April 15, 1946, p. 15; *Chicago Tribune*, April 14, 1946, part 3, p. 1 n.

12. *News-Sun*, April 29, 1946, pp. 1, 8.

13. *New-Sun*, May 2, 1946, pp. 1, 10. The bulk of the support came from the wealthier neighborhoods on the north side; the vote in other precincts was quite light.

14. Board of Education, "Minutes," Sept. 8, 1947, p. 205; *Chicago Tribune*, Nov. 23, 1947, part 3, p. 11 n.

15. League of Women Voters of Waukegan and the City of Waukegan, *Waukegan Illinois: Its Past, Its Present*. Ruth W. Gregory, ed., 3d rev. ed. (Waukegan, IL: The League of Women Voters, 1967), p. 14; *Suburban Factbook. Revised With New Tables and 1960–1961 Data*, table 4; Evelyn M. Kitagawa and Karl E. Taeuber, eds., *Local Community Fact Book. Chicago Metropolitan Area, 1960* (Chicago: Chicago Community Inventory, University of Chicago, 1963), table I-1, p. 4; "Waukegan Comprehensive Plan," p. 53. See Appendix, table 4.

16. Michael W. Sedlak and Robert L. Church, "A History of Social Services Delivered to Youth, 1880–1977," Final Report, National Institute of Education, 1982, p. 61.

17. Ann Greer, *The Mayor's Mandate: Municipal Statecraft and Political Trust* (Cambridge, MA: Schenkman Publishing Co., 1974), pp. 10–11. In 1950, census tract 5, on the south side, had a total population of 5,922 and a black population of 1,825. Tract 3, on the west side was 6 percent black: United States Census, *Statistics for Census Tracts*, "Table 1—Characteristics of the Population by Census Tracts: 1950," p. 72. By 1960, one tract on the south side was over 55 percent black: Kitagawa and Taeuber, *Community Fact Book: 1960*, p. 207.

18. H. R. McCall, "Daniel Webster Junior High School," *American School Board Journal* 136 (January 1958): 22; McCall interview. See Appendix, table 5.

19. Board of Education, "Minutes," May 2, 1946; McCall interview.

20. *News-Sun*, Sept. 9, 1947, pp. 1, 8; *Chicago Tribune*, Nov. 23, 1947, part 3, p. 11 w.

21. Reavis's views on education can be seen in a paper he had prepared a few years before he undertook the Waukegan survey. See William C. Reavis, "Problems in Educational Administration Created By Changing Population in Urban Communities," *Proceedings of the Thirteenth Annual Conference for Administrative Officers of Public and Private Schools*, 1944, vol. 7, *Significant Aspects of American Life and Postwar Education*, William C. Reavis, ed. (Chicago: The University of Chicago, 1944), pp. 153–66.

22. "Survey Report," pp. 22–29.

23. Those who opposed the referendum argued that this was a bad time to ask taxpayers to vote additional funds, that the program itself was too ambitious, and that success was unlikely: Board of Education, "Minutes," April 19, 1948, p. 295; *News-Sun*, April 20, 1948, pp. 1, 12; May 3, 1948, p. 1.

24. *News-Sun*, April 27, 1948, pp. 1, 5; May 3, 1948, p. 1; Board of Education, "Minutes," May 10, 1948, p. 309.

25. *News-Sun*, May 11, 1948, pp. 1, 8.

26. Board of Education, "Minutes," June 14, 1948.

27. Board of Education, "Minutes," July 19, 1948, p. 345; Sept. 7, 1948, p. 357; Sept. 13, 1948, p. 10; *Chicago Tribune*, Oct. 10, 1948, part 3, p. 9 n; *News-Sun*, Sept. 14, 1948, pp. 1, 8; Oct. 12, 1948, pp. 1, 12.

28. *News-Sun*, Oct. 13, 1948, pp. 1, 12.

29. *News-Sun*, Oct. 13, 1948, p. 12.

30. *News-Sun*, Oct. 8, 1948, pp. 1, 8; Oct. 12, 1948, p. 1; Oct. 13, 1948, p. 12; Oct. 14, 1948, p. 1; Oct. 15, 1948, p. 1.

31. *News-Sun*, Oct. 14, 1948, p. 6.

32. Board of Education, "Minutes," Oct. 25, 1948, p. 44; *Chicago Tribune*, Oct. 20, 1948, p. 19; *News-Sun*, Oct. 20, 1948, pp. 1, 10.

33. Board of Education, "Minutes," Feb. 7, 1949, p. 73; *News-Sun*, Feb. 7, 1949, p. 1; Feb. 8, 1949, p. 1; *Chicago Tribune*, Feb. 24, 1949, part 2, p. 1 n.

34. At the April meeting, supporters of the plan to build two intermediate schools took advantage of the absence of six members who still favored building a single intermediate school to vote for a referendum to build two intermediate schools as well as a new K–6 building in the southwestern part of the city: Board of Education, "Minutes," April 11, 1949; *Chicago Tribune*, April 21, 1949, part 3, p. 5 n.

35. *News-Sun*, May 5, 1949, p. 1.

36. Coulson's article on juvenile delinquency, published in *Harper's*, was described in the *News-Sun*, May 12, 1948, p. 3; Kottcamp's speech was reported in the newspaper on June 2, 1949, p. 6.

37. Board of Education, "Minutes," April 17, 1950, p. 213; May 22, 1950, p. 262; *News-Sun*, May 11, 1950, p. 32; May 12, 1950, p. 16; May 15, 1950, p. 5; May 17, 1950, pp. 1, 14. The board followed this success by scheduling another referendum for two new K–6 schools plus an addition to Washington School. This proposal, too, was approved by the voters: Board of Education, "Minutes," July 31, 1950; August 28, 1950, pp. 322–23; Sept. 11, 1950, p. 329; Oct. 9, 1950, p. 337; Dec. 4, 1950, p. 389.

38. Board of Education, "Minutes," Nov. 10, 1952, p. 384. Shortly after McCall came to Waukegan, 3,420 pupils were enrolled in the system's ten schools. By the fall of 1952, enrollment had reached 4,358. In 1948, experts had predicted that the baby boom would crest in 1955 with a total enrollment of 4,435. But in the fall of 1953, the schools had to find room for 4,667 pupils, and by 1959 with an enrollment of 7,873, Waukegan schools served 130 percent more children than they had in the spring of 1946. (Board of Education, "Minutes," May 13, 1946; Sept 8, 1952; "Survey Report," p. 15; Board of Education, "Minutes," Sept. 14, 1953, Sept. 8, 1959.)

39. Board of Education, "Minutes," Feb. 17, 1953, p. 3; March 9, 1953, pp. 7–8; June 25, 1953, p. 59; July 15, 1953, p. 83; Oct. 12, 1953, p. 114a; *News-Sun*, July 16, 1953, pp. 1, 20; Oct. 27, 1953, p. 1.

40. *News-Sun*, Nov. 3, 1953, p. 7; Nov. 9, 1953, p. 11; Jane Foley, "Letter to the Editor," *News-Sun*, Nov. 14, 1953, p. 4; *News-Sun*, Nov. 13, 1953, p. 1.

41. *News-Sun*, Nov. 12, 1953, pp. 1, 20; Nov. 14, 1953, pp. 1, 8; Nov. 16, 1953, pp. 1, 2, 8.

42. *News-Sun*, Nov. 18. 1953, pp. 1, 12; Board of Education, "Minutes," Nov. 20, 1953, pp. 144–45.

43. *News-Sun*, March 7, 1945, p. 2; March 13, 1945, pp. 1, 8; March 14, 1945, p. 2; April 10, 1945, pp. 1, 8; April 26, 1945, p. 8; Board of Education, "Minutes," May 14, 1945.

44. Board of Education, "Minutes," May 13, 1946, p. 367; May 9, 1955, p. 396; Nov. 14, 1955, p. 7; Feb. 13, 1956, p. 52; May 13, 1957, p. 288.

45. Sedlak and Church, "Social Services," pp. 78–79. It should be noted, however, that the new high school superintendent, J. Lloyd Trump, played a major role in bringing together the grade schools and the high school to devise the new counseling program.

46. At the time the articles were written there were ten principals and 140 classroom teachers in the Waukegan schools. In addition, there were fifteen special teachers of music, art, physical education, and household arts and three school nurses. Besides the superintendent and assistant superintendent, there was also a business manager. Student enrollment was approximately 4,100 (*News-Sun*, Feb. 1, 1952, p. 4). Ten of the articles were by Superintendent McCall, and seven were written by Assistant Superintendent Merle M. Kauffman. The rest were by classroom teachers, special teachers, librarians, and principals.

47. *News-Sun*, Jan. 29, 1952, p. 6.

48. *News-Sun*, Feb. 9, 1952, p. 2.

49. *News-Sun*, March 15, 1952, p. 5.

50. *News-Sun*, May 24, 1952, p. 2.

51. *News-Sun*, May 13, 1952, p. 5.

52. *News-Sun*, Feb. 25, 1952, p. 7; March 19, 1952, p. 12.

53. *News-Sun*, April 7, 1952, p. 4.

54. *News-Sun*, March 1, 1952, p. 3.

55. *News-Sun*, March 12, 1952, p. 11.

56. *News-Sun*, March 18, 1952, p. 17.

57. *News-Sun*, March 22, 1952, p. 4.

58. *News-Sun*, March 13, 1952, p. 15.

59. *News-Sun*, April 23, 1952, p. 7.

60. *News-Sun*, March 25, 1952, p. 13.

61. *News-Sun*, Feb. 18, 1952, p. 9; April 2, 1952, p. 7.

62. *News-Sun*, Feb. 27, 1952, p. 6.

63. *News-Sun*, May 1, 1952, p. 22. The quotation on drill is from an article on reading, published several years later (May, 11, 1955, p. 6).

64. The conservative *News-Sun*, in an editorial entitled "For the Whole Child," also supported a modestly progressive approach for children in the grade schools, arguing that the older ways of teaching "turned out too many students who had never learned the most important thing of all—how to live with their fellows." The aim of modern schools is to "combine the teaching of human relations with other classes . . . That is a sound idea" (Sept. 8, 1947, p. 12).

65. *News-Sun*, Jan. 30, 1952, p. 12.

66. James Capra, "Individualizing Instruction," *American School Board Journal* 137 (Dec. 1958): 18. On gifted education in Waukegan, see also Louise A. Osling, "A Special Interest Class for Bright Upper-Graders," *The Instructor* 69 (Nov. 1959): 28, 51.

67. James Kidney, "The Integration of Whittier School, Waukegan, Illinois" (senior honors thesis, Lake Forest College, 1969), p. 7 and passim. By 1963, McAllister was 89 percent black and Whittier was 77 percent black (*News-Sun*, Oct. 9, 1963, pp. 1, 4). McAllister was the last school in the system to get a school library. The 1968 survey of Waukegan schools was made by the University of Wisconsin, Milwaukee (*News-Sun*, Feb. 27, 1968, pp. 1, 4).

68. *News-Sun*, March 16, 1944, pp. 1, 12. According to the *News-Sun*, the campaign "featured . . . bitter charges and counter charges and distribution of campaign literature on a scale comparable with campaigns involving fat state, county or city political plums" (April 10, 1944, pp. 1, 8). Thalman resigned immediately, before the new board could act (*News-Sun*, April 11, 1944, p. 1).

69. *News-Sun*, June 13, 1944, p. 1.

70. In a speech to the American Association of School Administrators, Trump argued that as more and more students who would not go on to college entered high school, American high schools should devote about half their times to "common learnings" and "the content of the common learnings . . . should be devised in terms of the developmental tasks of adolescents . . . [and] the content should be organized in terms of meaningful units rather than the present courses" (*News-Sun*, March 14, 1946, p. 10). Trump elaborated on his commitment to democratizing the high school in two articles published in the *News-Sun*: Nov. 14, 1946, p. 19, and Nov. 15, 1946, p. 5.

71. *News-Sun*, Sept. 12, 1944, p. 1; Oct. 10, 1944, p. 1; March 13, 1945, pp. 1, 8.

72. *News-Sun*, Feb. 13, 1945, p. 4; March 27, 1945, p. 4.

73. Helen Cunningham and Elsie Katterjohn, "Life Improvement

Through the English Classroom, Waukegan Township High School," in Charles W. Sanford et al., *The Story in Nineteen Schools: Reports of Progress on Curriculum Developmental Projects Sponsored by the Illinois Secondary School Curriculum Program* (Circular Series A, no. 51. Illinois Secondary School Curriculum Program Bulletin no. 10. Springfield: Sept. 1950), pp. 343, 344.

74. Cunningham, "Life Improvement," pp. 348, 349, 350–51, 354, 362, 363.

75. Cunningham, "Life Improvement," p. 365.

76. *News-Sun,* March 12, 1948, pp. 1, 8; Sept. 12, 1947, p. 16. Of the school's graduates, only about one-third went directly to a postsecondary school (Cunningham, "Life Improvement," p. 344).

77. *News-Sun,* April 13, 1946, p. 1.

78. *News-Sun,* June 11, 1946, p. 6.

79. *News-Sun,* June 13, 1946, pp. 1, 16. The newspaper was probably quite wrong in attributing the board's defeat to the new curriculum. The major reason was that the board had done such a poor job of getting out the vote that an extremely low voter turnout gave the edge to those opposed to any increase in their taxes.

80. *News-Sun,* Feb. 20, 1947, pp. 1, 12; April 11, 1947, p. 1, 8; April 14, 1947, pp. 1, 6.

81. President Kuebler's speech, as reported in the newspaper, attacked progressive education in general. In an editorial, however, the *News-Sun* said that he specifically criticized the Waukegan high school program (*News-Sun,* April 11, 1947, pp. 1, 8; April 14, 1947, p. 14). The newspaper carried on its campaign against Trump's innovations even after he had left. See editorials on Sept. 12, 1947, p. 16, and May 10, 1948, p. 12.

82. *News-Sun,* Aug. 13, 1946, pp. 1, 8. By early 1947, the Waukegan basketball team was being described by the *News-Sun* as the best high school quintet in the state (Jan. 22, 1947, p. 13).

83. *News-Sun,* Sept. 11, 1947, pp. 1, 16. After leaving Waukegan, Trump had a distinguished career as a professor of education at the University of Illinois and published a number of influential books. He retained his youthful commitment to democratizing the high school, developing the "Trump Plan," designed to "bring about increased quality educational opportunities for a diverse school population." See David W. Beggs III, *Decatur-Lakeview High School: A Practical Application of the Trump Plan* (Englewood Cliffs, NJ: Prentice-Hall, Inc., 1964), p. xiv.

84. *News-Sun,* Aug. 19, 1947, pp. 1, 8; Aug. 20, 1947, p. 16.

85. *News-Sun,* May 7, 1948, pp. 1, 8; May 8, 1948, p. 1; May 10, 1948, p. 12; July 20, 1948, pp. 1, 8.

86. Clippings in Lake Forest College alumni files: *Libertyville Independent Register,* Nov. 4, 1937, and June 14, 1945; *Roselle Register,* Jan. 21, 1944; *Arlington Heights Record,* April 27, 1945.

87. "In the Matter of Albert Kroll vs. Board of Education of School District No. 75, In the Village of Mundelein, Lake County, Illinois." Hearing Before Appeal Committee, November 3, 1950. Typescript in the possession of Albert Kroll, pp. 18–19.

88. *Newsweek,* quoted in the *Independent Register,* April 4, 1957, p. 13; Northeastern Illinois Metropolitan Area Planning Commission, *Suburban Fact Book, 1950–1960* (Chicago: Northeastern Illinois Metropolitan Area Planning Commission, 1960), table 4a; *Suburban Factbook With 1960–1961 Data,* table 4. See Appendix, table 6.

89. Albert A. Kroll, "Survey and Long-Range Program for the Mundelein Elementary School" (unpublished M.A. Project, Northwestern University, 1949), table 1, p. 9. See Appendix, table 4.

90. Interview with Albert Kroll, August 26, 1988; *Independent Register,* Aug. 30, 1945, p. 6; Sept. 6, 1945, p. 3; Sept. 13, 1945, p. 1; Oct. 11, 1945, p. 4; May 13, 1948, p. 1; Aug. 22, 1946, p. 3; Sept. 5, 1946, p. 3; Oct. 7, 1948, p. 3; Nov. 4, 1948, p. 3; June 16, 1949, p. 1.

91. Kroll Interview; "Cella" to "Al" Kroll, Mundelein, April 11, 1950, Ms. letter in the possession of Albert Kroll.

92. The district did hire an eighth-grade teacher, so Kroll was relieved of one of his jobs. On the other hand, he had to give up his office for classroom space (*Independent Register,* Sept. 1, 1949, p. 3).

93. Kroll, "Survey," pp. 10, 24. My emphasis. The survey was conducted in the spring and summer of 1949.

94. Ibid., pp. 5, 25–28, 30–31.

95. Ibid., p. 16.

96. Figures derived from *Suburban Fact Book, 1950–1960,* tables 21a, 10a; Kroll, "Survey," pp. 10, 11–13, 16, table 3, p. 20. See Appendix, table 4.

97. Kroll, "Survey," pp. 2, 18–19, 8. Kroll's fellow students recommended that Lincoln be sold or used as a community center (p. 29).

98. Ibid., pp. 36–39, 51–52, 41–42, 45–48, 42–44, 30–31.

99. Kroll Interview; *Independent Register,* Aug. 25, 1949, pp. 1, 3; June 10, 1948, p. 3; Sept. 15, 1949, p. 1.

100. "In the Matter of Albert Kroll," pp. 16–33; Kroll Interview; *Independent Register,* May 4, 1950, p. 1; Aug. 17, 1950, p. 1; Aug. 24, 1950, p. 1; Aug. 31, 1950, p. 1; Sept. 14, 1950, p. 1; Sept. 21, 1950, p. 1; Oct. 5, 1950, pp. 1, 6.

101. Kroll's attorney, William Behanna, told Kroll: "I understand your attitude that you wish the case in Circuit Court to proceed to a final decision and adjudication by the Court. In my opinion, this would involve a needless expense both on your part and that of the School District." Since the newly elected board members opposed the dismissal, it would put them in the awkward position of having to authorize funds to support arguing a case they opposed: [William Behanna] to Albert Kroll, Waukegan, IL, April 18, 1951, unsigned copy of ms. letter in the possession of Albert Kroll. After running the family's gas station for a number of years, Kroll went back to teaching and became the principal-superintendent of another small school district (Kroll Interview).

102. "In the Matter of Albert Kroll," pp. 41, 60.

103. "Cella" to "Al" Kroll.

104. Jerome J. Kahn to W. R. Behana [*sic*], Chicago, Sept. 5, 1950, ms. letter in the possession of Albert Kroll. The letter was written for use in the

hearing before the board appointed by the county superintendent of schools.

105. Kroll Interview; *Libertyville Herald,* May 17, 1978, clipping, Lake Forest College alumni files.

106. *Independent Register,* June 14, 1951, p. 1; Aug. 23, 1951, p. 1; Nov. 15, 1951, p. 3; Sept. 3, 1953, p. 1.

107. Board of Education, "Minutes," ms., Board of Education Office, Feb. 15, 1955, p. 42; Mar. 27, 1956, p. 105; April 5, 1956, p. 107; Sept. 13, 1956, p. 143, August 17, 1957, p. 50; Aug. 27, 1957; Oct. 17, 1957; *Independent Register,* April 11, 1957, p. 13.

108. *Independent Register,* July 12, 1951, p. 1; Nov. 15, 1951, p. 3; Nov. 22, 1951, p. 3; Board of Education, "Minutes," Feb. 11, 1958; March 6, 1958; Aug. 28, 1958; Oct. 2, 1958.

109. Kroll, who became superintendent of another nearby school district, got to know Travelstead quite well. He depicts him as a man who was not highly dedicated to his profession (Kroll interview).

Chapter Nine

1. John Dewey, "Introduction," in Elsie Ripley Clapp, *The Uses of Resources in Education* (New York: Harper & Brothers, 1952); reprinted in *Dewey on Education: Selections With an Introduction and Notes by Martin S. Dworkin* (New York: Teachers College Press, 1959), pp. 129, 130, 131–32.

2. Joseph Calguire, "Union Township Schools and the Depression, 1929–1938, *New Jersey History* 93 (Autumn–Winter 1975): 122–25.

3. Ronald Lora, "Education: Schools as Crucible in Cold War America," *Reshaping America: Society and Institutions, 1945–1960,* Robert H. Bremner and Gary W. Reichard, eds. (Columbus, OH: Ohio State University Press, 1982), pp. 225–60; Frank G. Jennings, "The Revolution in Education: It Didn't Start with Sputnik," *Saturday Review* 50 (Sept. 16, 1967): 77–79, 95–97.

4. Dean John H. Fischer's speech as quoted in Fred M. Hechinger, "The Trends of 1960," *New York Times,* Jan. 1, 1961, p. 8e.

5. Robert S. Lynd and Helen Merrell Lynd, *Middletown in Transition: A Study in Cultural Conflicts* (New York: Harcourt, Brace and Company, 1937), pp. 225–26. What the Lynds reported for Middletown was true elsewhere. As Warren Sussman has pointed out, despite the decade's reputation for radicalism, even the ideologies of the era's intellectuals had profoundly conservative implications. See Warren Sussman, "The Thirties," in *The Development of an American Culture,* 2d ed., Stanley Coben and Lorman Ratner, eds. (New York: St. Martin's Press, 1983), pp. 215–60.

6. *Waukegan News-Sun,* April 14, 1952, p. 4. Another teacher, an advocate of the whole-word approach to reading, cautioned parents that children would be confused if parents urged them to sound out words. In any case, she argued, parents might "do more harm than good" if they attempted to instruct their child without first checking with the teacher (*News-Sun,* Feb.

2, 1952, p. 3). Ironically, these articles were published as part of an effort to enlist voter approval for a crucial referendum.

7. Lawrence Cremin, *The Transformation of the School: Progressivism in American Education, 1876–1957* (New York: Alfred A. Knopf, 1962), p. 350.

8. Bel Kaufman, *Up the Down Stair Case* (Englewood Cliffs, NJ: Prentice-Hall, Inc., 1964), pp. 54–56.

9. James Q. Wilson, *Bureaucracy: What Government Agencies Do and Why They Do it* (New York: Basic Books, Inc., 1989).

10. Roscoe George Linder, *An Evaluation of the Courses in Education of a State Teachers' College by Teachers in Service* (New York: Bureau of Publications, Teachers College, Columbia University, 1935), pp. 4, 110–11; Seymour B. Sarason, Kenneth S. Davidson, and Burton Blatt, *The Preparation of Teachers: An Unstudied Problem in Education* (New York: John Wiley and Sons, Inc., 1962), p. xii.

11. See chapter 2 and the report cited there from the superintendent of a small Massachusetts school district who noted that while the teachers in the district had "learned the words of modern education" they did not, in fact, carry out these ideas and their classrooms were "teacher-centered" rather than "child-centered." He speculated that this might be due to "faulty understanding," to conflicts between newer ideas and "old and thoroughly learned patterns of behavior," or a simple "failure of the teachers to recognize that what they do is not what they say is best." Willard Spalding, "Norwell: A Study of the Environment of School Children" (Ed.D. diss., Harvard University, 1942), pp. 329–30.

12. Richard J. Bernstein, *John Dewey* (Atascadero, CA: Ridgeview Publishing Company, 1966), p. 67.

13. Elaine Tyler May, *Homeward Bound: American Families in the Cold War Era* (New York: Basic Books, Inc., 1988), p. 14.

14. Office of Education, United States Department of Health, Education and Welfare, *Education in the United States of America*, Special Series, no. 3 (Washington, DC: United States Government Printing Office, revised, 1955), p. 16.

15. A. H. Lauchner, "How Can the Junior High School Curriculum Be Improved?" *Bulletin of the National Association of Secondary-School Principals* 35 (March 1951): 299–300, as quoted in Arthur E. Bestor, *Educational Wastelands: The Retreat from Learning in Our Public Schools* (Urbana: The University of Illinois Press, 1953), pp. 55–56.

16. Diane Ravitch points to the progressives' blindness to the "social implications of their separation of children into academic, general and vocational curricula" as a major symptom of the intellectual stultification that led to the demise of the movement. See *The Troubled Crusade: American Education, 1945–1980* (New York: Basic Books, Inc., 1983), p. 78.

17. John Dewey, *Experience and Education* (New York: The Macmillan Company, 1938), pp. 103, 111, 112.

18. For Dewey's ideas on value, see Bernstein, *John Dewey*, pp. 125–29, and Robert B. Westbrook, *John Dewey and American Democracy* (Ithaca: Cor-

nell University Press, 1991), pp. 402–18. See chapter 5 for a discussion of the ways in which progressive techniques were employed in the Cold War.

19. Henry May, *The End of American Innocence: A Study of the First Years of Our Own Time, 1912–1917* (New York: Alfred A. Knopf, 1959), p. 153.

20. Carleton Washburne, interview with Alex Baskin at Okemos, Michigan, Feb. 4, 1966.

21. Westbrook, *Dewey and Democracy,* p. 109. Westbrook also argues that Dewey "often underestimated the strength of the resistance to . . . democratic reforms by the 'vested interests' who were the 'particular beneficiaries of the existing social habits'" (p. 82).

22. See Appendix, table 5. Jonathan Kozol, *Savage Inequalities: Children in America's Schools* (New York: Crown Publishers, Inc., 1991), makes clear that the disparities between the financial resources of the wealthy suburbs and the impoverished cities is a major issue in the present urban educational crisis. Kozol explains: "Typically, in the United States, very poor communities place high priority on education, and often tax themselves at higher rates than do the very affluent communities. But, even if they tax themselves at several times the rate of an extremely wealthy district, they are likely to end up with far less money for each child in their schools" (p. 55).

23. Tracy Kidder, *Among School Children* (Boston: Houghton Mifflin Company, 1989).

24. Charles E. Silberman, *Crisis in the Classroom: The Remaking of American Education* (New York: Random House, 1970), pp. 122, 125, 220.

25. Larry Cuban, *How Teachers Taught: Constancy and Change in American Classrooms, 1890–1980* (New York: Longman, 1984), p. 2.

26. Reinhold Niebuhr, *The Children of Light and the Children of Darkness* (1944; New York: Charles Scribner's Sons, 1953), pp. 115, 118.

27. John Dewey, *The School and Society* (1900, rev. ed., 1915; Chicago: The University of Chicago Press, 1956). p. 29.

Index

Boldface page numbers refer to photos in the text.